Honor Me Honor You

Poore Pond Series Book Two

Kathy, thank you for appreciating my work.

Ruth Harwell Fawcett

Ruth Harwell Fawcett

Ambrosia Press
Cleveland

This is a work of fiction. The personalities, actions, and viewpoints of the characters are not the author's, but their own, within their fictional context. Any resemblance to actual persons, living or dead, is entirely coincidental.

HONOR ME HONOR YOU
Poore Pond Series Book Two

Published by Ambrosia Press LLC

Library of Congress Control Number: 2006909675

Printed in the United States of America.
For information address:
Ambrosia Press LLC, P.O. Box 7226, Eastlake, Ohio 44097-7226
http://honormehonoryou.wordpress.com

Paperback ISBN-13: 978-0-9729346-8-8
ISBN-10: 0-9729346-8-5

Hardcover ISBN-13: 978-0-9729346-9-5
ISBN-10: 0-9729346-9-3

FIRST EDITION

ACKNOWLEDGMENTS

I owe a great debt to many people for the birth of this book; the list given here is by no means inclusive. First, I thank my husband Bill for everything and, in this case, his constant support and respect for my work. I appreciate the significant contribution of cover artist Pamela Dills; the critical eyes and ears of Arlene Fenton and Roberta Smearman; the generosity of logistics facilitator Robert Dills; Teri and Chuck Hare for their technical magic; the patient advice and encouragement from SCORE Counselors at Cleveland Chapter 30, Eastern Branch; the publicity artfully arranged by Augusto Michael Trujillo of the Atlanta Journal-Constitution.

I must thank the Willoughby-Eastlake Board of Education for the opportunity to immerse myself for several decades in the teacher-administrator experience, which gave me the insight, inspiration, and imagination to create Poore Pond School and its inhabitants.

To my wonderful grandchildren: Sam, Peter, Mary Ruth, Sidney, Whitney and Bobby, Michelle and Jared, Nicole and Jon, who give unconditional love and who delight me with their remarkable sense of words and wordplay.

To teachers and their trainers who work tirelessly to improve education for the sake of better lives for children.

CHAPTER ONE—HOPE

Hope Fleming sat in her sun-filled kitchen, sipping tea and looking at a calendar. August 15, in block letters, stared back at her. She had marked the day principals were to report to their offices to prepare for the new school year, thus ending their summer break.

I began the summer with a funeral and ended it with a funeral. I am tired. My brain is barely functioning. Hope rubbed her forehead with her fingertips, thumbs resting on her cheekbones, elbows on the glass tabletop. She took a deep breath and turned to look out the wall of windows.

I must remember to water the new forsythia bush. Sighing, she thought of fellow principals who had sent it in remembrance of her sister, Frances. Her son George planted it the very next day, stopping just long enough to update her on his search for office space for the homeless foundation she was helping him establish.

She still felt convinced that giving her entire inheritance to George to fulfill his dream of helping the homeless was the right thing, the honorable thing, to do. But the overwhelming task of helping her son establish the foundation weighed heavily on her.

Hope looked again at the bare bush, impressive only in its symbolism; she knew she would see the yellow forsythia blossoms every spring and think of Frances, of her untimely and undignified death.

In some ways I wish I had not nursed her through those last weeks of life. It would have been much easier if she had stayed home in Seattle to die. Then I would not have to think of her—bald and gaunt from bone cancer and its equally horrifying treatment. Perpetually sick to her stomach, every organ—cruelly except her brain—malfunctioning.

I could just savor the memory of occasional emails, cards, and phone calls bristling with her sardonic wit if I had not "helped her die."

To stem the heartache, Hope forced herself to think of George's fledgling foundation and all the good it would ultimately do. She scoffed noisily. "Talk about the blind leading the blind. The inept leading the inept," she heard herself say as she rose to carry the empty cup to the sink.

But she laughed to herself when she recalled his first response to the news that she had inherited all that money and was donating it to a foundation he would establish for the homeless.

"Why can't I just take small bills and hand them out on the street corner every week. Give them instant relief from their misery. Those poor dudes would think they'd gone straight up to Heaven."

The two of them had laughed until their sides hurt at the vision of whiskered, toothless men in tattered clothing, pockets and fists overflowing with cash.

George described his mental picture of Schuyler, one of his street friends, who was intrigued by television. He would park himself in front of appliance stores that had multiple television sets running in their show windows and watch for hours, often until the manager chased him away. George imagined Schuyler carrying a switched-on, six-inch portable TV around all day, watching "radio people," as he referred to them.

She walked into her study and looked at the neon pink index card with her to-do list crowded onto it. She dialed Theodore Keller's number and left a second message. *He's never in. How can he run a consulting business that way?*

Theodore said we need to file for certification of incorporation now that we've decided not to have a membership organization. The processing takes several weeks. Must we have this incorporation before we recruit the board of directors? It's all so confusing. Where will we find responsible people who care about the homeless? It would be so much simpler if we could just do it George's way, just hand out cash on the street.

Hope replaced the receiver, letting her eyes rest on the red-leather journal on the shelf beneath the telephone. Surprised by her sudden courage, she flipped through the pages, sadly noting how Frances' handwriting had evolved from uniform penmanship in earlier entries to a jagged, uneven scrawl angled on the pages of later entries.

She read a few lines near the end of the journal and immediately felt guilty for wanting to have missed helping Frances die. "Hope is steady and calm even when I am beastly with upchucking and complaining. Being with her has given me courage I never knew I had. But what are sisters for if not to see one another through the door of death? I wish we'd spent more time together over the years. Why didn't we?"

Her last comment, entered the day before she died, was barely legible. I think it says, "So long, World. It's been a gg…" The last word was incomplete.

The telephone rang sharply. Hope checked the caller-identification window and saw Michael's name. What does he want? She dabbed at her eyes with tissue as if to conceal the state of her emotions from him. The ring repeated. Hope, unable to lift the receiver, waited. It rang again. This time she willed herself to answer the phone.

"Hello, Michael, George isn't here." She tried to keep the distaste she felt from spilling into her voice.

"I know that; he's here at work with me. It's you I want to speak to."

Silence filled the wires as Hope waited for his next comment. She was proud of her calm but wanted to finish the call quickly. She took quiet, shallow breaths.

"About this ridiculous stipulation you've put on the money you're giving George." Hope flinched at Michael's strident speech. "Why can't he buy himself a partnership in Polyflem with it? Why does he have to throw it away on a bunch of homeless derelicts. We all know they'll waste it on booze or drugs or whatever owns them. Makes no sense."

Hope had not the stomach to respond. She thought of Michael at Frances' memorial service. Alec's eyes were sad, his face pale, appropriate for a bereaved ex-husband. Michael wore the face he always wore: cold eyes, set jaw. But then, she was surprised that he had come at all. George had sat next to his mother, his shoulder braced against hers. Thank God he is capable of caring; he is not his father's son in that respect.

"Hope! Are you there?"

"Yes, Michael."

"I'll stop over at the house tonight. Talk about rerouting that inheritance that dropped in your lap. Give George a solid future in this company. That was something, wasn't it? After all these years? How long has old Mary been dead? Must be twenty years."

Hope turned the receiver away from her ear and closed her eyes. She could not listen to that loathsome voice another moment.

"She came to our wedding, didn't she?" Michael's strong voice projected from the earpiece. "She never liked me. I could feel it. Did you know that? Never warmed up when I was around. Tough old bird. How about tonight?"

"Tonight what?" Hope's civility was rapidly diminishing.

"I'll stop over tonight. Haven't you been listening?"

"I don't think so, Michael. No. The money has already been put in trust for the foundation. It won't be changed. Do not come to this house. Goodbye." She replaced the receiver softly, loathing her inability to deflect the distaste she felt at the sound of Michael's voice. *I must stop giving him this power over my emotions.*

Hope took a hunter green pocket folder and went to the porch, oblivious to the heavy midsummer air and lack of breeze. She propped chintz pillows behind her and spread the contents of the folder on the sofa. Theodore's hand-written list gave her pause. She read through his twelve steps for establishing a foundation and felt immediately exhausted. *Is it better for George to muddle through this process on his own, or should I keep doing what I'm doing to help? I don't mind the extra work so much now, but when I'm back at school next week...*

All the responsibility of Poore Pond rained down on her. Where was the old relish she felt for opening school, welcoming staff, greeting parents and students?

There was also the matter of a new secretary. After she'd read of Bella's transfer in summer board-meeting minutes, Hope had received her note announcing the job transfer to central-office bookkeeping. Just yesterday she had a letter from Roger Russo, personnel director, stating that her new secretary was to be Corinne Tompkins. *The departure of an employee is a chance to improve your staff. Where did I hear that?*

Hope sighed heavily, feeling too warm and acutely aware of her exceptionally low energy level. She knew she would have to be George's active partner if there were ever to be a foundation. *And I must keep up my guard if Michael is to be kept out of the till.*

In uncharacteristic fashion, she abruptly gathered the disheveled pile of papers and stuffed them into the folder, carrying them back to her desk in the study. She looked around aimlessly then tidied the papers next to the computer. She replaced two novels on the shelf and took a magazine from the ottoman, dropping it in a rack beside the red leather chair.

In the kitchen, she scooped a handful of pistachio nuts from an earthenware bowl. Savoring the air conditioning, she stood at the counter, shelling and eating the sweet nuts. *It's after 11:00. I should be thinking about food.* She opened the refrigerator and looked for something appetizing.

Why don't I ring Belva and see if she's free for lunch?

Over chicken Caesar salads, Hope listened to Belva Carmichael describe Corinne Tompkins, her secretary when she was Director of Federal Programs.

"The ultimate professional," Belva said, stabbing the air with her fork for emphasis.

"What I want to know is," Hope looked at her friend with mischievous eyes, "can she spell? Does she care about pronouncing names correctly?"

"One-hundred percent," Belva said, buttering a piece of crusty roll.

"That's one less thing I have to worry about then." Hope poured tea from the tiny pot. "Tell me, Belva, are you ready to go back to work?"

"I suppose I am; I've been lazy long enough. I didn't accomplish one thing on my list for around the house this summer. I need to get back under pressure. Then I'll get more done." She perused the dessert menu.

"I'm not up to it yet. I'm so fragmented. Haven't even sorted out all Frances' business yet. Well, Alec is taking care of most of it, her property, that is. But I promised my sister I would take her ashes back to Roseville and have them interred next to our parents." She opened the dessert menu. "Want to split something?"

"How can you do that? You have to have a whole plot, don't you?" She frowned at Hope. "I'll split the strawberry shortcake. Or the double-chocolate-fudge brownie."

"Frances told me about a new service; it's called shared interment." She looked at Belva's aghast eyes.

"Somehow I don't think you mean adjacent plots."

"No. Apparently cemeteries are now selling one-foot-square parcels of occupied plots—reselling, I should say—expressly for burial of loved ones' ashes." She leaned forward as if about to divulge secrets. "Get this: just below ground, over the top of the original occupant's casket." She sat up again and sighed. "Can you believe that?"

"Sort of like renting out your spare room?" Belva scoffed. She shook her head. "You've got to hand it to those marketing types. They think of everything. But don't you already own that square foot?"

"Well, yes. They call it an accommodation fee. I think that's the correct term. But you can't put just anybody's ashes there. You have to certify that the person had a loving relationship with the original occupant of the burial plot."

Belva burst into sardonic laughter.

"No, wait." Hope thrust her hand, palm-side, at Belva. "This is the best part. That's why it's called Loving Partners Plan."

"And you are actually considering it?"

The waitress appeared and Hope ordered a double-chocolate-fudge brownie. "We're splitting, so we'd like an extra plate, please." She smiled at the young woman who smiled back.

"Well, yes. Yes, I am." Hope took another bite of lettuce. "What are my options? Rent a shelf in the mausoleum? Purchase an entire plot? I don't know."

"Tell me, how do you certify a loving relationship?" Belva pushed her salad plate to the center of the table.

"I have no idea, just document the parent-child relationship, I suppose. Who would challenge it?" Hope frowned at Belva.

"The way you heap scorn on your parents, your childhood, I should think you might." Belva looked warmly at her friend.

"That was I. Frances has fonder memories, always called me an ingrate. Miss Grandiose, she would say when I wrote her from college about my posh friends, as she referred to them." Hope lowered her chin and raised her eyes. "We were poles apart in our lifestyle preferences.' She lifted her chin. "Frances' idea of well dressed was a flannel shirt with jeans. Her idea of quality clothing was L.L. Bean. That was her designer." Hope pulled at her hair and looked away. "She made it a point to be different from me." She met Belva's eyes.

"And you made it a point to be different from your parents?" Belva smiled through closed lips.

"That's right." Hope stretched her shoulders. "I was obsessed with it. Like Jonathon Franzen's character in The Corrections. Only I didn't write about it; I just lived the corrected life. My version, that is." Hope, regretting her self-disclosure, reddened and swallowed.

The chocolate dessert arrived already split onto separate plates. The two women spooned large bites, both welcoming an end to the unsettling conversation.

As Hope pulled into Poore Pond parking lot, she waved to Ray, teetering on a small stepladder as he polished the glass window on the school sign. She parked her car and walked toward him.

"Glad you stopped, Hope." he smiled warmly. Eldon was here to service the copier, the big one in the office. Said to tell you he has to order a part for it, takes a couple days." He climbed down from the ladder and stood back to inspect his cleaning job.

"Did he leave paperwork?" Hope moved forward to scrutinize the glass.

"Yes, it's on Bella's desk. Well, I guess it's not Bella's desk anymore, is it? Will you have a secretary next week?" He wiped vigorously at a dull spot on the window.

"Corinne Tompkins bid on the job. She's from Federal Programs. Do you know her?"

"I think she's Ty Tompkins' wife. You know, Coach Tompkins at the high school. Soccer coach." Ray folded the ladder and gathered his supplies.

"Corinne is coming here tomorrow at noon. I've heard good things about her; I'm anxious to meet her."

"I miss Bella though. She was a lot of fun." Ray began to walk away. "Always had a smart remark for me. Lightened things up."

Hope joined him to walk into the building. "She did, didn't she?" They moved in silence. "How is your cousin Ralph getting along, Ray? Is he managing on his own?" She stopped at the boiler-room door.

Ray looked at the ground. "Oh, okay, I guess. He tries to go to Chamber meetings and that, the way he and Millie always did. But says he misses her more at those things than he does when he's alone at home. She was the chatty one."

Ray glanced at Hope then opened the heavy door for her.

Hope slipped through the door and was surprised by a new green velour chair parked at Ray's desk. It stood out like a mink coat at a garage sale.

"What a good-looking chair, Ray. How do you happen to have it?" She rubbed her hand along the padded arm.

"In the right place at the right time, I guess." He smiled broadly. "I was in Steve's office talking new cafeteria tables and this guy from data came rolling it in. Said he had to have a straighter chair for his back problems. Wanted to give it away. So I put it in the van." He laughed and slid it away from the desk. "Try it, Hope. It's really comfortable."

Hope unloaded her briefcase and armload of folders onto an adjacent file cabinet and sat down gingerly. She squared her elbows on the wide arms and leaned back, breathing deeply. "Why, you're right! It is very comfy, Ray." She smiled up at him. "You really needed a new chair; that tattered old thing you had was a disgrace, not to mention how bad it must have been for your back."

She stood and gathered briefcase and folders. Looking around the factory-like boiler room, Hope noticed for the first time, Ray's stark, cold environment. The new chair emphasized the lack of even basic office amenities. "Have you ever thought of partitioning off an area for your desk, Ray?"

"Uh, well, no. It's always been like this. Just a boiler room."

"But if we boxed in that corner where the worktable is, you could have a private office." She placed briefcase and folders again on the file cabinet and walked to the table, extending her arms to mark a corner. "Like about here." Her body still facing the table, she turned her head toward Ray. "What do you think?"

Ray could feel his smile widening at the idea of a private office. "I never really thought about it before. But, yeah, it would be great."

"I'll speak to Steve about having the carpenter build a partition. You are the plant manager; you should have a proper office." She retrieved her belongings and walked through the doorway to the corridor.

"By the way, Ray," she stopped again. "How are Heather and Jeremy? Are they gearing up for her to start training? Is everything okay?"

Ray rubbed the top of his head. "Yeah, she's all set. Picked up her books yesterday after orientation. I guess she's excited."

Does he have reservations about Heather's starting pharmacy assistant training? "That's good." Hope walked away.

Hope's inbox, placed for the summer outside her door, was piled high with envelopes, catalogs, and flyers. She entered a musty office and put her briefcase on the floor, folders on the table. She opened the window into the courtyard and waved to the job corps worker tending plant beds. *Ray's really behind schedule out there. He usually finishes these courtyards before the end of my break.* She rubbed her temple and wondered if there were a problem about which she should know.

After sorting the contents of her box into piles and the trash can, she took a letter opener and slit the envelopes. Recognizing Melanie Armstrong's energetic handwriting, she read her brief letter first.

> Dr. Fleming,
>
> It's just been confirmed, and I wanted you to be among the first to know. Jay and I are pregnant, due in February. We are so excited!
>
> I will be in next week to work on my room. See you then.
>
> Melanie

Hope pondered the news and thought of Mia. *I wonder if Mia has kindergarten experience. She did such an outstanding job for Millie Blackwell last spring, before Millie lost her fight with cancer.*

She glanced at the shelf holding a small photograph of a smiling Millie with the Stamp Club kids crowded around her. Her hand rested on the shoulder of a child who proudly held a blue ribbon, partially obscuring the title, Commemorated Minority Americans, attached to the front of a cumbersome display box.

Her eyes clung to Millie's tiny photo face for a moment as she said a silent prayer for the departed teacher's soul. *What a happy time that was. And it was after she had started cancer treatments, so the good news gave a lift we all needed.*

After all envelopes were opened, Hope's new charges were several: arrange long-term substitutes for two pregnant teachers, due in December and February, and for a third whose adopted infant would arrive from Iraq in November. *Oh yes, the Board implemented the new federally mandated family leave last year. As I recall, restrictions on family leave were somewhat different from those on maternity leave. I will have to check the contract.*

Hope found she must also identify a fourth-grade teacher willing to work with a college student for September experience. She needed to accommodate high-school art teacher Dale Feltham's request for a fifth-grade class to buddy with his students as part of their senior project requirements. Parent Elinor Fisher asked to be partnered with a first-grade teacher for fieldwork in language arts to complete the teacher-recertification process with the State.

Hope pulled out a teacher roster to scrutinize. She noted first, second, and third choices for each request and dialed the phone. Energized by the task, she smiled in gratitude for the familiar surge of adrenaline.

CHAPTER TWO—RAY

Caroline cleared the dishes as Ray finished the hot-fudge sundae she had served him.

"Sit down, Ma. I'll do that. You just relax a little." He was worried about her shortness of breath and slow movements around the kitchen. "What time is your appointment tomorrow?" He sought her eyes.

"One thirty, Ray. But don't you worry. Claire's coming to take me. She's adjusting her lunch hour." Averting her eyes, she sat down heavily.

"Aw Ma, I can take you. School hasn't started yet, so it's no problem getting away. And I want to hear what Dr. Crider tells you. I'll call Claire and cancel her."

"All right, Son." Caroline said weakly. Ray thought she wanted to lay her head on the table, she looked that weary.

"Come on, Ma. I'll help you get ready for bed." He placed his dish in the sink and came to her chair, bending over and offering his arm. She took it and braced her other hand on the tabletop for support as she rose. At the bathroom door, she stopped and told him she'd finish on her own.

"Aren't you supposed to take Heather and Jeremy shopping tomorrow for school clothes? Didn't you tell me that?" She looked at him with confused eyes.

"You're right. You're right, Ma. I am." He forced a smile. "Your memory is still sharp as a saber. But we're not going until four-thirty. Heather gets off at four, so I'll pick up Jeremy from Latchkey and we'll go get her. Then on to the mall!" He hoped his smile belied his concern for her.

"Well, dragging me to the doctor will leave you too tired to traipse around the mall with the Bakers. Claire can take me." She waved her arm at the wrist for finality and closed the bathroom door.

Ray wiped the counters and table and rinsed his ice cream dish. He thought of Marty and wondered how he was coping with his layoff.

He decided to work on the new task plan for Rosie and him. Hope had requested it in order to "maximize their efficiency," she had said, now that they no longer had two night custodians. She had asked Rosie to come in for a morning meeting this week while she was still on days. *It's just as well if Claire does take Mom to the doctor. That meeting is day after tomorrow, and the plan has to be ready.*

Ray sat at the kitchen table with a legal pad that bore an incomplete job chart. *Only thing to do is alternate the rooms. Clean each one every other day.* He knew it would be only a matter of time before the teachers would fume.

How could he and Rosie do just enough cleaning in every room, every day, to make them feel clean? Shine a little. With thirty classrooms, they each had fifteen, plus adjacent halls and two sets of restrooms. Ray was responsible for the office and clinic; and the night shift, which now consisted of Rosie only, cleaned the library and front and rear lobbies. There could be no shirking on the restrooms and clinic; State law required daily cleaning and sanitizing. *Twenty minutes per room, that's five hours just for classrooms. Then we each have our common areas, trash, repairs, paperwork, ordering, unpacking.* He sighed heavily. *And we have to work around all those outside groups.* Ray began to tense up and knew that he would never fall asleep if he thought about this now.

He glanced at a yellow post-it note on the chart. Hope had notified him that the parent group would be starting a new fundraiser, Market Night, the third week in September. That meant at least twenty-five volunteers in the building, unloading the truck full of frozen foods a half hour after dismissal, spreading it all out in the small gymnasium, and helping parents pay for and pick up their orders. *Where would they all park? And what would that foot traffic do to the floors?*

He threw down his pencil and shoved the legal pad onto the coffee table. "Cripes! It can't be done!" his voice rose more than he intended.

"What's wrong, Ray?" Caroline's weak voice cried from the bedroom. Ray heard her stirring and walked in as she was trying to steer her swollen feet into thick slippers.

He tucked her legs under the covers and tried to make his voice soothing. "Nothing, Ma. I'm just belly-aching because we lost Marty. He was laid off." He managed a smile. "But don't worry; we'll work it all out. Rosie's a real workhorse." He switched off the lamp.

"Well, you've never been afraid of hard work either, Ray. The Sellers have always been workers." She turned on her side toward him. "But I sure hate to see you having to work harder than you already do. Everybody has his limit, you kn…" Her voice trailed off.

"I'll just have to work smarter, Ma." He chuckled. "I'll figure it out." He tiptoed toward the door and quietly closed it.

For half an hour, he drew and redrew an alternate-days chart. No matter how he adjusted the chores, there were not enough minutes.

He rubbed his temples. He stretched thoroughly, his arms above his head. He poured a glass of milk, grabbed a couple graham crackers, and sat down facing the television set. The newscaster gave unemployment figures and announced another plant closing. Shocked workers with haunting faces appeared on the screen. They had not seen this coming. Many of them had just spent money on school clothes and school supplies and expected to have the means to pay for them.

One man said he had five kids starting school. He and his wife had joked that very morning that they were really doing their part for the economy, even bought a computer for the eldest child. The man's desperate eyes did not match his casual remark, "Maybe the kid will start an internet business and support the whole family."

Ray, heartsick, turned away. He switched to a sports channel and finished his milk. He felt small, complaining about extra work. He still had a job, didn't he?

A professional soccer game appeared on the screen, immediately reminding Ray of Jeremy. Now ten years old, he had joined the YMCA Soccer Program. Ray had been taking him to practices Tuesdays and Thursdays and would continue to do so after school started, to give Heather study time when her classes began in two weeks. He looked forward to it and knew how much it meant to Jeremy. He had overheard his bragging to another student when they both joined a group of neighborhood boys volunteering to pick up litter around the schoolyard in preparation for opening of school.

"Mr. Sellers takes me to soccer practice two days a week." Jeremy boasted. "We always go to Bumper's for ice cream after. He lets me have whatever I want." The boy looked at Jeremy with envious eyes and scornful lips.

Ray had chuckled to himself at Jeremy's exaggeration. Out of four practice sessions, they had gone to Bumper's once. He laughed now as he recalled the incident.

Rising while pressing the television remote-control off button, Ray went to his bedroom. He undressed and washed, thinking the entire time of tomorrow's shopping expedition with Heather and Jeremy. He knew he would enjoy himself and fairly tingled at the thought of his surprise for them. He would use the gift card Aunt Peggy had given him for his thirty-ninth birthday, to treat them to dinner at the new Pearl Grill, across from the mall.

It will be a celebration of Heather's brave new venture. I hope it works out for her. She needs the security. Jeremy needs it, too. But part of him felt uneasy about her entering this new phase, about the fact that it may change her. It may distance her from him. *Stop it! You sound like Davey, talking concern for his son, Jeremy, and then throwing obstacles in Heather's path when she tries to make a better life for them. You're pathetic.*

He pulled back the plaid comforter and crawled into bed, reaching to turn the switch on the alarm clock. He snuggled into the pillow and pulled the comforter around his shoulders.

I hope Heather wears that white turtleneck tomorrow; she looks so pure and fresh in it. Like an angel. He had a fleeting vision of the next time he'd seen her after helping get her car going one day. She was wearing the white turtleneck with a red miniskirt. *Was that really a whole year ago?*

Ray entered the office and was greeted by a slender woman with sleek, brown hair. "You must be Mr. Sellers," she smiled. "Dr. Fleming told me you would be here. I'm Mrs. Tompkins, the new secretary." She extended her hand.

Ray's hand met hers and they shook firmly. "Call me Ray," he smiled back at her. "Welcome to Poore Pond." He noticed that she was quite well dressed, in expensive clothes like one of Hope's professional friends.

"Thank you, Mr. Sell—Ray. This is a stately school. And I understand that you are responsible for the beautiful landscaping." She pulled new pencils from a long box.

Ray dropped his eyes and chuckled. "Well, I have a lot of help from the kids here. They all like to dig in the dirt."

"That's kids for you," she laughed softly. "I should know; I raised three rowdy boys." She pointed to the triple frame on her desk. Three well-scrubbed, freckled faces in neckties beamed at him.

"Good-looking kids. Aren't you—are you Coach Tompkins wife?"

"No, but you're close. He is my brother-in-law. I'm married to Ty's brother Thad. Thad's sort of a coach, too; he's a fitness trainer at Farley's over in Snellville."

They chatted briefly about the two brothers sharing an interest in physical development. Corinne began unpacking a carton on her desk.

"Is Hope in?" he asked looking toward her closed door.

"Yes," Corinne replied, lifting the phone to her ear and pressing the intercom button. "Mr. Sellers is here to see you, Dr. Fleming." She looked away for a few seconds then replaced the receiver.

"Dr. Fleming will see you now, Mr. Sellers." She looked at him with a business-like face.

"Thanks, Corinne." Ray opened Hope's door gently. He found her facing the computer monitor.

"I'll be right with you, Ray," she said. She clicked print and a swooshing sound began.

Ray sat down and waited until she joined him in the opposite chair.

"How may I help you, Ray? Hope smiled widely.

"About this Market Time schedule," he waved the green paper in his hand. "That starts the third week of school and takes place the third Thursday of every month through May?"

"That's right." Hope uncapped a bottle of water and drank. "Would you like water, Ray?"

Ray shook his head no. "But I would like a little more information about this Market thing. He looked at the green paper in his hand. Let me get this straight. The truck comes at 3:45? And the parents come to pick up their food orders starting at 4:45? Is that right?

"That's right, Ray. And don't you worry about that truck. A crew of twenty volunteers will be here to unload it. And to give out the items to the customers. You don't even have to be down there." Her wide smile bored into his dubious eyes.

Well, that doesn't sound so bad. "Great." He smiled back. "Great. Thanks, Hope." He rose to leave. Corinne nodded to him as he passed.

That doesn't sound so bad. He whistled softly down the hall, ignoring feelings of trepidation.

Ray drove along in silence, aware of Heather's subtle fragrance. Tension hung in the air as it never had between them before.

Why the heck does Davey have to meet them at the mall? He'll spoil everything. Heather turns into Tough Mama around him. She's a different person when he shows up.

Ray did not like to recall his first meeting with the man last spring. Heather had made Ray a nice dinner to show appreciation for his helping her with the move to a new apartment, and they were celebrating.

He was drunk as a skunk when he came looking for Jeremy. Heather had immediately become a mean drill sergeant and cut Davey no slack at all.

Ray glanced sheepishly at Heather, as if she could read his thoughts.

I know it's hard on her, what she's been through with him. So why did she allow him to be part of this shopping trip today? She obviously does not enjoy his company.

"I'm sorry, Ray." He could feel her eyes on him. He turned to meet them and she looked away.

"No need to be sorry." He sighed involuntarily. "If that's the only way he'll meet his obligation, what choice did you have?" Ray wanted to be understanding, but a small knot of resentment tightened in his stomach. "I just wish he would have sent you the money for Jeremy's school clothes, that's all. It would have been a lot easier on you." He met her gaze and immediately regretted his words.

"You're right, Ray. It would have been so much easier for me—and Jeremy. And for you." She turned an angry face toward him. "But Davey's not that kind of man. Davey likes to make it harder on us. It's all about power and control. He knows that I know I would never see that money if I didn't accept it his way. He does meet his financial obligations to Jeremy , but he always tries to do it in some complicated way." She sat up straighter and looked out her window. "That's just how he is."

"Davey had a terrible childhood, Ray." Her voice softened to normal. "He has no idea how to be a father." She glanced at the empty rear seat. "I hated letting Jeremy ride with him. But he was at the bus stop and charmed him into wanting to go. Said they'd stop for ice cream on the way. That was all it took."

Ray forced a chuckle. "Well, it's just a few blocks. What can go wrong in that short a time?" His eyes begged her to smile back at him.

"You're right. He deserves that much. He is Jeremy's father." She relaxed her shoulders again.

Maybe it won't be so bad. Ray knew that Heather would never agree to Jeremy's riding with Davey if he had been drinking. *Davey's not such a jerk when he's sober.*

In the end, the shopping excursion went smoothly despite the tension. Davey looked scrubbed and well dressed in khakis and a pressed plaid shirt and was pleasant, almost charming. He and Ray sat talking over coffee while Heather and Jeremy looked for clothes and shoes. At one point, Jeremy invited them to help him decide on which sports-logo jacket to buy. Davey voted for his favorite team's jacket, an expensive, reversible style that suited Jeremy best. He even handed Heather an extra twenty dollars to help pay for it although he had already given her $350 cash. Ray warmed to him for that.

When they were ready for dinner, Davey declined, saying he had promised to meet Desiree at The Steakhouse on highway 109. So Ray, Heather, and Jeremy ate at The Pearl Grill. They needed to laugh and made spectacles of themselves, giggling endlessly at each other's jokes, whether or not they were funny.

When Ray pulled into their driveway, Jeremy invited him to come inside and see all the new clothes. Ray accepted at once.

Reluctant to leave their company, he asked Jeremy to model a few shirts and the camouflage pants he had bragged about all the way home.

He and Heather admired all the choices.

"Why, you'll be the best-dressed kid at Poore Pond," Ray said to the boy, who, chin against chest, unbuttoned a red-cotton shirt with pockets on the front and on one sleeve. Jeremy looked at him with sheer delight in his face. Ray patted his shoulder and said good night.

Heather walked him to the door and stepped outside. "Thanks, Ray, for being such a good sport. And for dinner. It was great." She touched his arm lightly.

Ray put his hand over hers, meeting her eyes just before she turned away. "I enjoyed it. Davey's not such a bad guy. You can see how much he cares for Jeremy." *And for you, Heather.* He removed his hand.

She waved at him from the window as he drove away. The excitement of her touch lasted all the way home.

Ray, surprised that his sister was still at the house, maneuvered his van around her small car. He entered the quiet kitchen, fighting back anxiety. Claire sat before the living-room television with the volume so low it could barely be heard.

"Hey, Ray," she said, not quite smiling.

"Claire, what's up? What did the doctor say? Is Mom in bed?" He looked toward the hallway.

"Sit down, Ray." Claire patted the sofa beside her.

Ray sat, not sure he wanted to hear what she had to say.

"Mom's heart is getting weaker." She said it so matter-of-factly that Ray did not grasp the seriousness of her news. "Dr. Crider wants to try a new treatment. Some sort of chemical-electronic mix. It's a six-hour treatment which will strengthen her heart. If it works on her—it does not work on every patient—she could gain weeks of life."

Weeks of life? Weeks? "What does that mean Claire?" He looked at his sister for signs of the desperation closing in on him, but her face was closed. She smoothed the arm cap on the sofa with deep concentration.

"It means," she took a deep breath. "It means Mom's heart is so weak now that Dr. Crider needs to use whatever he can find to try to help her."

Ray opened his mouth to speak, but Claire waved him silent.

"The best results his patients have had from this new treatment have been a gain of close to six weeks of a stronger heart for each six-hour treatment." Claire's voice began to crack.

When would treatment start? How soon will we know the results? Side effects? Is it painful? Ray could not get the questions out, his heart was so full of fear.

The next morning Dr. Crider returned Ray's call at school and told him exactly what Claire had told him. He added the fact that he had scheduled Caroline for her first treatment next Tuesday, providing the results of her pre-procedural tests indicated that she was a good candidate. He would call Ray or Claire by Friday.

CHAPTER THREE—THE BRADFORDS

Dylan rushed to the car, and Ian closed his phlebotomy textbook with an unconscious sigh. He reached over the back seat to grab his son's hand.

"Hey, Dylan." He managed a wide smile. "How's it going at your new school?" His eyes searched the boy's sober face.

"It was okay, Dad," Dylan said, looking past him to wave at a slow-moving boy with a huge note pinned to him. Ian saw that the note read:

My name is Clark Foster. I go to my Granny's house today, not home.

In silence, Ian and Dylan watched Clark, urged on by children at windows and driver at the door, calling "Come on, Clark, Come on!" The boy labored his way to the mini-version yellow school bus. Ian stifled a desire to carry him to the driver.

A pleasant-faced aide guided him onto the bus as the driver climbed behind the steering wheel. Minutes passed before the bus finally pulled out, gears shifting loudly at the stop sign. The few small passengers stared with vacant faces at Dylan and Ian as the bus passed. Both driver and aide waved and smiled, and they waved back.

"Is that your bus, Dylan?" Ian asked as he looked to see that the boy's seatbelt was fastened.

"No, Dad. My bus already left. Didn't you see the number on the side? It's number 14; my bus is 28."

"Oh, well, you know your bus number already. Great, Dylan." In the rear view mirror, he studied his son's face. "Clark looks like a nice boy. He's your friend?"

"Sort of." Dylan shifted impatiently. "I don't want to talk about school now, Dad. Let's just go to Dr. Walley's. Get it over with. I hope he doesn't give me Novocain. I hate that stuff."

He's not happy in his new school. I was afraid of this. How can I fix things for him? Maybe I'll talk to Dr. Fleming.

Ian pulled onto the boulevard, his heart bleeding for his small, silent passenger, only seven years old and already careworn.

The warm greetings Dylan received from both receptionist and dental assistant cheered him and Ian as well. Dylan went in willingly when Dr. Walley met him at the door with a smile and a "Hi Sport."

Ian opened his textbook and began reading, actually rereading, the section he had finished earlier. Annoyed, he struggled to comprehend the technical language. *Why can't they write in plain English?*

He unfolded pages of reading notes and reviewed them, stimulating his recall somewhat. Taking a deep breath, he resumed reading, stopping now and then to make notes.

"Dr. Walley will see you now, Mr. Bradford. Dylan is finished."

Dylan was rummaging with gusto in the children's treasure chest when Ian entered the room. He smiled at his father. "Dr. Walley has cool stuff, Dad."

Ian, conferring with the doctor, felt himself relax. He enjoyed the good report on the condition of Dylan's teeth as well as Mark Walley's interest in his progress in the Physician's Assistant Program at City College. They had a lively conversation regarding the science of human blood and the utmost importance of knowledge of the subject to any medical practitioner, at every level.

"Mr. Bradford, there's a phone call for you," Wilma, the receptionist, announced. Ian lifted the phone she indicated he should use.

"Hi Ian," Helsi said in that clear voice of hers. "Sorry to track you down at the dentist's office, but I need your help."

"What is it, Hon? Can't it wait until we get home?"

"Well, it can, but I wanted to catch you while you were en route, save you a trip. Or me."

Ian felt heat rising in his chest. *Not another stop at the grocery store. I've done that three times this week.* "What do you need, Helsi?" He tried to filter from his voice, the irritation he felt.

"Lucy needs to be collected from school. I'm trying to get dinner in the oven. She and another girl were disrupting volleyball practice, so the coach kicked them out. They're both suspended from the team for two weeks."

"Lucy? I can't believe she would do that. She always follows every rule." Ian needed a target for his anger. "What is the matter with that coach? She knows Lucy is a good kid."

If I pick her up, that will mean at least a fifteen-minute conversation with the coach. By the time I get home, it will be dinner time. Then homework time. I won't get my hour-and-a-half study time before dinner. And I have class tomorrow night.

"Why can't you pick her up, Helsi? I really need to hit the books before dinner." Wilma walked through, pretending not to notice Ian still on the phone. He knew it was time to go. "Oh all right. I'll go now to get her. Which door do I go in?"

"Boiler-room door," Helsi's icy voice retorted. "And Ian, we really need to get a cellular phone."

The dial tone rang in his ear.

"Dad, do you know what amphibians are?" Dylan called from the back seat. "They can live on land and on water, too. Frogs are amphibians. So are salamanders." He rocked his small body as if to make a point.

"Dylan, you're interrupting us." *How does he know all that science?* "I just asked your sister a question." He glanced back at Lucy. "Are you ready to tell me now, Lucy? What were you and Deidre thinking, carrying on like that? Disrespecting Miss Becker."

Lucy stared straight ahead through the windshield.

Dylan looked over at her cautiously. "Dad, amphibians start out in the water. As tadpoles. Remember those tadpoles we brought home from scout camp? A whole jarful!" He looked from Lucy to his father and back again. "Only they didn't make it."

"I know, Dylan. We'll talk about amphibians at home." Ian said, despising his detached voice. "Right now I need answers from Lucy." *No wonder Dylan is babbling on like that. He can't stand the tension in this car. I can't stand it either. But I want to know why my daughter, A-student and holder of good-citizenship certificates for every year she's been in school, suddenly turns into a disruptive kid. In volleyball practice of all places!*

"We'll discuss this at home, Miss Lucy, with your mother," Ian said emphatically and checked the rear-view mirror for her reaction. She stared at her father's back with cold eyes, her face closed.

Ian pulled into the driveway and stopped the van sharply. The unfastening of seatbelts was the only sound heard as all three Bradfords climbed out. Dylan grasped his father's hand, struggling to keep hold of his book bag with his free one. Ian intertwined his large fingers reassuringly around his son's. Lucy quickly cut a wide path to the back door.

We will get to the bottom of this if it takes all night. He helped Dylan set the heavy bag on a small, red child's chair by the door. He gingerly placed his textbook on the counter, ignoring the urge to carry it to his desk in the bedroom and escape into it.

Helsi came downstairs. "How was the dentist visit, Dylan?" She opened the oven, releasing delicious smells of roasting meat. She closed the door and looked at him.

"It was okay." Dylan looked at his father.

"Where's Lucy?" She avoided Ian's eyes.

"In the bathroom," Ian answered, eyes seeking hers as he dried his hands on a paper towel.

"We have to talk about this, Ian." She finally looked at him.

"I know. I know. But let's do it after dinner. Give us all a chance to cool off." He took plates from the cupboard and began to set the table. "How soon do we eat?"

In the end, it seemed that Lucy had acted out at volleyball practice from frustration with changes at home. "You and Mom are always snapping at each other." Her face reddened. "You used to treat each other nice and help each other. I loved it when I caught you hugging. Now—." She threw up her hands.

Helsi tried to embrace her daughter. But Lucy shook her head wildly as if to shake off the tears filling her eyes. Helsi held fast and Lucy melted into her arms, sobbing.

"What are you afraid of, Honey?" Helsi stroked Lucy's long, straight hair.

"That you and Dad will get divorced." She stepped away from her mother. "We're all afraid of that. Ask Sean. Ask Robbie." Grimacing, she looked first at Ian, then at Helsi. She sat down hard on the sofa and covered her face with her hands.

After repeated reassurances that they had no intention of divorcing, Ian and Helsi enfolded each other and then pulled Lucy into a three-way hug.

"Neither of us is going anywhere, Lucy. You're stuck with us. For the rest of your life." Ian laughed, and Helsi joined him. Lucy began to laugh, sending such joy to her parents that their laughter grew loud and raucous.

"Quiet! We'll wake Rachel and Dylan!" Helsi ordered, forcing herself to stop.

They composed themselves and said their good-nights, Lucy promising to apologize properly to Miss Becker tomorrow.

"Think I'll study for an hour or so," Ian told Helsi as she pulled a bulging plastic bag from the trash bin under the sink. She knotted the ties and handed the bag to her husband. He ran it out to the garage while she placed a fresh bag in the bin.

Darn, I really wanted to cuddle on the couch with Ian, watch a movie or something, tonight of all nights; it's been so crazy. But I know he has class tomorrow, and he needs to study.

Ian returned. "Go ahead and study at your desk, Ian. I'll stay out here and watch a little television." Helsi's warm voice belied her disappointment. She ignored the tiny knot of resentment forming in her stomach.

"Thanks, Babe." Ian smiled at her. "But we do need to talk soon about Dylan. He's unhappy at that school." He stretched his arms above his head and groaned. "And I didn't like the looks of the other kids either. We should talk to Dr. Fleming."

Helsi nodded and flipped through the TV guide. *The last thing I need right now is another problem to think about. What I really need is an emotional movie, one of those slit-your-wrist stories on the Women's Channel to get lost in.* She picked up the remote and began surfing.

"Are you quite sure you want to disrupt Dylan again?" Hope sat down after checking the Special Services Roster. "The intervention specialist does have space for him, and federal law allows us a little flexibility in the way we serve him, if it is in his best interest."

"How much time would he spend with the intervention teacher, Dr. Fleming?" Helsi asked. "Would she be his homeroom teacher?"

Hope smiled at her. "She would not be his homeroom teacher, but she would be the one grading him in the subjects in which he qualifies for service." She looked at Ian.

"That's everything, isn't it? Dylan qualifies for help with everything." Ian ran his eyes down the Intervention Plan on the table. "Reading, spelling, writing, language, math." He looked up. "What else is there?"

Hope explained the concept of reading in the content areas; in this case, social studies and science. The homeroom teacher would be teaching those subjects and would be expected to adjust assignments for Dylan to align with his emerging reading comprehension skills, as supported by the intervention teacher. He would also have music, art, physical education with his homeroom class.

"What I want to know is." Ian touched Hope's wrist lightly, "I don't mean to revert to my old bull-headed ways of dealing with the school, Dr. Fleming." She laughed as did both Bradfords. "But why didn't we do this in the first place? Instead of uprooting him and all? Is that a fair question?"

"That is, indeed, a fair question, Ian. Mr. Bradford.

"Please, call me Ian. You've been working with us on Bradford kids for how long?" The three of them laughed warmly.

"Ian, many children who are developmentally delayed, as is Dylan, achieve better in classrooms of children just like them. The team thought that might be the case with your son. The security of the self-contained, special-education classroom with like classmates, few students, and a teacher's aide keeps those children focused. The opportunity for more one-on-one attention from the teacher and the aide provides the repetition they need to learn." Hope stretched her shoulders and smiled at Mrs. Bradford.

"Helsi, you know what I'm saying, don't you?"

"Of course, Hope." She smiled. "It makes perfect sense."

All agreed that Dylan would return to Poore Pond classes the following Monday. He would be in Mrs. Cooper's first-grade class with intervention services from the new specialist, Mrs. Pruett.

Helsi pulled into the driveway just as the Poore Pond bus rambled up the street. She waited near the curb and thought of Dylan. Next week he would be riding this bus with his sister and brother.

Robbie and Rachel got off last. Robbie's shirttail hung to his knees, and Rachel had lost her hair ribbons.

"Are those ice cream sandwiches all gone, Mom?" Robbie asked in a desperate voice. "I'm boiling and starving." He fanned the stiff collar of his new plaid shirt. She patted his head.

"There are a few left, Son. Go ahead and get one. But change your clothes first." She followed him toward the back door.

"Mom, Mom." Rachel tugged at Helsi's jacket. She kissed her daughter's hair. "Mrs. Armstrong gave me a job today, Mom." Chin uplifted, her eyes searched her mother's face.

"Did she now?" Helsi asked, overdoing her enthusiasm. What sort of job?" She looked directly into Rachel's eyes.

"Line leader. I lead the girls' line." She beamed with pride.

"That's a big job, isn't it?" Helsi asked. "You have to set a good example, don't you?" She held the door open while Rachel dragged her book bag over the threshold. "Well, I am sure you will have other turns to practice." Helsi checked the oven controls to see if the automatic setting had worked. She opened the door slightly and saw the lasagna beginning to bubble.

"No, no. I get to be line leader for a whole week. Every job is for a whole week." She began digging furiously in her book bag. Out came a hand-colored, laminated rectangle that bore the words LINE LEADER next to a small drawing of a girl's profile. She smoothed it with her hands and showed Helsi the velcro backing. "I have to take good care of this badge. It has to last." Helsi smiled at her daughter.

"Did Robbie get the only ice cream left?" Rachel whined as she opened the bottom freezer and happily pulled out a chocolate ice cream sandwich. Taking a napkin from the holder on the counter, she announced, "I'm going to eat this while I watch my show," and joined Robbie on the living-room floor.

The hissing of air brakes sounded, and Helsi rushed outside to watch Dylan disembark the Center bus. He walked the mandatory bus length from the tires and then ran to her. She took his hand and waved at the driver and aide. Dylan did not look at the bus but slumped toward the house without a word, pulling his mother with him.

I will tell him soon that he's going back to Poore Pond. I just do not know if it's the right thing for him. Why didn't we give the new school more of a chance?

"How was your day, Dylan?" She smiled brightly at him.

"I don't want to talk about school, Mom. I want a snack."

"Later then." They went inside.

CHAPTER FOUR—HOPE

A cold rain fell against the window, drawing Hope's eyes from her word processing task. She rose and gazed at the grey courtyard. Lifeless flower stalks brushed puddled cement walks in a sudden fury of November-like wind. She shivered and hugged her shoulders.

This weather. It's not even October yet. We certainly don't want to drive to Rosedale in this. Not on those winding, two-lane roads.

She looked at the calendar. Day after tomorrow.

Her eyes returned to the September page and widened with realization that school had been in session a month already.

She felt grateful that George had agreed to accompany her to Rosedale this weekend to inter Frances' ashes at their parents' gravesite. Belva Carmichael had decided to go with them although she had known Frances only the last few weeks of her life.

Belva had found instant rapport with her friend's sister and enjoyed her wry sense of humor. Frances assumed a matter of factness about her encroaching death. "Stepping up to the turnstile," she had called it. "It's the only time I've managed to move quickly to the head of the line—any line," she had said with the inflection and timing of a professional comic. All three had laughed, Frances the heartiest. Hope found their behavior eerie.

Though more interested in fashion and appearance than Frances was, Belva did share her attraction to natural elements, a sort of earthiness that Hope disdained. They both liked hiking and nature walks, could spend hours on the banks of a river or pond, soaking in the sounds of small animals, thrilling at occasional sightings of the creatures. Hope had to have with her, a good book to read if she were to tolerate more than a few minutes in such a setting.

She almost envied them their affinity for nature. While she found a certain comfort in the outdoors, she could take only small doses when she had need for a brief respite during times of particular stress.

Belva was a godsend those last days, agreeing to meet Hope and Frances at the arboretum where they would spread blankets and soak in the green countryside. Hope would soon tire of the wind in her hair and all the talk of wild creatures and their habits, conversation to which she could barely relate. Belva would nod approval when Hope opted to go to the car where she would tune the radio to soft classical music and read the novel she had knowingly brought along. Those times made her feel indebted to Belva and a little jealous of the fact that her friend had more in common with her sister than she ever had.

Guilt was part of her feelings, too. Very aware that she would have had no choice but to stay with Frances and indulge her need for these small retreats if Belva had not come along, Hope never arranged to bring Frances on her own.

A loud thunderclap accompanied by a quick spark of lightning interrupted her thoughts, and she quickly stepped away from the window. The lights flickered briefly, sending Hope to the outer office.

Corinne looked skeptically at fifth grader, Emmylou Parks, whose thin elbows leaned on the counter facing the secretary. Corinne looked toward Hope, eyes serious. She looked back at the girl, then again at Hope.

"Dr. Fleming, Emmylou has a request. A going-home change. But she has no note from a parent."

"Have you phoned Mrs. Parks?"

"Not yet." Corinne narrowed her eyes and looked cautiously at the girl. "Emmylou tells me their home phone number has been changed to unlisted, and she is not allowed to give it out." She looked at Hope, her face signaling suspicion.

"What about her parents' work numbers? Have you tried those?" Hope turned to smile at Emmylou, who did not smile back.

"Well, according to Miss Emmylou, her father is in Chicago on business; and her mother does not work on Thursdays."

"What is the change, Emmylou?" Hope asked kindly.

"Oh, just that someone else is picking me up today." The child did not look at her principal.

"And who is that, Emmylou?" Hope moved closer to the girl while Corinne wrote hurriedly on a square of paper.

"My uncle, my Uncle Kurt. He's picking me up since Dad is out of town and Mom's working late. He's picking me up and taking me to soccer practice. So I don't have to miss it. That's all. Not early release or anything. Just at regular dismissal." Her eyes riveted to the floor, her tense body belied the casualness in her voice.

Hope stared at the girl. *I thought she just said her mother does not work on Thursdays.*

The silence was deafening.

"I'll just go out when my bus is called and meet him—meet Uncle Kurt—in the parking lot." She looked toward the door.

"Let's go into my office, Emmylou, and sort this out." Hope gave a gentle push to the girl's back.

"Here's an important message for you, Dr. Fleming," Corinne said, quickly rising and handing her a folded note. "You had better read it now; you need to take care of it right away."

Hope's eyes met hers in utter understanding. Corinne handed her the fifth-grade records binder. "You may need this."

Hope took a chair at the round table, opposite Emmylou and unfolded the small square of paper to read Corinne's neat handwriting:

> **Emmylou changed her story to me a few times. First she said her neighbor, Bob, was picking her up. Then she changed it to Uncle Kurt. Mr. Mathews' note is attached. He fears she will just run out when we start calling bus numbers, she seems so focused on the end of the school day. Has not had her mind on her work at all, and you know she is usually a solid, average student.**

Hope flipped the stapled paper and recognized Boris' bold hand. He requested that if Emmylou does go home on the bus, the principal escort her to it. The girl had given him a long, unclear explanation. She refolded the note and tucked it into her blazer pocket.

"All right, Emmylou, let's see how I may help you." She moved her chair next to the child and looked into her face. Emmylou dropped her chin and scrubbed her hands.

"Let's call Mom to verify this so you don't miss your bus." She glanced at the wall clock.

In the end, Mrs. Parks, reached at the number on record, returned Hope's call in a matter of minutes. She did, indeed, expect Emmylou to come home on the bus.

"She does have soccer practice but not until 6:00 o'clock. We take her after supper." She shared Hope's concern for the child's motives and agreed to pick her up in the office.

A sullen Emmylou left school with her mother, who promised to get back to Hope with any explanation she could glean from the child.

She and Corinne watched them walk to the parking lot.

"Did you see that article in the Sunday paper, Dr.Fleming, about sexual predators on the internet?"

"I'm still working my way through the Sunday paper, Corinne. I saw the byline, but I did not read the article." She looked at Corinne's open face and took a quick breath. "You don't think—." A sense of dread came over her. She turned toward her office.

"It's just that Emmylou is nearly the same age as some of the victims in the article. She's maturing physically, too." Corinne blushed slightly. "And those predators can be brazen." Corinne's eyes widened. "Picking children up from school or on the way home from school was not unusual."

She sat down heavily in her desk chair and began sorting papers. "I'm probably jumping to conclusions. Emmylou has good parents."

Corinne's head swung sharply toward Hope. Hope lingered at her office door, her face expectant. "But so did some of the victims in the paper. One thirteen-year-old met a man using the name Monty, in a chat-room called barelylegalfemales. Can you imagine that?"

"We've made such a point of warning our kids about all that. Why do you suppose they take chances anyway?" Hope asked, collecting envelopes from the inbox outside her door.

"Well, it turned out one day that a detective went to that chat-room, impersonating a 13-year-old. He was out to catch predators trying to lure young girls. That's how they're caught." She handed Hope a reference-letter draft.

"Entrapped, really." Hope laughed and took the letter. "What a good strategy." Corinne laughed with her.

"Maybe you could get a detective to come in and talk to our kids, Hope. One that works on cases like that."

"Your point is well taken, Corinne. I'm going to look into it." She took the pink message note the secretary handed her. George wanted her to return his call.

George told his mother that Theodore had asked to have a meeting regarding board members for the new foundation, and he had set it tentatively for tonight after dinner at Hope's Canterbury Road house.

"Why not meet before dinner, about 4:30, George?" Hope asked, thinking she could manipulate a rare meal with her son. He worked such long hours at PolyFlem that she seldom saw him these days. And it was always difficult to schedule him for foundation meetings with Theodore.

"No, no I can't come that early." George said with a trace of impatience. "Dad's got me working late with him on this big Korean order we just landed. We'll eat while we work. You know how he is. Nothing is negotiable." He coughed and cleared his throat.

A chill pierced Hope's heart. Ill thoughts of Michael floated vaguely through her mind.

"Actually, I don't mind it. I know that's how businesses succeed. And I enjoy working with Dad. We make a good team. He is so smart." George chuckled convincingly.

Hope agreed to expect George around 7:30 though Theodore planned to arrive at 7:00.

She replaced the receiver, congratulating herself for not reacting to George's defense of his father. *No racing pulse, no heat in my chest, just a small spark of admiration for George's optimism.*

Corinne buzzed Hope's intercom. "Boris is waiting to see you, Dr. Fleming," she said in elegant voice.

Hope opened the door, and an excited Boris entered. They shook hands and sat in opposite chairs at the small table. He spread on the tabletop, a stack of envelopes addressed in children's manuscript, explaining that they were the first letters to his students from children he had worked with all summer at an orphanage in Mexico.

The students had become pen pals, both groups showing off their written-language skills for extra credit in composition.

Boris and his Mexican counterpart had organized the project, beginning with child-to-child email correspondence and growing to letter writing. The two teachers had led their classes through comparative discussions of the uses and structure of both forms of communication.

The culminating activity would be a conference telephone call, another form to be included in the study.

Boris' forehead gleamed with perspiration as he stood to punctuate his words with expansive hand gestures.

Hope, dazzled by the success and creativity of the project, exclaimed, "Congratulations, Boris. The project in implementation has so much more life than I gleaned from your outline." She smiled sincerely. "You have really outdone yourselves, you and Mr. Gloria, is it?"

"Mr. Patri. Nino Patri." Boris smiled. "Thank you, Hope. I knew you'd like it."

Second-grade teacher, Katrina Davis, slipped into the office as Boris left. "I have just a quick question, Hope—well actually a request."

Hope stood and approached the pleasant, wholesomely attractive teacher. "What sort of request, Katrina?"

"Artie Omark wants to help with daily announcements tomorrow; he's got a new necktie. And you know how much he likes to feel important." She chuckled.

"Of course I do." Hope laughed. "How he loves wearing a tie. Do you have an announcement in mind?"

"Why can't he tell everyone about the new school sign you ordered? Student Council kids are not part of that, are they?" Katrina dropped her bulging canvas bag to the floor.

"That's a good idea. Send him down at first bell." She rummaged in a file folder and handed the teacher a color brochure.

"Let Artie look through this and work up a description of the sign. He won't be stepping on any other group's toes."

"That will be right up his alley: first with the scoop." Katrina's smiling eyes turned serious. "Do you have word on his grandmother? Is she still in the hospital?"

"She's home now, Katrina. Mr. Omark stopped in and told me. She was given a new M.S. drug that's supposed to help her regain strength in her limbs."

"Those grandparents are amazing, raising their grandchild, running that mail-order business out of their tiny apartment, and dealing with Mrs. Omark's disease." Katrina lifted her bag and stepped away.

"Well, most of it falls on the grandfather; his wife's in a wheelchair. Multiple sclerosis can be such an up-and-down disease." Hope opened the glass door for the teacher and waved goodbye.

The enticing smell of sausage croissants filled the car as Hope drove home with George's favorite from the French Bakery. He will probably not have had a proper dinner when he gets here. He can munch on these and the leftover fried peppers in the refrigerator.

She checked her watch. It was already six o'clock. She just had time to eat and change into lounge clothes before Theodore arrived.

Hope hurried to answer the doorbell, adjusting the zipper on her blue cashmere sweater as she walked. Theodore's speckled-gray hair filled the peephole until he turned. When she saw him, her breath caught briefly, surprising her. She inhaled deeply and opened the door.

"Well, Theodore, hello," she said, an unstoppable smile widening at him.

"Hi, Hope," he smiled back. "Am I late? Is George here yet?" Hope nodded amicably, and he stepped inside.

"May I take your jacket?" she asked though doubtful he would remove the camel hair blazer she could not help but admire.

"No. No, thanks. I'll leave it on. I'm wearing a ratty old sweater under it." They both laughed. "I'm sure you don't want to look at that all evening,"

"Wearing such a beautiful camel-hair jacket," she motioned toward the study, "it does not matter what you wear under it. It's impossible to look anything but sensational."

She gestured toward a chair at the square library table where several folders lay in a neat stack. They sat opposite each other and smiled for a silent moment.

"I hope you don't mind meeting here, Hope. I know it was presumptuous of me to suggest it, but I just did not want to go back to the office. Once I do, I can never get out again." He pushed back from the table and placed one ankle on his firm thigh. "You must have that problem, too, all those teachers and parents needing to see you." His eyes implored her to agree.

"Oh gosh yes," Hope said. "But I'm my own worst enemy. I try to be always accessible, and sometimes it is just not possible. My supervisor, Brian, says to simply walk out the door when you need to. If you're due at a meeting, you're due. Just go."

"Do you think we will find board members who are as dedicated as you are, Hope?" He pulled a black, zippered organizer from his briefcase.

Hope opened the top folder on her pile. She glanced at the mantel clock and said, "George will be along in a few minutes. He's coming straight from work." She looked down at her list of questions then at Theodore. "Would you like a cold drink, Theodore, or a hot one?"

"Maybe I'll have one later. Let's go over a few points before George comes. I'm confused about the lines of authority here. Is George the founder, the on-the-record founder? Or are you both co-founders?" He met Hope's penetrating gaze head on. "You understand, I need to be clear about this before George gets here. It affects all decisions, and frankly, eliminates a lot of ego problems if everyone knows and accepts the hierarchy."

Hope knew that George would not care who was on record as the founder, so long as help for the homeless became available. But it was important to her that he take ownership early on. She did not want to dedicate her life to this foundation; it was his dream, after all. But neither was she ready to leave important operational plans to him. He saw the homeless through idealistic eyes and was too inexperienced to know the pitfalls. If left on his own, he would surely fail to build in protections for himself and the fund. Hope could see him insisting on random cash handouts to any tragic-talking vagrant who asked.

"I'm sensing that you feel a problem with George's being sole founder. Is that right?" A knot of resentment began in her stomach. Though she did not think George should be sole founder, Theodore had no right to be so biased. He hardly knew George.

"Of course, it's not up to me. It's your decision, yours and George's. But it could be awkward working this out in his presence."

What is he insinuating about George? I'm not sure I like this man. "I understand." She squared her shoulders and looked at him. "Is it feasible to designate George as sole founder with stipulation that I have input on key decisions?" She felt her mouth tightening and forced a thin smile, the best she could manage.

Theodore frowned. He shifted in his chair. "But, Hope," thrusting his face near hers, "you told me you wanted only minimal involvement. That you were too busy with your work at Poore Pond. You cannot have it both ways." He leaned back.

The front door opened noisily and both their heads swiveled toward the foyer. They listened silently to George's heavy footsteps echoing through the house.

"Hi Mom, hi Theo." He stood in the doorway in a rumpled sweatshirt and thick-toed boots, smiling widely.

The three of them struggled with the mission statement. George wanted it to simply say: to help the homeless have a better life. "That's really the crux of it," he said through oily lips as he forked fried peppers into his mouth.

Hope, though she had no experience with private foundations, knew the statement was too broad, not to mention the fact that it should read: ... to have better lives. She thought of the school district's mission statement, a bit lofty but clear.

She remembered leading the parents in revising their group's mission statement for Poore Pond School. They had no difficulty making it literal and clear.

The parent group had moved readily from an abstract, ...to enrich the education of all Poore Pond children..., to more specific language. With the smallest bit of guidance, they edited and re-edited their statement, finally agreeing upon: ...to fund and implement, with approval of school officials, extra-curricular activities and the purchase of supplemental classroom programs and materials.

Theodore patiently explained that the mission statement must be, not only clearly stated, but also narrow enough to prevent applicants from sandbagging the board with requests the foundation could not fund.

"Homeless persons need everything," he said with kind eyes. "But you can't fix all their problems for them. The foundation cannot change them from unwashed, unfocused, unproductive, mentally ill vagrants into squeaky clean, clear-minded, middle-class contributors just by throwing money their way."

"They may all be unwashed derelicts; but they are not all unfocused, unproductive, and mentally ill." George said passionately, missing the point. He bit off a piece of sausage croissant with a vengeance.

What have I gotten us into? How are we going to do this? Hope felt tired and brain dead.

"Who wants a cup of tea?" She rose and put the kettle on, then took three red-patterned cups and saucers from the glass-door cupboard. Trying not to listen to Theodore and George's debate, she arranged the tea tray. She ran hot tap water into a white ironstone teapot and placed small spoons, caramel crystal sugar, and shortbread cookies on the tray.

She filled a small white creamer with milk and heated it in the microwave oven.

Theodore left the table and walked tensely to the window. George dug through a frayed envelope full of newsprint, pulling out a creased copy of *The Homeless Grapevine,* which he thrust at Theodore.

The kettle whistled. Hope watched it boil for another minute then emptied the water in the teapot into the sink. She dropped the knotted bundle of teabags into the preheated pot and lifted the kettle, refilling the pot with fresh boiling water.

The weary group managed to close the issue with a sketchy version of a tentative mission statement. They agreed that each of them would put thought into fleshing it out according to their own ideas. They would meet again Thursday evening, same time, same place, and share their draft statements.

To help put tension from that issue behind them, they brainstormed a list of possible board members then set out composing an introductory paragraph to pitch when recruiting them. George outdid himself with an appeal for potential board members to "be among the first Samaritans to answer the call to address, with this solid funding, the most despicable and rapidly spreading social malfunction of the age." He finished with a boyish, self-satisfied smile in the manner of a candidate for political office.

Theodore added the magnanimous premise repeated by sociologists, theologians, and authors of spiritual works, "Service to others is the highest form of human development." The dignity in his voice and bearing mesmerized Hope and George for a moment.

Hope wanted heavy emphasis on the damage done to innocent children. Riveting her eyes on first George, then Theo, as if imploring them to share her passion, she continued "They could not help but be permanently scarred by the experience of living on the streets, out of cars, in and out of temporary shelters. Their young psyches are so assaulted by trying to cope with the never-ending series of changing settings, each more impersonal than the last, that their chances of developing trust and a healthy sense of self are forever lost." She stopped for breath.

"In fact, perhaps this foundation should assist only homeless families," she suggested, her voice ringing with conviction.

A white-faced George cajoled, "But Mother, there are already so many county and church-sponsored programs for homeless families. Ours would end up being just a carbon copy of those."

She knew he was right. She had a referral list of such agencies in her office. In truth, she preferred not to see children in their shelter; it would be too heart-wrenching.

He began pushing papers into his frayed envelope. "Let's sleep on it. We'll be fresh for the next go-round." He went to Hope and kissed her on the cheek.

"You are right, George." Theo said. "We need to give ourselves space. The work of this foundation is too important for us to structure it on anything less than clear minds and open hearts." He rose and zipped his organizer, stuffing it into a black leather briefcase.

Looking squarely at Hope, he asked, "Do you see the good that comes from these discussions?" She studied his face. "The fact that we each have a different view of the needs of homeless souls will help us consider every aspect." He waved and caught up to George, patting him on the shoulder warmly.

Hope followed them and switched on the outside lamp. She hugged George's back and shook Theodore's hand. "You are quite right, Theo," she whispered. "These heated exchanges are part of the process, aren't they? But now I see why you wanted to air certain structural points before the meeting.

"See you Saturday morning, George. Early," she called after him. George waved over his shoulder as he climbed into a white van with the PolyFlem logo on the door.

Hope watched Theo race off in his black sports car, closed and locked the door, and switched off the outside lamp. Her head was swimming with thoughts of the countless needs of homeless families.

Not wanting to fill her heart with the sadness of Frances, she stifled thoughts of the trip to Rosedale.

Visions of EmmyLou at the computer floated through her mind.

I need positive thoughts tonight if I'm ever to relax and fall asleep. Her mind scrolled through the events of the day. *Boris and his Mexican orphans, what a wonderful program for building awareness of other cultures. And for keeping children interested.*

CHAPTER FIVE—RAY

Ray opened the door to Mr. Taylor's fifth grade. "Okay, the multi-purpose room is ready now. The floor is a little wet, but the fan is on. It will dry in no time." The teacher smiled and asked the group of twelve high-school students sharing desks of various children, to take their supplies down and set up for work.

"Thank you, Mr. Sellers. Class." He nodded amiably toward Ray.

"Thank you, Mr. Sellers. That was nice of you," a chorus of young voices chanted.

Ray smiled back at their happy faces and waved. He slid quickly to the hall. *Thank you, Hope, for buddying those high-school kids with Chuck Taylor's class. He keeps his students in line. Less work for me.*

Ray hurried to finish putting away the supplies he had unpacked before lunch. *If I can get the burned-out lights replaced in Room B-1 before the class comes back from its field trip, I won't have to use up my classroom-cleaning time after dismissal doing that.*

He loaded five one-gallon jugs of blueish disinfectant solution onto a cart along with thirty packs of coarse, brown paper towels and three cartons of quart-sized liquid-soap refills. Rolling down the hall, he headed for storage rooms in each wing.

"Hello, Mr. Sellers," two students chorused as they walked alongside Hope. Ray smiled and nodded.

"Do you need help with that, Mr. Sellers?" a tall, lanky boy in khaki cargo pants supported by monstrous athletic shoes, asked respectfully.

"Well, it just so happens," Ray looked at Hope.

"These boys are office helpers, Mr. Sellers." She smiled. "They donate part of their free-choice time to the office every Tuesday." She smiled at the boys, squirming with embarrassment.

"They are available if you need them, for the next oh, 20-to-30 minutes." Looking at them, she asked, "Are you interested, boys?"

"Yes," they replied fervently.

"I can use them, Dr. Fleming. I can use them." Ray asserted, noticing their strong bodies. *They could lift those big boxes of garbage bags with no trouble at all. There are fifty of them on the four wheeler.*

"Great. Mr. Sellers, this is Gerald," she indicated the tall boy, "and this is Marc," she gestured toward the shorter boy, muscular and sturdy with a broad face and thick, dark hair.

"They earn free-choice minutes by consistently turning in quality work, on time. Aren't they good role models?" Hope's face shone with pride.

Ray shook hands with each and wondered why he had not noticed the boys around Poore Pond before. He thought he knew all the kids.

After instructing Gerald and Marc in delivery of supplies on the cart, Ray rushed to Room B-1, carrying fluorescent tubes in two long boxes

"There you are, Ray." Hope came into Room B-1 and began talking to Ray's feet, planted halfway up the ladder.

"It's good you had jobs for Gerald and Marc. They are both transfer students from the new charter school that closed." She looked up at Ray, who urged her to stand back as he came down the ladder with a fragile fluorescent tube. He leaned it carefully against the doorway.

Hope held a new tube ready for him, so he ascended the ladder and reached down to take it. She waited silently while he guided it into the fitting.

Hope touched a ballast, propped against a chair, sending small beams of dust into the air. "Oh, you have not dusted these yet, have you, Ray?" She wiped her hands together and brushed off her skirt.

Ray sprayed the plastic ballast with cleaning solution and began wiping it, the clean cloth quickly filling with dark soil.

"Charter schools?" Ray looked at Hope, watching him work. "Are those the ones started by business people?"

"That's right." Hope pointed to a dirty spot Ray had missed on the ballast.

"They get the State money and claim they can do a better job than the public schools?" Ray turned the ballast, inspecting it.

"That's exactly right. They claim they can not only do a better job, but they can make a profit doing it. They're business minded."

"But this one closed. Did I read in the paper that it ran out of money? I rest my case." Ray laughed and balanced the long ballast as he climbed the ladder. Hope shifted her weight as if balancing for him.

"But some of the charter schools have been successful." Hope added. "They've run efficiently and stayed in the black financially. So apparently, they can succeed, given the right circumstances."

She walked toward the door as Ray descended the ladder.

"I'll go check on the boys before I do that other ballast," he said, following Hope.

"Let me know how they work out. We may do this again."

Hope headed for the office. She stopped and turned once more toward Ray, "We need to sit down and discuss your new hours, too, Ray, how they are working for you."

New hours? Working from 6:00 to 3:00 instead of 7:00 to 4:00 hasn't changed anything. I just end up working on my own time until 3:30 – 3:45. It's just as hard to clean classrooms before school as it is after. Well, not exactly. I can work without interruptions in the early morning. After school, that's another story.

Ray managed to leave school at 3:20, having cleaned Room B-1 nonstop. The teacher had planned ahead, and the students went straight from field-trip buses to dismissal. Only two children came back to the room to retrieve forgotten belongings.

Heather stood at the top of the outside staircase, waiting for Ray. He had offered to help her rip out the old carpeting in her apartment. She had lobbied landlord Tommy Draco for new carpeting; and he finally agreed on condition that she remove the old, which he admitted had been used carpeting when installed. "You look nice with that scarf tied over your hair, Heather. Like a little peasant wife." They laughed.

Ray followed her into the kitchen, crowded with furniture, and tried inconspicuously to sniff his armpits as he walked. He had not bothered to change his shirt after work since he would be doing a dusty job at Heather's. He would just have to keep his distance from her.

"Where's Jeremy?" Ray looked across the empty living room.

"I sent him to Latchkey today. So we could get this done without worrying about him."

The worn tacks pulled easily from the floor, and dust streams filled the air as Heather tugged at the heavy carpet. "I'll pick him up at six."

By 5:30 Heather and Ray had all the carpeting removed and tied into bundles, which Ray carried down the stairs to the rubbish shed. *I wish I could take her to pick up Jeremy and then out to eat. But I am so smelly and dirty.*

He suddenly remembered that he had promised his mother he would clean windows after work. She had spent three days cleaning them inside, doing a window at a time then resting before tackling the next. It was important to Caroline that the outside windows were cleaned before the insides became dirty again.

I wish Ma wouldn't push herself like that. It's not necessary. Doc wants her to be rested when she has her first treatment tomorrow.

Ray pulled into the driveway and waved at Caroline as she lolled on the porch swing. All thoughts of going straight to the shower vanished as he saw her waiting there, her face expectant and compelling. He would drag out the ladder and make those windows shine and then have his shower.

"Where's the small ladder, Ma?" Ray asked, coming around the house from the garage.

"Claire has it, Son. She's round back getting at the bedroom windows. Says she has time off from work so thought she'd come over and help us." Caroline smiled with pleasure.

"Where's her car? I didn't see it in the drive when I pulled in."

"Oh, she parked it in the garage, out of the sun." Caroline replied with nonchalance. *Why did she take off work to help clean over here? She knows I can manage. I'm a custodian for cripes' sake. Cleaning is what I do.*

"I'll take over now, Claire. You go sit down with Ma." Ray held the ladder firmly, waiting for his sister to descend. Claire kept polishing glass. "Geez, Claire. I'll do those. I promised Ma."

"Just let me finish this one, Ray. Then you can do all the rest." She wiped nonexistent smears fervently before climbing down.

"Why did you take off work? I told you I would finish these windows today." *Why does she get her kicks from showing me up? Always trying to make me look bad in Ma's eyes.*

"Take off work? I wish." Claire's voice dripped with sarcasm. "I've been laid off. No notice, no nothing." She brushed the hair from her eyes. "Just pink-slipped on the spot. About ten o'clock this morning."

Ray looked at his sister with compassionate eyes. "What was their reason?" He moved the ladder to the next window.

"Heck, they don't need a reason. But they told us—five people in my department were let go—the big D-word."

"D-word? What's that? Desperate?" Ray sneered.

"Downsizing, you fool. Downsizing." Claire spat the word.

"Is business that bad? I thought people were borrowing money again. The papers are full of talk about job growth and an economic upturn." Ray checked his pocket for the special chamois and started up the ladder.

"Humph!" Claire smirked. "That economic upturn is true. They just forgot to mention it's in India. My job has been outsourced to India. Indian computer techs are going to manage First Bank's records.

"That's bizarre. Where did you hear that?" Ray's voice trailed into a squeak as he stretched to reach the farthest point on the window.

"It's true. Freda brought in an article from the Wall Street Journal." Claire pulled a creased photocopy from her pocket and waved it at Ray. "Read this. Spells it all out. Indian workers will work for pennies on the dollar of what we earn. College graduates even. A lot of big companies are outsourcing. IBM is outsourcing." She used the word like a curse word.

"Does Ma know you're laid off? She thinks you took some sort of leave."

"No, I,—." She looked up at him through tired eyes. "I didn't think she should know. She'd just stew about it." Claire walked toward the front porch.

Ray moved to the fourth side of the house; two bedroom windows and a small bathroom window to go, and he would be finished. He could not wait to soak in a hot shower and get into clean clothes.

"I'll pick you up at 11:00, Ma." Ray could hear Claire's words from the porch. "That will give you plenty of time to get settled in for your twelve-noon treatment. Do you have anything good to read? A magazine or something? Dr. Crider said most people feel like reading or watching TV for the six hours."

I was going to take Ma. What's Claire doing?

"Ray wants to take me, Claire. He's already arranged to leave work. Said he'll get me started. Then you can spell him when you come." She struggled to take a deep breath. "Let's just leave it like that."

"But I'll be off anyway. I'll take you. Ray can stay at school."

He was both relieved and annoyed. Hope had planned a big assembly, speakers and everything, for Citizenship Day. He knew she needed him to help troubleshoot although she had not hesitated to approve his afternoon leave. But to stay at work and have Claire accompany their mother for this first-time treatment—drastic treatment at that—did not seem right.

Nevertheless, when Claire came to announce her plans, Ray muttered, "Okay. I'll come by there after school."

The assembly was a big hit with students and teachers. More parents than usual dropped in and stood at the back of the multi-purpose room. The keynote speaker, Get-It-Now-Gordon, a successful musician with a one-man band, entertained the kids with sing-alongs and a demonstration of types of musical instruments. He invited several children to play them on stage. Ray saw Jeremy wildly waving his hand to be chosen and not making it.

But when Gordon talked about his rule-breaking days of childhood and law-breaking adult days, he had the full attention of every person in the room. The audience was stone silent. At both assemblies, not one child had to be reprimanded and no teachers or parents socialized. Gordon described his days in detention centers, jails, and rehab houses with a touch of humor, but more so, the grim reality of incarceration. No one missed the point.

As he listened to Gordon's speech from the lobby where he polished floor-to-ceiling windows, Ray forgot his guilty feelings about not being at the hospital.

Cleaning up after the last assembly, he asked Hope what she thought about Gordon.

"He could not have been more appropriate, could he?" She smiled at Ray as she packed the cordless microphone into its cradled box. "The fact that he ignored the rules as a child really hit home with our kids. You could tell by the way they hung on his every word."

"He was perfect. Broke rules as a kid and kept right on doing it as a grownup." Ray laughed and coiled the speaker cord.

"We are fortunate to have the parent group pay his fee. They work so hard to raise their money. And he's a national figure; he does not come cheaply." Hope gathered extra programs from the table. "Perfect specimen for Citizenship Day, wasn't he?"

So much better than those super–successful types who talk about how they've always done the right thing, and that's why they are where they are today. "Sure was. I think most people are drawn to sinners and their stories. Why is that?"

Hope laughed heartily. She took a deep breath. "You need to leave for the hospital now, don't you, Ray?"

"Yes, but I'll wait until after dismissal. Want to make sure Gordon gets his van out ahead of the buses." Ray placed the speaker and lectern on the four-wheel cart. He folded the small table and loaded it before maneuvering down the hallway. Getting to the hospital was now in the forefront of his mind.

Claire helped Ray settle Caroline into bed after a prescribed meal of toast and tea. She snuggled gratefully into the blankets.

Ray started a pot of coffee and pulled a bag of cheese Danish from under the cake cover. He took out two mugs and the sugar dispenser, two spoons from the drawer.

Claire came in with a heavy sigh. "Coffee. That's just what I need. How'd you know that, Ray?" She smiled at him through closed lips.

"Try this cheese Danish, Claire. It's from that fancy new bakery on Trane Street. Best I ever had." He filled the coffee mugs and sat down at the table.

Claire joined him. She took a small, skeptical bite and washed it down with black coffee. "Oh yum," she said with delight. "But what were you doing on Trane Street? Don't tell me that's where you and Heather hang out." She slapped his arm.

"Heck no," Ray laughed. "The library-club kids brought them to me. They wanted to thank me for helping them mount a banner on sticks for the book fair." He took a large bite of Danish. He blew on his coffee and took a sip. "That's steaming hot! How did you gulp it down like that, Claire?"

"My mouth's been on fire since yesterday's news; I was so mad. Guess I didn't feel how hot it was."

"We put a huge, long banner next to the school sign outside, so no one could miss it." He spread his hands widely apart. "Those kids sure do work hard on that book fair. Make a ton of money, too, for Library Club."

Claire nodded before tiptoeing down the hall to check on Caroline. Ray listened to the quiet opening and closing of the bedroom door.

She returned and sat back down at the table. "You really get a kick out of working at that school, don't you?" she said in a low voice. "You love those kids and all that activity."

Ray looked thoughtful. "Yeah, I guess I do. They kind of grow on you." He chuckled.

"I envy you sometimes, Ray." His sister looked at him with serious eyes. "A job you enjoy. You have standing at that school. That must feel good."

Ray, detecting emotion in her voice, asked gently, "What are you going to do, Claire?" He brought the coffeepot from the counter.

"I don't know. Collect unemployment until I find another job, I guess." She held up her cup for a refill. "Trouble is, that won't even cover my rent and car payment, not to mention my consolidation-loan payment." She stirred the black coffee.

"You'll find another job, Claire. You always could find a job when you needed one." He cut another pastry in half and placed a piece on her plate. "Have you read the ads in the paper?"

"Yes and not a bank or savings-and-loan job in the whole classified."

"Then try something else."

"I won't make the money I was used to. I was a manager, Ray. If I go outside my field, I'm not worth snuff." She stirred her coffee fervently.

Ray, ready for pleasanter talk, stood. He smiled at his sister. "I'll see if Mom wants anything from the store. We're all out of lunchmeat. I need to get some."

Not hearing her brother, Claire blurted, "Well, I can always move back here if I have to. Until I get on my feet." She looked somberly at Ray. "I'm going now. Call me later and let me know how Mom's doing." She hurried out the kitchen door.

Ray listened to Claire's engine start and wondered how it would be to have her back in the house. A small knot formed in his stomach.

CHAPTER SIX—THE BRADFORDS

The warm autumn breeze billowed through the windows of the van, matching the exhilaration Ian felt. He had found tonight's class fascinating.

The first two sessions the instructor had droned on and on about the syllabus, her requirements for outside readings, and the importance of class participation, which counted one-third the grade for the course. She spent hours explaining various types of laboratory equipment and how it was to be used; she gave repetitive warnings about thoroughness, double checking procedures, and never delegating the checks to others. She emphasized all the work and rigor of the program.

While Ian had found it interesting, tedium set in after so much time spent explaining how the class would run.

But today the topic was Liability, and Ian listened with every fiber of his being. Although he was well versed in the liability of a paramedic, he had no idea how little he knew about the subject in regard to the role of physician's assistant. Apparently, maintaining an office to which patients come involves another long list of compliances with state regulations for sterility and cleanliness, disposal of wastes, record keeping, inspections, and on and on.

Anxious to get home and share his exuberance with Helsi, Ian drove too fast. *Was I supposed to stop at the store for something? I can't think of anything. Oh well, guess I'm so used to picking up things lately, it seems as if I ought to stop every time.*

"Hi Buddy!" Ian, pulling into the driveway, called to Robbie who was sitting on the step. Robbie ran to him, his green Conflict Manager's pinny flapping in the wind.

Ian climbed out of the van. "What are you doing up so late? And why are you wearing your uniform? Managing conflict at night now?" Laughing, he bent down toward the boy.

"Notice anything different, Dad?" Robbie beamed at his father while his fingers absent-mindedly stroked the new badge sewn onto the apron-like pinny. The shiny embroidery stood out from last year's badge, which was now dull from wear.

"Wow! A new badge." He stroked it carefully. "That's right, you're a second-year Poore Pond Conflict Manager now." He knelt down and looked admiringly at the boy.

Robbie laughed. "Hey Dad, remember how you didn't want me to join last year? You said I'd be miserable." He looked deeply into his father's eyes.

Ian dropped his chin and stood. "Yes, well, I was wrong, Robbie." He looked at his watch. "You need to get to bed, Son. It's nearly nine thirty." He walked toward the house.

"You were really wrong, Dad. Mrs. Sutton said she's glad I stayed in this year because I'm the most responsible CM on the squad." He ran to keep pace with his father's long legs. "She calls us CMs now. That's cool, isn't it, Dad? CMs. You could be a PM, couldn't you? PM for paramedic?" They entered the quiet house.

Why isn't Helsi here to greet me? Why is Robbie up alone? He looked in the laundry room and the living room then back to the kitchen. "Where's your mother, Robbie?"

"She's taking a hot bath. She told me I could wait for you in her place." He began to yawn.

"You need to get to bed, Son. Can you get that thing off by yourself?" He began unbuckling the left side of the pinny while Robbie worked on the right side.

"I can do it, Dad; I've done it a hundred times," he said proudly, squirming out of his father's reach.

Ian helped ease it over the bulky pajama top and his large head. "Go on to bed; I'll come tuck you in." His eyes followed Robbie up the stairs. He listened for sounds from the bathroom at the top of the stairs and thought he heard faint strains of music.

"Come on, Dad."

"In a minute, Son." He walked to the kitchen and opened the freezer. Taking a bran muffin from a square plastic container, he put it on a paper plate which he placed in the microwave. He touched the auto-defrost button and removed the butter dish from the refrigerator.

He climbed the stairs and knocked on the bathroom door. "Hon?" *There is music playing in there. What the heck is she doing?* "Helsi?" He raised his voice. "Helsi!"

"Yes." He could barely hear her.

"I'm home, Hon. Are you coming out soon?"

"In a little while, Ian."

He went down the hall to Robbie's room where Dylan slept soundly in the opposite twin bed, and shuffled quietly across the carpet. Robbie lay under the covers, leaning on his elbow, waiting. Ian patted his arm gently down and tucked the blankets under his chin. He switched off the lamp and kissed his son's forehead.

"Good-night Robbie," he whispered. Robbie smiled up at him, his white teeth gleaming in the dark. "Keep up the good work, Son."

Ian walked past the closed, silent bathroom feeling tense and unsure. He knocked rhythmically on the door and called, "See you downstairs, Hon."

There was no response, but he could hear water running in the tub.

Ian rolled over and looked at the clock. It was only 5:45, and Helsi was already out of bed. *She always gets up at six thirty. What is going on with her?*

He pulled on a tee-shirt and went downstairs, flannel lounge pants slipping at their loose waist. He could hear Helsi setting the table.

Ian caught her from behind as she stood at the open refrigerator. She smelled of the lilac body lotion she always used. Hugging her waist, he kissed her hair. "Did you even come to bed last night? I fell asleep alone and woke up alone, Helsi. I didn't like that."

Helsi shrugged him off and carried a jug of milk to the counter without looking at him.

He tried again. "Was that music coming from the bathroom last night? What did you do, hire Usher to serenade you in your bath?" He laughed.

"As a matter of fact, that was Usher you heard. I borrowed Sean's CD player and had a long, luxurious soak. I needed it; I needed something uplifting." She looked toward him, not at him.

Ian did not miss the tension in her voice. *What the heck's bothering her?* He filled a mug with coffee and opened the refrigerator.

"Ian, the milk is in the pitcher on the table. You saw me carrying it."

What's this all about? She's cold as a fish.

He sat at the table with his coffee and waited for her to join him. She busied herself rearranging cereal boxes in the cupboard. The sight of her sweet figure in baggy flannel pajamas clutched his heart.

"Come have coffee with me, Hon. It's early. The kids won't be up for another hour. Helsi without turning toward him, mumbled something about needing to do the cupboard.

Ian, trying to think of an appropriate glib remark, noticed on the table, a folded card with a child's drawing of a bundle of balloons. To Mom, written unevenly in black-crayon letters, caught his attention. He opened the fold and found written in the same childish scrawl: I hop yur aniverzry is nice.

Ian pounded his forehead with his palm. So that's it. Yesterday was our anniversary and I didn't do a darn thing about it.

He rushed to his wife, took her reluctant hand, and led her to the sofa where he sat down, pulling her onto his lap. His hand on the back of her head, he guided her lips to his and kissed her long and hard.

"Happy anniversary, Girl of My Dreams," he said squeezing her too tightly.

"My anniversary was yesterday," she said cooly, her eyes a bit coquettish.

"So was mine," he laughed. "I am so sorry, Helsi. I had every intention of bringing you flowers last night. But I got so caught up in that class, my pea brain couldn't handle anything else."

"Me thinks that means thee did not remember until the very day."

Ian laughed at her olde English accent.

"Could that be true?" A smile played at her lips.

"Guilty as charged." Ian put his forehead to hers.

"You are herebyeth sentenced to another year of bondage, all privileges rescinded." Helsi lifted his arm from her lap and rose. He stood after her and took both her hands in his.

"Helsi," his eyes transfixed hers. I love you more than anything. I love our family. I love our home, the way you make it a home. Thank you for another year of rapture. Happy anniversary, Hon." He kissed her smartly. She kissed him back.

"There's just one more thing." She gave him a sly look. When am I getting my flowers?"

"Did we get more bananas, Mom?" They turned to see Dylan padding in with sleepy eyes. Rachel slipped in behind him

"I'm off to the shower, Family." Ian swept toward the stairs, swatting his wife's derriere on the way.

Before leaving for work, he made a date with his wife to have early dinner at The Bistro, the area's one upscale restaurant.

"Lucy is old enough to babysit now," he said. They both agreed that since Sean would be away at practice so would not be there to taunt his sister, this would be a good test run for Lucy, who had been asking to be left in charge. They would be home early as well.

"Get a little dolled up, Helsi," Ian said, hugging her goodbye. "I'll make a reservation." She smiled at him, waiting to wave at the door as he drove away.

I'll borrow the money from my book fund for next term.

Helsi deserves a special night. Get her flowers, too. Maybe chocolates. It's the end of the month; there should be a chance for overtime when we do equipment inspections again.

Excited about the special evening and happily recalling the joy of last night's class, he tuned loud music on the radio and drove gratefully to work.

Few diners were in the restaurant when the hostess seated them, so they were given Ian's choice of table away from the kitchen and near the fireplace. A waiter approached and lit candles flanking a small bowl of red baby carnations on the snowy white tablecloth.

Ian ordered a decanter of merlot and sat back in his chair. He looked at his wife, appreciating how lovely she looked. She wore the closely fitting, black dress she always wore for their rare special occasions; and she had pinned up the sides of her hair in a very enticing way. The v-neck of the black dress framing her creamy white skin emphasized her chiseled features. Ian drank in her beauty and realized how precious she was to him.

Helsi watched him ceremoniously sample the wine as the waiter graciously stood by. My Ian is a handsome man. He looks so right in suit and tie.

How many times have I ironed that shirt? Seeing the collar caress his neck, she felt very close to him.

We must hold tightly to what we have. Why was I cold to him last night? He works so hard. He's a good man. She ignored a small wave of unidentifiable fear darkening her heart.

"Cheers," Ian offered, holding his wine goblet toward her.

"Happy anniversary, Hon."

She lifted hers to his and echoed, "Cheers," returning his smile. "Happy anniversary to you, Ian; and thank you for this expensive treat. It's great to have a real date with my husband." She lowered the glass to her lips and enjoyed the smooth, warming drink.

They worked away at their juicy steaks and chatted about how tender and delicious they tasted. They reassured each other that leaving Lucy to babysit Robbie, Dylan, and Rachel had been a good decision.

Helsi heard soft background music and looked around for its source. Her eyes lit on a small piano tucked into a corner. The white-haired, tuxedoed man manipulating the keys cut a slight figure on the bench. She estimated his age to be late seventies and wondered if he had to depend on the income from this job. She felt sad to think that might be the case.

Helsi leaned forward and whispered, "Ian, how old do you think the pianist is?"

Ian looked toward the music, his eyes lingering long enough to make her uncomfortable.

"Don't stare, Hon."

"Oh, sixty, seventy-something. Why?" Ian asked loudly.

Whispering even more softly, Helsi said, "I just think it's sad that a man his age has to be out here working. And at night yet." She glanced his way again and then back to her husband.

"The guy probably enjoys it. It's better than lying on the couch, watching TV. Besides, he's a musician. Musicians usually love their music. It's their lifeblood. And they work at night."

He refilled their glasses, took a last bite of dinner, and drank heartily of the wine. He looked into his wife's eyes.

"I can understand how a man's work can get into his blood, especially if he's doing what he most wants to do." Ian looked across the dining room. He swallowed and cleared his throat.

"I'm enjoying this class so much I can't get enough of it. That instructor is so good. She really knows her stuff." His eyes searched Helsi's; but she kept her head down, toying with a last bit of baked potato. "She makes you want to learn everything about the subject." Helsi raised her eyes without lifting her chin.

"That kind of learning can get into your blood," he continued.

Helsi saw that Ian's eyes were shining and felt happy for him. She felt resentment, too. *He wants me to be as excited as he is about this. Well, I'm the one stuck picking up the slack with the kids and the house. While he studies two hours every night and goes to class twice a week. How about me? What's my lifeblood?*

She forced herself to smile into his eyes and prayed that he did not sense her mixed feelings. "You've had paramedicine in your blood ever since I first met you, Ian Bradford." She reached for his hand. "So don't give the teacher all the credit. She is preaching to the choir with you. Lucky her."

They laughed together, Helsi giving it all she had.

"How about dessert, Hon? We'll ask to see the dessert tray."

Fearful of the size of the dinner check, she did not want to increase it. She wondered how he was managing to pay for this night.

"Let's go home and have coffee and those heavenly chocolates you brought. We don't want a whole rich dessert." She saw relief in Ian's eyes.

"Guess we should get home to the kids." He signaled the waiter.

Every light in the house was on when they pulled into the drive. Lucy ran frantically out to meet the car.

Ian and Helsi rushed from the van.

"What's wrong?" they asked in unison. Helsi hugged Lucy.

Rachel ran out of the house, followed by Dylan and Robbie, all sporting wet hair and wearing pajamas.

"The gerbil's dead!" Robbie screamed. "He can't move or anything."

"What gerbil for Pete's sake?" Ian asked. "We don't have a gerbil, do we?" He looked at Helsi.

"Robbie brought the classroom gerbil home for the weekend today. There's no school tomorrow, you know. So the kids take turns caring for the animals on long weekends and breaks. Today it's Robbie's turn."

"That's just great. Whose idea was that, Robbie?"

"Miss Lape's. Our student teacher." Robbie's voice ran at fever pitch. "She promised everyone in the class would get a turn. Said we had to be responsible and care for him as if he were a member of our family." Tears crept into the boy's voice.

"Where is the little rodent?" Ian asked, heading toward the front door, his arm around Robbie. Lucy led the way

"In a box. On the coffee table," Dylan said with authority. "It was my idea. We put wood shavings in first." He stayed at his father's side.

"And I put a nice cover over him," Rachel chirped. "So he wouldn't be cold." Helsi took Rachel's hand.

The family hovered around the lifeless creature, each offering a kind word in its behalf.

"What am I going to say to Miss Lape?" Robbie wailed. "She trusted me." He wiped the back of his hand over his eyes.

"I know! It's a family tribunal. Lucy's been court martialed!" Sean burst through the door. "Flunked your first babysitting assignment, did you, Little Sis?"

Lucy glared at him. "Have some respect for the dead, will you?" She sniffed the air. "You smell like sweat; get out of here!"

"Who died then?" Sean wiped his face with his tee-shirt.

Ian explained the late gerbil's plight to Sean before sending him to the shower. The boy lumbered up the stairs with as much noise as he could muster from his slight figure.

Helsi rolled her eyes at Ian. "Okay, children, off to bed.

"But what will I tell Miss Lape?" Robbie grimaced at his mother.

"We'll talk about that tomorrow. Remember tomorrow is Teacher Workshop Day; no school. You have three days to work it out, Robbie." Slipping off her heels and carrying them, she ushered the children upstairs.

"I'll be there in a minute, kids," Ian called from the kitchen. He filled the pot with water, spooned coffee into the basket, and pressed the start button. He removed his suit jacket and hung it on a doorknob, mentally tallying the cost of the evening. *Seventy dollars for the dinner, twenty-five bucks for flowers, twenty-eight for candy. That's one twenty-three. If I get three hours overtime, I'll be covered.*

Relieved, he set out coffee mugs and spoons. He took the elegant gold box from the refrigerator and placed it on the table. He wanted to sample a piece of chocolate but saw that it had not yet been opened. *It is Helsi's gift. I'd better let her open it.* Looking toward the stairs, he muttered, "What's keeping her?"

Helsi, barefoot and wearing a plaid robe, came in on silent feet. She returned Ian's coffee mugs to the cupboard and brought china cups and saucers in their place. "It's been such a lovely evening, Ian. Let's try to make it last a little longer." She slipped her arms around his neck. "That coffee smells good."

"Did Robbie settle down?"

"Yes, yes. After we thought of several options. Apologize to Miss Lape and offer to buy another gerbil? Or just go ahead and buy another gerbil?" She filled their cups with steaming coffee. "Then Robbie had to know if we would tell her the gerbil was not her Crenshaw or just let her think it was."

"So there was a deep moral discussion going on up there?" Ian laughed. "Thanks for leaving me out of it." He filled the tiny creamer Helsi had ready.

"I don't know." Helsi mumbled through a mouthful of dark-chocolate trifle. "Oh Ian, these are heavenly."

They savored the coffee and exquisite chocolates, the quiet house, the temporary peace.

When they were finished, they lounged before the television, their legs entwined. Helsi was bored by the documentary on the health-care crisis. *I know Ian spent at least a hundred dollars tonight. Where will we get that money?*

Maybe I should get a job. A part-time job to pay for those extras. I could work on his study nights. That's every night he's not in class. Or maybe mornings when Rachel's at school. She looked at Ian; he stared intently at the screen.

Thank God we have good health insurance with the city. Those poor souls without it. Parents who can't afford to take their children to the doctor. Ian sighed.

He glanced at Helsi's closed eyes, her head resting on the sofa back. *She's tired. It's been a long day for her. At least she had a nice anniversary dinner even if she did have to get supper for the kids first. No wonder she's exhausted.*

He thought again of the $123. *Sure hope I get that overtime. Otherwise, where will I get money for textbooks next semester?*

CHAPTER SEVEN—HOPE

"I tell you I won't have it!" Mrs. Egan stated flatly, her voice raised. "My son is a good boy." She swallowed, digging into her bag and pulling out a citrus cough drop, which she unwrapped and popped into her mouth. She began again.

"Frances doesn't bother anybody. He follows the rules and gets his work—"

"Please, Mrs. Egan, sit down," Hope interrupted and guided her to a chair. She set a fresh bottle of water on the table in front of the woman. Taking a seat opposite her, she placed a small pad and pencil on the table.

"Do you mind backing up a bit, so I can get the details down clearly, Mrs. Egan?" Hope took pencil in hand. "I need to know three things: one, the nature of the bullying—specific acts, please. Two, where and when it took place. And three, the name—or at least a description—of the perpetrator." She looked directly into Mrs. Egan's eyes.

"Just get Frankie in here and let him tell you," Mrs. Egan instructed in a tired voice.

"It would be helpful if you could tell me again what he's told you, Mrs. Egan." Hope softened her voice. "That way I can do a little investigating before we bring in Frances. It will be easier on him if I can verify a few of his points, so he can feel we really intend to help." She watched Mrs. Egan shift in her chair, disdain on her face.

"Where do you want me to start?"

Hope spent lunch recess talking to Jimmy Connor about Frankie Egan. Jimmy said they were good friends and always played together. Their favorite game was "kil—catch the man," he had told her, quickly correcting himself. He went on to say they "played alone, no other boys; and they never played rough. To "catch the man, they simply tapped his shoulder or arm, never grabbed or hit." He looked at his principal with innocent, ocean-blue eyes; and Hope wanted to believe him.

During afternoon recess, Hope observed the playground from a second-floor window. The children, open jackets flapping in the breeze, scurried around like colonies of ants. After a few minutes, she was able to discern individuals. In the clearing near the primary swings, she saw Jimmy and Frankie run to each other and speak briefly before each rushed to other third-grade boys. Jimmy led Terry Cutler toward Frankie who approached them with Adam Menske in tow.

The four boys began to run around and fall about, stopping periodically to look toward the nearest supervising teacher. They were all quite adept at slowing down their action when a teacher blew the whistle or looked their way.

The only visible pattern to the game was in the running, the falling about, and the changing of roles. It seemed that Jimmy would chase and fall on Terry, then move to Adam, while the other boys rotated as well.

Those boys are clearly violating the No-Body-Contact Rule, and they know better. She continued to watch, hoping a teacher would catch them off guard, in the act. Suddenly, the rotation changed to Jimmy versus Frankie. Hope watched with revulsion as a bigger, bulkier Jimmy forcefully threw a compact little Frankie onto the ground. He then fell on top the boy just as Frankie was getting up, butting his head into Frankie's chest. The shrill sound of a teacher's whistle caused all four boys to freeze as two teachers rushed toward the little group.

A resolute Hope hurried to her office to meet the boys for adjudication.

At 2:18 Hope finally managed to get a bit of lunch. She sat at her desk with half a tuna-salad sandwich and perused the shortlist of substitute teachers available for long-term assignments.

Vicki Perry, who had replaced the late Millie Blackwell as third-grade teacher, would begin family leave in two weeks. She and her husband planned to fly to Baghdad to pick up the Iraqi infant they had adopted. Vicki had requested six additional weeks off to settle in with the baby. All details were set, and the leave had been approved through the personnel department.

Seven names were on the shortlist, three of whom had removed themselves from consideration once they learned the class had four students identified as learning disabled and another child with a hearing loss as well as a boy-girl ratio of two to one.

Normally, Hope would not have permitted a class of that makeup, but there were special circumstances for this one. Learning disabilities teacher Marla Sutton and Vicki Perry had agreed to a pilot program in which both teachers work closely together with a group of children having similar learning traits. The plan provided systematic practice of particular skills in both the classroom and the LD resource room. Children worked at a much more intense and focused level than they did in the usual arrangement between classroom and special-education teachers. It represented the newest theories in the treatment of learning-disabled kids.

Because of Vicki's experience in teaching deaf children, Hope had placed Hilary Butler in her class. She had interviewed other teachers in the third-grade department and found them anxious about using the lapel microphone and monitoring the receptive device Hilary wore. They felt ill prepared and were reluctant to take on the extra responsibility; whereas, Vicki agreed readily.

The Butlers, sophisticated in their ability to secure the best possible advantage for Hilary, felt confident that Mrs. Perry's class was the most reasonable placement for their daughter.

The two-to-one, boy-girl ratio of students simply reflected this year's third-grade enrollment.

To Hope's great relief, the class had run smoothly. When Mrs. Perry brought news that the infant she and her husband had been awaiting had finally been cleared for their custody, she kept her concerns quiet. But she secretly worried that the delicate balance Mrs. Perry and Marla Sutton had created so masterfully would disintegrate with even the best of interim teachers.

She desperately needed to find that best interim teacher and to find her or him as soon as possible. Hope recognized the names of the remaining four, all of whom had worked successfully at Poore Pond in the past. But she wanted to find a trait or two in their credentials that would tell her a particular teacher had the right stuff, so to speak, to meet the needs of this unique class.

She pulled four folders from the stack of applicants and began re-reviewing resumes. One of the candidates, Bluewave Stonecipher, had worked three summers at a special-needs camp and had glowing letters of reference from camp officials. "Caring, creative, energetic, loved by children and parents," the letters stated. "Responsible and mature," "Spiritually open."

Hope dialed Ms. Stonecipher's number and left a brief message. She refused to let herself be put off by either the name, Bluewave, or the unexpected voicemail greeting, "Bluewave's spiritual oasis." She put the Stonecipher file aside and rose from her desk.

Corinne buzzed her and she pressed the intercom button.

"Call for you, Dr. Fleming, from Theodore Keller. Will you take it?"

"Yes, of course, Corinne."

"Very well. Line two, please." Corinne's smooth voice and professional manner thrilled Hope anew each time she experienced them.

Hope pressed the line button and took a deep breath, mentally filing through her memory bank for the latest issue she and Theo had discussed. "How are you, Theodore?"

"Great, Hope, just great. I have good news for you." His rich voice caused her breath to catch.

"Good news? Just what I need at this moment," she murmured, willing a smile through the wire.

"Well, Doctor." He laughed. "Theodore has your best medicine. Two more people have agreed to be on George's board." He cleared his throat. "Well, tentatively agreed."

"Tentatively?" Hope asked.

"Well. They just want to wait and see what sort of organization we come up with. Who the rest of the board members are. What sort of building we house the foundation in and where it is located. Typical information."

"Is this customary, Theo?" Hope felt uneasiness rising in her chest.

"Oh yes," Theodore sneezed. "Excuse me, Hope." She could faintly hear him blowing his nose. "I'm sorry. Now where were we? Oh yes. You asked if it was customary for potential board members to want detailed information before agreeing to serve. Well yes, it is typical. That is, it's typical of those who make a serious commitment to the position. And rightly so, Hope."

"I understand, Theo. It makes sense that they would not want their names connected to any questionable boards, any with poor potential for succeeding, I guess." She sighed.

"You're not getting cold feet, are you, Hope? Because if you are, George could always just donate the money to existing agencies that help the homeless. That would be a lot simpler."

"No, no. My feet are not cold. I want to go through with it." *Is he trying to get out of this project? Is it looking hopeless to him?* "It's just that I feel so out of my element. Starting a foundation is an entirely foreign area to me. I feel inadequate."

"Everything will fall into place once we have a good, committed board." Reassurance filled his voice. "And things will move faster as well."

"That's what I want to hear from you, Theo." She inhaled deeply. "But I would not blame you if you lost heart. George and I require so much spoon feeding through this process. You must find it tedious."

"Not at all, Hope. Not at all." His voice grew softer. "I always enjoy our meetings. You—and George, of course—are good company. In fact, I wanted to ask you to have dinner with me tomorrow night, just the two of us."

Hope's heart skipped a beat. "Do you mean a business dinner or a social evening?"

"Entirely social. What about it? Are you game?"

"I am game, but I have a previous engagement." *It would be rude to cancel my plans with Belva.* "May we make it the following night?"

Silence. Hope could visualize Theo punching through his palm pilot.

"No, I'm not free." Let's just make it Friday night. The weekend. How about that? Are you free?"

"Yes I am. And Friday night will be more relaxing, don't you think?" She jotted his name in her pocket calendar under her 5:00 o'clock hair appointment. "What time, Theo?"

"Six thirty? I will pick you up at your place. Does that work for you?"

"Yes, of course. See you then."

A lighthearted Hope gently placed the phone back on its base.

She walked to the public-address-system board and scanned announcements taped near the microphone. The getting-ready bell sounded, and she flicked on the all-call button. "May I have your attention, please."

At that moment, Artie Omark rushed to her side and held out a carefully written card. "I'm supposed to read this," he whispered. "Mrs. Davis said so."

She glanced at the card, the words exhibit and barnyard sculptures jumping out at her, and began reading through the list of reminders for upcoming activities. Feeling Artie poke her arm, she looked his way while trying to keep her mouth toward the microphone and continue speaking.

"I'm supposed to go first. My teacher said."

Flustered, Hope announced, "Now we have Artie Omark from Mrs. Davis' second grade with a special announcement.

He moved closer to the microphone, bending it down to his level. "Students in Room E-3 invite all homerooms to our exhibit of orj-nal barnyard sculptures. Come to Room E-3 this Friday to see the awesome art exhibit. Sign up on the sheet in the office to reserve your time choice. Please come. Thank you."

He bowed and stepped away. Hope took his place. Stifling a laugh, she adjusted the mike and opened her mouth to begin again. Just then, Artie jumped back to the microphone with a quick, "Excuse me, Dr. I forgot something."

Looking cherubic in a red bowtie which set off his round face, he positioned his mouth to speak into the mike. Corinne's eyes met Hope's and they exchanged doting grins.

"Oh, and there is going to be a dress code. Boys have to wear neckties. Girls wear skirts. Or—you will not be allowed into the exhibit." He pointed his chubby finger at the system board and shook it forcefully.

Howls and laughter flooded the wires from classrooms throughout the school. Then raucous applause broke out.

Hope shrieked. Corinne burst into laughter. A parent waiting at the clinic door clapped her hands and fell into side-splitting guffaws.

Second bell sounded. Hope gathered herself and began reading the names of students who were to be picked up from the library holding point, and two changed bus numbers. "Have a lovely, safe evening and a good night's sleep, everyone."

She grabbed her trench coat and portable microphone before hurrying out to the buses. A smiling Corinne thrust a note at her as she rushed past.

Patrolling lines of children awaiting their respective buses, Hope used her principal's voice to redirect stray students who visited other lines or to intervene with those who engaged in horseplay. Two girls fighting over a folder were sent to separate benches inside the doors.

She noticed intimidation on the face of a small boy in line next to his big sister and moved toward them. The sister's face reddened as Hope stood closely, brushing the child's sleeve as she fumbled innocently in her book bag.

"Diana, are you still helping David learn his math facts?"

"Sometimes," the girl replied, her voice husky with embarrassment.

"Good for you."

She turned to David. "David, is your sister a pretty good math tutor?"

"Sometimes," David said with cloudy eyes. "Sometimes she's mean when I don't know the answer." He bravely made eye contact with Diana.

Hope looked from David to Diana and back again. "Diana is one of our leaders here at school. She's on Student Council, isn't she?" David shook his head in affirmation.

"I am sure your sister will try harder to be patient with you, David. You are her special brother and she cares about you, don't you, Diana?"

Hope looked straight into the girl's eyes. "I am so proud of you, Diana. You are one of our best role models at Poore Pond. But good citizens are nice at home as well as at school. That's the hard part." Hope smiled at her. "Be kind to your brother."

Diana swallowed and responded with false confidence, "Yes, Dr. Fleming. I will be more patient with my brother." She averted her eyes and put her hand warmly on David's shoulder.

"And, David," the princpal leaned into David's face. "Make sure you pay attention when you are being helped with math. You must try your best." She smiled at each of them and walked away.

Hope unfolded the message Corinne had given her and read the neat writing:

New student registering tomorrow. Home-schooled until now. Fourth-grader. Over-aged, over-sized. Martin Purdue. Call Marjorie Purdue at 982-3000. She wants to fill you in on her son's weak social skills and a few other problems.

Family moving to Tudor House Townhomes.

Hope pushed the note into her coat pocket and waved the last departing bus down the drive. She thought of her dinner date with Theo and wondered about Martin Purdue. *I cannot wait to get Belva's take on all this.* The workout and swim exhilarated Hope, and she welcomed the quiet supper with Belva afterward.

"This is such a relaxing club, Belva," Hope said as the two of them took a table in the café overlooking the pool.

"Isn't it? I tried others before I found this place. So many clubs are filled with younger, gorgeous people in designer fitness wear, showing off their toned bods. The hunters are all over those places, too.

"No hunters here? What about those two fellows over there?" Hope gestured toward the adjacent bar where two tall men with perfectly coiffed hair sipped drinks while their eyes scoped the room.

"Oh those two. That's the tennis pro and his partner. They're harmless." Both women laughed. "Rugar, the tennis pro, the one with the ascot, is always on the lookout for wealthy older women to sign up for private lessons. His fees are enormous, but the really lonely and desperate ones pay them."

A black-shirted waiter handed them green leatherette folders. They asked for a few minutes to peruse the menu, and he strode away.

Belva recommended the eggplant sandwich, and they both ordered it, Hope, with a side of cottage cheese; Belva, with onion rings. "I cannot resist those things," Belva confessed. "I swam five extra laps, so I wouldn't feel guilty about having them; I'm ready."

"You stay so trim and fit, Belva. I can't imagine that the occasional onion ring would hurt you." Hope took a large drink of water then pressed the lemon slice against the glass with a spoon.

"The occasional onion ring? How about weekly blossoms of onion rings? That's probably how often I indulge myself."

With a flourish, the waiter placed a perfectly round, golden onion-ring cluster in front of Belva and swirled off.

The mouth-watering aroma enticed Hope to pick up a fork. She stopped herself just short of attacking her friend's food.

"Go ahead, try some, Hope. You're skinny; you can afford it."

Hope dabbed at her mouth with a stiff napkin. “That is sinfully delicious. Why didn’t I have that? Cottage cheese solves nothing.”

Belva finished chewing, swallowed, and pronounced, “Onion rings and chocolate solve everything. Have another go, Hope.”

The two women ate their sandwiches and onion rings with a relish unusual for Hope. Obviously, the swim and workout had stimulated her appetite.

The conversation turned, as it often did, to high-profile students needing frequent discipline. It turned out that Belva had had experience with Jimmy Connor since he had attended Shakerag School for kindergarten and first grade.

“The boy has a serious problem. Starting in kindergarten, he was a chronic bully. I must have spent twenty-five percent of my time trying to modify his behavior that first year.”

Belva looked at Hope with beautiful brown eyes full of warmth. “His parents were really supportive of the school. We tried everything: daily reports, incentives at home, incentives at school. Extra-Step Program. He made a little progress by the end of the year. But after summer break when he came to first grade, we were back at square one.” Belva shook her head sadly.

“Was there an obvious family dynamic contributing to his aggression?” Hope suspended her last forkful of eggplant in the air, waiting for Belva’s response.

“Did I know of any weird family situation, you mean?” Belva pushed her plate away and took a drink of coffee.

“Exactly.” Hope stirred her tea and sipped it.

“I was never sure, but I had a hunch that the grandmother, maternal grandmother, was not a good influence on Jimmy. And he spent most of his time in her care.” Belva signaled the waiter for more coffee.

“Why did you feel that way toward the grandmother?”

“I don’t know exactly. She just never seemed to dote on Jimmy, the way most grandparents do, you know.” Belva looked at her watch.

“We should go, shouldn’t we?” Hope asked, rising and gathering her things.

Belva waved good night to the hostess and followed her friend out the door.

In the cold car, they waited for the heater to do its job before resuming their discussion of Jimmy Connor.

“You were saying that Jimmy’s grandmother did not dote on him in a typical way,” Hope recapped.

"That's right. She was always tense around him at school, even during music programs and awards assemblies, functions like that. You know the type." Belva fed a parking ticket into the gate box. The bar rose slowly and the car kept pace. They pulled onto the main street and Belva resumed talking.

"She was never comfortable with herself, could not relax and just enjoy her grandson. I had a tendency to over-analyze her behaviors but never came up with anything concrete." She looked toward Hope.

"Are you saying the woman had no apparent capacity for enjoying life?" Hope's eyes met Belva's.

"Precisely." Belva yawned widely and apologized.

They identified various ways in which a child can be affected by living with constant negativity. But both were too tired to deal with the matter in any depth. They rode home in silence.

"Are you game to go again next Wednesday?" Belva asked as she pulled into Hope's driveway on Canterbury Road.

"Of course. I'll drive next week." Hope climbed out of Belva's low sports car. "Same time?"

Hope laid out paper and pencils, water bottles, and mints for the conference. She counted the chairs to make sure there were enough and noted that the coffee had brewed.

Corinne had put reminder messages in the teachers' boxes and had received confirmation calls from Jimmy's father, Mr. Connor; Frances' parents, Mr. and Mrs. Egan; and Terry's mother, Mrs. Cutler. Only Adam Menske's parents could not confirm. Mr. Menske would be en route from out of town and would try to make it in time; Mrs. Menske would be there if or as soon as her replacement arrived at work.

The boys, Jimmy, Frankie, Terry, and Adam would wait in the media center with librarian Mr. Knowles until called to join the meeting. It was agreed that Adam would not participate unless his parents arrived and would go to Latchkey if they did not make it in time.

Mrs. Egan arrived first with a pleasant-faced, robust man whom she introduced to Hope as her husband, Frances senior.

"It's good to meet you, Mr. Egan." He returned her smile warmly. "Always helps to put the child in context when I know the rest of the family."

"Oh no. Now you can see where Frankie gets all his bad traits." He laughed heartily. Infected by his obvious enjoyment of his own remark, Hope laughed, too.

Mrs. Egan shot them a surly look and glanced at a tall, handsome man approaching them.

"Hello," Hope stepped toward him.

"Michael Connor. It's good to see you, Dr. Fleming. I met you the evening of Open School." He extended his hand to Hope then to each Egan in turn.

"Would you care for coffee while we wait for the others?" Hope gestured toward the table where cups and shortbread cookies surrounded a large urn.

The group made small talk and drank coffee.

Mrs. Cutler arrived, looking smart in a black business suit and carrying a trench coat and notepad. Hope made introductions and pointed out the coffee. She promptly served herself.

Hope noted the time at 3:48. "Let's wait a little longer for the Menskes." She looked from one parent to another. "If they're not here by 4:00, we will go ahead and start." She backed toward the door. "I'll check with Mrs. Tompkins in the office."

Corinne met Hope in the hallway with a message from Mr. Menske. He was five minutes away.

Ed Menske arrived and Hope opened the conference by thanking the parents for coming and reminding them that their attendance sent a signal to their sons that school behavior was important.

Choosing her words carefully, she summarized the problem of rough play on the part of the boys. She emphasized the dual names the boys used for the game: Catch the Man to her and Kill the Man among themselves. The parents laughed at that, except Mrs. Egan, who remained poker faced.

Mildred Menske rushed in, announcing her name. Chairs shifted to make room for her next to her husband.

Hope welcomed her and thanked her for coming.

She outlined the playground incident she had witnessed, feedback the duty teachers had given her about recent behavior patterns of this group of boys, and playground rules at Poore Pond.

Some parents asked questions; others shared their own conclusions. For the most part, their faces remained unreadable.

Without identifying the words of individual boys, Hope shared their remarks made in private hearings with her.

When she paraphrased one boy's description of his play with another child as merely "tapping the shoulder of the other boy in a game of tag for two, called Catch the Man," Martin Connor surprised her with an outburst.

"That sounds like my kid. He's a master at euphemism." He flashed a small smile around the table, then turned a serious face to Hope. "Was that Jimmy? Were you quoting my Jimmy?"

Hope inhaled sharply. "Mr. Connor, this is a group conference. I am not at liberty to identify the remarks of individual children made to me in a private hearing."

"How on earth can we get to the bottom of this then?" Mrs. Egan asked. "If we can't discuss the boys' opinions?" She looked at Hope with disdain.

With deliberate calm, Hope looked at Mrs. Egan. "During this phase of the meeting, we try to clarify as closely as possible, the behaviors of specific children by considering the evidence. Then we call in the boys to testify."

"Oh my heavens!" Mildred Menske blurted. "Testify? We are talking about eight-year-old boys, for crying out loud." She turned an aghast face from her husband to Hope. "We are not having a formal deposition. This is not as serious as all that; it's a little rough play on the playground."

"I beg your pardon," Mrs. Egan countered. "My son has been bullied at recess for the past two weeks. He's very upset. In my opinion, this is a serious matter." She folded her hands and looked at her husband.

"Let's bring in the boys and let them have their say," Mrs. Menske asserted.

"Are there any questions about the information covered before we do that?" Hope asked brightly.

Mr. Connor asked what Hope meant by evidence.

"Our only form of evidence consists of accounts of adult eye witnesses and, to some extent, child eye witnesses. Of course, we must keep in mind the nature of children's accounts." Hope broke eye contact with Mr. Connor and glanced around the table with smiles for all the parents.

"Their views are very narrow. They tend to try to please the questioner. They may try to either protect or indict their playmates and," she looked directly at several parents, hoping to discern their response to her remarks. "Most children are easily intimidated by adult authority figures."

"Just one question," Mrs. Cutler interjected. "What are the ages of the children on the playground with Terry's class's afternoon recess?" She smiled.

"Only third graders are out at that time, Mrs. Cutler." Hope smiled back. Each of the primary grades has a separate time for recess." She looked around the table. "Any other questions?" She waited briefly. "Very well. I will get our boys. It would be helpful if you would arrange a vacant chair by your sides for your little adjudicants." Hope's light manner belied her formal language.

The boys filed in roguishly. Seeing so many adults, they grew quiet and serious. Each took a seat next to his respective parent and sat down stiffly.

Hope noted each child's body language to get a sense of his comfort level. She knew that the first child to speak in his own behalf would have the most intimidating task. Look at Jimmy Connor. Why he seems a bundle of nerves. She looked at Frankie.

Frankie looks cool and calm. How can he when he's been more brutalized than the others? Terry and Adam were unreadable, but Terry wore a natural smile. Adam's expression was neutral, quite adult-like. *Adam's our boy; he speaks first.*

"Jimmy, Frankie, Terry, Adam, do you know why we are here for this meeting?" Hope met the eyes of each child in turn.

"We broke rules," Jimmy chirped.

The other three, without looking at one another, nodded collectively.

"That's right." Hope kept a serious face. "After we discuss your behavior with your parents, I'm going to ask each of you what rule or rules you think you have broken."

Each lad's account was fairly close to what he had given the principal first round but also echoed bits of confessions she had elicited from them during their private hearings.

"I know I made a bad mistake. I will never have body contac' again. I will respect the rule against it." Adam fired off, dropping his voice with his eyes.

"I wasn't playing rough, but I broke the rule just because I played with rough boys." Frankie chimed. He looked at his fellow students. "Well, maybe I did play a little rough. One time. That day we were sent to Dr. Fleming." He avoided his parents' eyes.

"What about you, Jimmy?" Hope asked with compelling eyes. "What do you have to say about your behavior?"

Jimmy swallowed, his face and neck reddening noticeably. He cleared his throat and looked down at his hands. "I got a little rough in the game." He brushed his nose with thumb and forefinger, keeping his chin down.

Mr. Connor looked at Hope.

"A little rough, Jimmy?" Hope's eyes burned into the boy's.

"Uh yes." The boy lifted his eyes to Hope's. "Well, a lot rough. It was uh. Uh. Not safe. I could have hurt someone." He sent a sidelong glance to his father.

"You were very rough, Jimmy." Mr. Connor said, his eyes riveted on his son's. Jimmy looked bravely at his father. "Dr. Fleming told me she saw you, she saw you slam into Francis and knock him down." Tears filled the boy's eyes but he stoically held his father's gaze.

"So your consequence will be stronger than some of the other boys, Jimmy." Hope had his full attention. "Your father and I will talk with you about that."

"Terry." Hope looked at the cherubic boy sitting beside his attractive mother. His calm and reverent demeanor matched hers. "Terry, do you have anything to say about your part in this?"

The boy's small smile faded when his mother nudged his arm. He stood and looked at his principal. "We played too rough." He thrust both hands into his pants pockets.

"We can't play Kill the Man it's body contact." He looked at his mates. "Can't even play Catch the Man it's body contact, too." He pulled his hands from his pockets and spread them in front of him, palms upturned.

"We don't deserve recess cause we don't help keep the playground safe. We're not good Poore Pond citizens," he continued in a remarkably steady voice. He looked at his mother and sat down, completely unruffled.

All six parents broke out in applause, surprising Hope with their generous spirit.

In the end, after each boy had managed, some with prompting, to verbalize his guilt clearly, sentences were imposed.

All four boys would spend three afternoon recesses in detention (Due to prior infractions, Jimmy would spend six).

They would write letters of apology to their homeroom teachers, the playground-duty teachers, their parents, their principal.

They would view educational, anti-bullying videotapes. They would write summaries of the main points in the tapes. Only then would their afternoon recesses be reinstated.

In the privacy of Hope's office, Mr. Connor agreed to arrange professional counseling for Jimmy. Hope sent him off with permission forms to be signed, authorizing the sharing of information between school officials and the counselor.

The support these parents showed for due process she so carefully provided encouraged Hope. She had spent a great deal of time and thought in order to get it right. The fact that they accepted the consequences she imposed on the boys further encouraged her.

But she fully expected a disgruntled Mrs. Egan, in typical fashion, to visit her a few days later with an issue about the outcome.

She really is a dear person. Struggles so with her tendency to take everything literally. She puts all her energy into parenting Francis, though. We have to give her that.

Hope vowed to have positive contact with the woman as soon as possible. In the context of a friendly, personal conversation, Mrs. Egan may set aside her concerns and simply vent.

Perhaps she would agree to volunteer at the science workshop next month. She's such a detail person. That's what it takes to run one of the hands-on stations.

Hope opened the office door and glanced at her inbox. A note from fourth-grade teacher, Brad Kushner, grabbed her attention. She stepped back into her office and unfolded the lined paper.

Hope, I am working late in my room. Please buzz me or come up after your meeting. Problems with Martin Purdue.

Thanks, Brad.

Brad Kushner appeared in her office immediately after she summoned him. Fairly bursting with youthful energy, he sat down and placed a legal pad filled with notes in front of him. Without waiting for Hope to seat herself, he began.

"Hope, you know I always make it a point to handle students myself." He shot serious eyes at her. "I have involved you in only the gravest situations, do you agree?"

Willing herself not to mirror his intensity, she smiled and said, "Of course." How does he have such energy this late in the day? He must be nearly forty, and teaching is hard work.

"Jacque Mullins, I believe, was one of the few students I asked for help with, and that was because she was bi-polar and none of us knew it. Remember?"

I do, indeed, remember Jacque. My first month at Poore Pond, before anyone trusted me. She almost got the best of me.

"I remember her well, Brad. I especially remember the wonderful teamwork that went into writing her behavior plan." She sipped briefly from a water bottle. "Are you seeing symptoms of deeply seated problems in Martin?"

"Oh yes. I do. I mean, the boy is not at all concerned about being accepted by the other children; he is completely oblivious to them." He threw up his hands. "He's oblivious to me. And he's much larger than the other kids; I think they're afraid of him."

"Is he respectful to you?"

"Respectful? I have no idea. He makes no eye contact with me. Or with anyone else, for that matter." Brad ran his finger around the inside of his collar.

"Didn't his parents say he sees a private therapist for his lack of social skills?" Hope began to recall the registration conference.

Brad nodded. "Remember, we were promised a list of strategies from the therapist? Tips we could use in the classroom to help him succeed and be accepted. That list has never come through."

"Well, Martin's only just arrived. Let's give everyone a little settling-in time."

"But I want to get off on the right foot. Set him up for success, you know. Martin has so many strikes against him, and I don't want the other kids to start closing ranks on him." Brad's brow furrowed. "You know how negative they can be."

"Yes. Yes. Herd mentality. But I also know that getting a classroom of kids to like each other is one of your strong suits."

She raised her forefinger. "And the report his parents gave us contained helpful information, don't you think?" Brad nodded unconvincingly.

Hope pulled out Martin's file, and they pored over it together. Though hand written, the report had an official look to it because it was written on a standard behavior-plan form. Brad stood next to Hope. Both bent uncomfortably at their waists and silently read through the document.

It contained a brief paragraph describing his "inability to make friends and his undeveloped social skills, in general."

Another rather lengthy paragraph touched on the boy's tendency to ignore his classmates and his teacher, the very trait that had frustrated Brad.

"Though a happy child, Martin is uncomfortable speaking to children or adults; and while this tendency may be seen as rudeness, it is simply his reluctance to talk, for whatever reason.

Martin is seeing child-development specialist, Dr. Eli Cornelius, who advises us to treat him like a verbal child by consistently reinforcing our expectations that he can and will speak."

"I'm not sure this is an official behavior plan, are you?" Brad asked, his brow furrowed.

Hope turned the page and ran her finger down to the three signatures at the bottom. "Look at this, Brad."

There were three signatures: Martin Purdue, Marjorie Purdue, and Cornelius Eli. Hope's index finger, the nail neatly lacquered with clear polish, underscored tiny manuscript beneath Dr. Eli's "signature." The words, Martin Purdue as attorney-in-fact, had been written in precise, microscopic lettering.

Hope and Brad looked knowingly at one another.

"We need a conference," they said in unison.

In the end, Brad agreed to let the world turn a few more days; keep careful, objective observation notes; and let Martin and his parents reach a comfort level with the new school. Next week, Hope would schedule a conference with the Purdues.

She had every confidence in Brad's ability to manage Martin while patiently gathering data. His parting words were optimistic.

She felt suddenly tired and noticed that it was nearly six o'clock. She stretched her shoulders and walked through the Latchkey room, typically quiet this time of day. Pockets of students completed homework; others watched an animal video.

Coordinator Celia Youngblood sat with two third-graders awkwardly wielding thick plastic knitting needles. She adjusted their short rows of stitches then modeled the next step for the girls, who gave their all to listening and watching.

Hope waved softly as she passed and heard running feet from games in the upstairs gym.

Oh, the good sounds of after-school care. All's right with the world. I can go home now.

Hope heard the phone ringing repeatedly as she approached the office; she hurried to answer it.

Corinne's smooth voice came over the line. "Hi Hope. I'm glad I caught you; I don't like to bother you at home."

"Hi, Corinne. What's up?"

"I just wanted to tell you about Emmylou."

Hope's breath caught as she focused all her attention on Corinne's words.

CHAPTER EIGHT—RAY

Ray guided the heavy carpet cleaner back and forth, back and forth over the wet pile, trying to do the best possible job for Heather. *She's been looking pale and tired lately. Working, going to school, running this place; I'm afraid it's all too much for her.*

Hope had annoyed him when he asked if he could borrow the school's cleaner over the weekend. Her face filled with distress as she muttered misgivings: "it is unethical to use public equipment for private benefit," or something to that effect.

In the end, she had approved his using it, on the condition that he place it back on school property no later than early Monday morning, preferably Sunday night. He could "check the boilers and return the equipment at the same time."

Why does she always get so technical about everything? Ray refused to acknowledge a part of him that understood why taxpayers might be upset if they knew. *Heck, I'm a taxpayer in this district.*

But now the fuss seemed worth it: the carpeting cleaned up nicely. Heather had taken Jeremy for wrestling tryouts in the city recreation program, and Ray wanted to be finished with all her carpets before they returned. He looked at his watch and stepped up his pace.

A loud pounding at the door interrupted his thoughts. He turned off the machine and walked toward the kitchen door. He could not make out the bulky figure darkening the curtained window. *Who is that? Tom Draco maybe?*

The door opened before he reached it, and in walked Davey, Jeremy's father.

"Hi Davey. How's it going, Buddy?" Ray called, trying to mask surprise guilty feelings. He offered his hand.

"Hi R—." A sneeze drowned Davey's voice, and he pulled out a handkerchief to cover his mouth. Ray lowered his hand.

"Is that a cold or are you allergic to carpet cleaners?" Ray asked, laughing. He so wanted to keep the conversation light and avoid revealing the resentment he felt.

"I don't know, could be," Davey looked around the apartment. "Where's Heather? Where's Jeremy?"

"They went to wrestling tryouts." He looked at his watch. "They should be back anytime now."

Ray motioned toward a kitchen chair. "Want to sit down?" He walked toward the machine. "I'm just finishing up here, won't be but a few minutes." He switched on the cleaner and began to guide it back and forth, wishing the tension would leave his body.

Back and forth, back and forth he pushed, concentrating more than necessary. *Has he sat down yet? What the heck is he doing?*

Ray hurriedly finished the last section of the living-room carpet and shut off the machine. Davey, his long, wiry body leaning over the counter, seemed to be reading a paper from a pile of Heather's mail. *What does he think he's doing? It's against the law to read other people's mail.* Heat rose in his chest.

"Well, that's it. All done. Heather has clean carpets throughout." He smiled to himself, pleased with his accomplishment. He discreetly looked at his watch. *I'd better go. Though I sure hate to leave him here for Heather and Jeremy to deal with. But now that I think about it.* Ray looked hard at Davey. He walked over to him.

"Do you want something to drink, Buddy? Heather's probably got soda or something."

Davey turned toward him. "Maybe I'll just have a glass of ice water." His eyes turned toward the refrigerator. "Where does she keep the glasses?" He scanned the upper cupboards.

Wanting—but not wanting—to show him, Ray watched the man open three cupboard doors until he found a glass. He watched him walk to the refrigerator and open the door.

He is. He is. He's stone-cold sober. I'll be dad gum.

"That ice water looks good." Ray grinned widely. "Mind if I join you in a drink?" He helped himself, and they both sat down at the shiny-clean table.

"Heather sure does keep a clean house, doesn't she?" He asked Ray. Ray nodded, looking forward to her delight with the carpets.

Davey cleared his throat. Ray coughed.

"Notice anything different about me, Ray?" Davey's eyes locked his.

"Different? Well, you look taller." He laughed. Davey, stone-faced, stared at him.

"You know, you've seen me only a few times; and I was two sheets to the wind every time." He straightened his shoulders. "Don't tell me you didn't notice." He frowned at Ray.

"No, no." Ray grinned again. "I guess I did notice. I guess I did." He glanced away, remembering the night Heather had cooked a lovely dinner for the two of them; and Davey had crashed it, looking for Jeremy. He could still see Davey weaving down the staircase, girlfriend Desiree guiding him slowly. *He was pathetic that night, tried to drive drunk.*

"I quit drinking, Ray." Ray shot wide eyes at him.

"That's great, Davey." He smiled broadly. "That is just great."

"And I'm going to try to get back with Heather." He lowered his chin. "If she'll have me; I don't know if she will."

"A kid needs his father." Davey exclaimed, straightening his back.

A sinking sensation rose low in Ray's stomach. "Well, all you can do is try, Davey." He tried to warm his eyes as he looked across the table at him. "We just do the best we can. That's all anybody can ask." He wondered if Heather would go back to Davey just to lighten her load. *No one could blame her if she did; she might do it out of sheer exhaustion.*

Ray rose and walked to the window. His mind teemed with conflicting thoughts. "Did you just quit cold turkey?" He did not look at Davey, but gazed out the window, seeing nothing.

"I'm going to AA. Taking the Twelve Steps; you know, the meetings, prayers, public confessions, the whole bit." He pulled out a pack of cigarettes and walked to the door. "I'm smoking five times as much since I quit drinking. "And coffee. We get drunk on coffee at those meetings." He shook his head and went out the door. Through the curtain, Ray watched him inhale deeply, following the cloud of smoke into the air.

No sense waiting around for Heather now. He wrapped the cord neatly across two hooks on the cleaner and rolled it to the door. He methodically placed the jug of solution in the holder attached to the cleaner, taking time to place it exactly. Slowly, he pulled on his jacket and gloves.

Davey, lighted cigarette between his lips, helped carry the heavy machine down the outside stairway and into the van.

The sound of rubber rushing over pavement surprised them, and they both turned to look. A small silver sports car stopped abruptly behind the van, just short of the two men.

A tall, dark-haired woman emerged in the darkness.

"Well, Claire. What are you doing here?" Ray stepped toward his sister. She handed him a small, white paper bag.

"Here's Mom's prescription. She needs it for her morning dose." She looked nervously at Davey.

"But what are you doing on this side of town? And at this hour?" He peeked into the bag and saw the familiar plastic vial full of large yellow capsules.

"It's a long story, Ray." She glanced at Davey. "I'm sure your friend does not have time for it." She turned toward him and raised her eyes to his. "I'm Claire Sellers, Ray's sister." She offered her hand.

"Oh, sorry." Ray grinned sheepishly. "Davey, this is my sister, Claire. Claire, this is Davey, Jeremy's father."

"Glad to meet you, Claire." Smiling down into her face, he subtly tossed his cigarette onto the ground and took her hand. He held the handshake a little long, in Ray's opinion.

She beamed up at him as if he were a heartthrob movie star. Ray watched and grimaced.

"I still don't get it, Claire," Ray blurted, wanting to break their moment.

"Do you live around here, Claire?" Davey asked as he released her hand.

"Actually, not far from here," she murmured through the widest smile he had seen on his sister since the wedding to her ex-husband. "I live over on Fullerton. Those garden apartments near Kroger strip mall. Do you know the area?"

"No. Well, maybe. I did go to a Kroger here once with Jeremy. Is that the closest one?"

"It would be, yes." She laughed warmly. "That Jeremy of yours, he is really something else. Smart kid, knows what he likes."

"Oh, you know Jeremy?"

"Yes, he's been to Ray's house. To see our mom. "Ray lives with her." She glanced at her brother. "Takes care of her actually. She loves kids, always wanting her own grandkids."

Ray's brow furrowed. They don't even know I'm here.

"Do you have time for a cup of coffee, Claire? There's a funky little coffee shop on the street behind us." He shifted his weight to one leg, showing off his tall, lean frame. Ray, feeling a twinge of envy, noted how confident Davey seemed to be with women.

Claire checked her watch. "Maybe a short cup," she laughed. "I was on my way to the Y to work out, but that can wait."

"So that's what you're doing over here! Ray nearly shouted, determined not to be ignored again.

She looked at her brother as if he had just arrived. "Well, yes. I saw you and your car as I passed, so I circled back to give you Mom's medicine. Save myself a trip over there after my workout." Seeing Ray's confusion, she continued. "I went to that discount pharmacy over here. Remember, I told you about it? Cost thirty percent less there. Big savings." She smiled at Davey.

"Now I get it," Ray said. He turned to go. "I'll see you later."

"Bye, Ray," Claire called over her shoulder as she hurried to her car. Davey, already positioned to pull out into the street, nodded to Claire to follow him. He half-waved to Ray and drove off.

Ray, his heart filled with trepidation, watched his sister's car follow Davey's and thought of Heather. *What business does he have taking Claire for coffee when he's trying to get back with Heather?* He felt sick to his stomach. *Boy, a sober Davey is nothing like a drunk one. I don't think I want my sister smitten with him.*

Ray, reluctant to go without seeing Heather and yet anxious to separate himself from tonight's events, climbed the stairway to lock the apartment. He turned out all the lights but the one above the kitchen sink.

He closed and locked the door, looking around to gauge his privacy before placing Heather's key beneath the soil in the large terracotta pot. He recalled having helped her plant daffodil bulbs in that soil when she first moved to the apartment. That had been a happy time for him. *I did a lot for her and Jeremy then. But I wanted to. I did it for me.*

Ray dragged the heavy carpet cleaner over the pavement as quietly as he could. There were lights on in many of the surrounding houses though it was not quite 6:15 A.M. He would have it safely returned to the storage closet before Hope arrived.

I'm glad I cleaned Heather's carpets for her. But I won't use that machine again. Hope was right. It's wrong for me to borrow school property for personal use.

He switched on half the overhead lights and maneuvered down the empty corridor. Colorful Buddy Day posters dotted every other span of wall space.

Dad gum. Today's Buddy Day again. He moved close to a poster to check the week's schedule. *Oh good. It's Chuck Taylor's fifth-graders with Trudy Cooper's first. Those teachers watch their kids. I don't have to clean up their spilled juice and finger paints all over the lavatory sinks.*

He looked again at the schedule. Tuesday's buddy classes were Boris Mathews' fifth and Ali Cantrell's first. *I will get to Hope before tomorrow. She has to put a stop to the sloppy way those two classes buddy up on Tuesdays. She'll ride herd, I know.*

The milk-order count matched the delivery sheet Ray found on the cooler lid, with the exception of a shortage in the number of chocolate milks. As expected, the quantity of white milks exceeded the order by the same amount as the shortage. *I hope that Hapwell girl gets her chocolate milk. Last time we ran out of chocolate, so Helen gave her white. She wasn't having it.*

She complained to her mother, working in the library. Went straight in there with her tray. Sat down and refused to eat until her mother produced chocolate milk.

Laughing to himself, Ray headed toward the boiler room. He remembered Mrs. Hapwell's refusal to indulge the child. She ended up sulking over her tray all through lunch period and recess, not eating a bite. *I do not want to put Mrs. Hapwell through that again. I had to hand it to her. She didn't give in to her daughter. I wish there were more parents like her.*

Ray passed the dark office where he noticed two overflowing school bags on the floor near the door. He could tell by the worn red canvas that they belonged to Hope. Picking them up, he carried them through her half-open door and set them on the round table. He found the principal stooped under her desk in an undignified way.

"Good morning, Ray," she called in a muffled voice. "I'll be with you as soon as I get this plugged in."

"I'll do that for you if you want." She uttered sounds apparently refusing his offer, so he stood by helplessly.

A deep sigh sprang from her. She backed out and rose awkwardly, holding onto the desk for support. "There, that's done." She dusted her hands. "Belva gave me a new warming tray and insulated tea mug." She held up a shiny black mug bearing a pair of pink stiletto-heeled pumps above the caption, The Trappings of Authority.

"Oh thanks, Ray, for bringing in the bags. Those leaflets are for the buddies. Today Mr. Taylor and Mrs. Cooper's classes buddy. Did you see the schedule?" She took a colorful leaflet from one of the bags and handed it to him.

"Yes I did." He shuffled the leaflet pages, seeing nothing. "As a matter of fact, I needed to talk to you about that." His eyes sought hers, but she was looking at the leaflet she held.

"These are great tools, Ray." She pointed to a page of questions in large print. "Look at this; it's a bully test. There are questions kids ask themselves to see if they might be bullies." She ran her finger under a question, reading it aloud. "Do you ever try to keep a friend from playing with someone else? A bully test, isn't that a good idea?" She looked at Ray's impatient face.

"Oh yes. You wanted to talk about Buddy Day." Her eyes penetrated his. "What do we need to discuss?" She waved him toward a chair.

"Oh, by the way, is Heather managing her schedule any better? You had mentioned how tired she looked."

"If anything, it's getting worse for her. Her job, studying every night, keeping up with Jeremy, she tries to do it all perfectly." He rubbed his forehead.

"There must be some way we can help her." Hope fixed her eyes on Ray, but with a far-off stare. He busied himself looking around the room, anxious for an idea from her.

"We cannot help her do the coursework or her job." Hope's mind was back in the room. "But we can help her care for Jeremy and run the home. Do you agree?"

"You're the expert, Hope," Ray chuckled. "I do take Jeremy whenever I can, so she can study." *Of course, that will all change if she goes back to Davey.*

"I know you do, R—wait! I have a woman who needs a job." She thrust spread hands, palms out, in the air. "It's a real shot in the dark; she's homeless, one of George's cronies." She rolled her eyes. "But she did a little work at Polyflem, cleaning and packing, that sort of thing. And he thought she did a good job."

"We could try her out, maybe have her clean while Heather's home, see how she does." Hope's eyes stared off again. "I wonder if she cooks."

Ray squirmed in his chair. "Heather can't afford to pay her, Hope. Were you thinking minimum wage? Maybe I could pay her something."

"No. No." Hope shook her head vigorously. "I want to pay her. I need to give something back." She smiled at Ray. "You give your time to her and Jeremy. I can certainly give a little money for their benefit."

If that's solved, now we can talk about Buddy Days.

"All right. Will you ask Heather about this, Ray?" Her eyes sought his. He looked at her squarely. "I'll talk to George about Adelaide, that's the woman's name." She took out a pocket calendar and wrote in it.

"Can we talk about Buddy Days now, Hope, before everything heats up here?"

"Yes, of course. But let's put a time frame on this."

They agreed that Ray would speak to Heather this week and Adelaide would be offered the job by Friday.

In the end, Hope agreed to take extra copies of Buddy Day Guidelines to Boris Mathews and Ali Cantrell and speak to them about sticking to the rules. Ray knew she could be heavy handed and would be firm about all cleanup taking place in classroom sinks, not lavatory ones. She would insist that no refreshments be permitted in the common areas. They would be limited to the corner snack table in the cafeteria or to the classrooms.

He knew she would lay down those rules as if they had not heard them before. He just hoped she would monitor the kids and teachers; he hated policing them.

Safety-patrol students and Mrs. Ricci's audition candidates began to arrive, bringing puddles of water from streets still wet after an overnight downpour. Ray wheeled his ever-ready mop bucket to the door. He mopped the puddles thoroughly and cranked the mop through the wringer. He reapplied the mop to the area, then placed a yellow caution sign over the center.

"Good morning, Mr. Sellers," a small voice called. Ray turned to see Jeremy Baker standing before him.

"Well, how are you, Sport?" Smiling widely, he offered his hand; and the boy took it, shaking forcefully as Ray had taught him. "How was your weekend?"

"It was okay." He put down his heavy book bag and looked up, his face filled with anticipation, not lost on Ray.

"How did you do at tryouts?"

"I made the rookie team!" he said proudly. "I used those holds you showed me." He beamed at Ray.

"You did? They helped you?" The boy nodded vigorously. "And how's Mom? Did she have a good weekend?"

Jeremy's face fell. "No. No she didn't. There was trouble." He locked his thumbs and twisted his waist.

That darn Davey. "What kind of trouble? Did your dad come over?" Ray adjusted the mop handle more securely.

"Yes, he came over, gave Mom some money, too." He grinned sheepishly.

"Did he give her a hard time about it?" Ray felt heat rising in his chest.

"Not about the money." He looked down the hall at the approaching safety patrollers.

"What then? What did he give her a hard time about?"

"About Mr. Draco." Jeremy did not look at Ray.

What's that slimy Draco doing now? Heather knew he would be a problem. "What about Mr. Draco, Jeremy? What's he done?"

The first bell sounded and Jeremy picked up his book bag. "I have to go now, Mr. Sellers." He hurried to his classroom.

Ray wheeled the mop bucket back to its corner for use after all the students were in classrooms. He made the rounds of the lavatories, making sure there were plenty of paper towels and soap.

As he approached the intermediate boys' lavatory, he heard assertive voices.

"Stop it!"

"Make me, Cool-Boy. Make me!"

Nearing the door, he heard scuffling and heavy breathing.

"Stop that or I'll—"

"You'll what, Fashion Boy?"

Ray entered the lavatory and nearly stepped on a pair of fifth-grade boys brawling on the damp floor.

"Hey, what's going on here?" Ray pulled them apart. "On your feet." He glowered at them. "Okay, let's go see Dr. Fleming."

The boys remained planted.

"I said let's go!" Ray's raised voice startled them, and they marched through the door and down the hall. Ray stayed closely behind, following them to Hope's office.

Corinne stood at her desk. She gave the boys a wary look.

"These boys need to see Dr. Fleming. They were fighting in the lavatory. Is she free?"

Corinne buzzed Hope on the intercom, and she opened her door. "Come in, Mr. Sellers. Bring your cohorts, please."

Ray described the boys' behavior and left them with Hope just as the second bell sounded. Crossing the lobby, he noticed large puddles of water and soaked mats near both front doors. He pulled the water vacuum from the storage closet behind the stairway and pushed it toward the entrances.

I wonder what Tom Draco did? And Davey? I suppose he went back to Heather's after he had coffee with Claire. The nerve of that guy.

Ray finished removing the water and brought two dry mats from the boiler room. He spread the wet ones on a wire crate near the warm boilers, knowing they would be dry in twenty-four hours. He stopped at the six other entrance doors and repeated the tasks. By the time he finished, it was nearly ten o'clock.

He would just have time to unpack the six-box shipment waiting on the four-wheeler before he would have to set up the lunchroom. Though too busy to stop, he wanted to call Heather and ask what happened with Tom Draco. But he did not like to call her at work, and he was not sure he wanted to hear it. *Maybe Jeremy just thought there was trouble. Kids follow their senses and they sometimes get the wrong idea. Besides, Joyce is back in town. She keeps a tight rein on Tom when she's home.*

Ray finished mopping the lunch-room floor and set the drying fan on it. He headed to the teachers' lounge for hot coffee to eat with the chocolate donut Boris Mathews had kindly brought him. He looked forward to a quiet break at his desk.

He found the coffee pot half full and still steaming hot, just the way he liked it. The only thing he disliked more than the last cup in the pot was a cup of lukewarm coffee. He carried the over-filled cup carefully, not wanting to sip it until he had a bite of donut.

He sat down at his desk and unwrapped the sticky donut, took a large bite, and savored it. He reached for the hot coffee. Mid-air, his hand stopped.

"Mr. Sellers, telephone call. Are you in there?" Corinne's clear voice carried over the soft hum of the boilers. Not wanting to interrupt his moment, Ray stared at the speaker high on the wall.

"Ray, Ray, are you in there?"

"Yes, I'm here, Corinne," Ray replied, his voice dull.

"Telephone, Ray. I believe it's Heather Baker. Line two."

"Thanks, Corinne." Ray sighed. He looked at his coffee.

He picked up the phone. "Hi Heather. How are you?"

"Hi Ray." He thrilled at her sweet voice. "Thanks for cleaning all my carpets. They look just great. I owe you a dinner." She laughed in her child-like way.

"No you don't, Heather. I didn't mind doing them."

Suddenly serious, she snapped, "Ray, Davey said he stopped at my place and talked to you. Is that true?"

"Well, yes. He did. He came looking for you and Jeremy. Why?"

"Well." Her voice grew thin. "He asked me to get back together with him." She cleared her throat. "And when I said I didn't think you would like that, he said he'd already talked to you; and you were all for it."

Neither spoke for a moment.

"That part's not true, is it, Ray," Heather whispered. Ray could hear the emotion in her voice.

His heart pounded. He swallowed. "Of course not, Heather." He had to force the words out of his mouth. "I mean, well, it's partly true, I guess."

Heather said nothing. Ray's full heart pained him. He looked at his coffee, getting cooler by the second. He looked at his chocolate donut. He thought about Davey. He thought about Jeremy.

Ray inhaled deeply. He exhaled slowly. "Heather, don't take this the wrong way. But I can't come between you and the father of your son."

"Okay, Ray. Thanks for leveling with me," Heather murmured in a voice so low he could barely make it out. "Bye."

The dial tone hummed in his ear.

Ray stuffed the donut in his mouth and gulped the cold coffee, tasting neither. *Dad gummit!*

CHAPTER NINE—THE BRADFORDS

Helsi laid the shopping bag on the kitchen table and ran to answer the telephone. It was Betsy Petersen, asking her to bake for Conflict Managers' Night next week. Betsy thought there should be savories as well as sweets, so Helsi agreed to make cheese squares. *That's a great idea; it starts so early—6:30. Most families will be lucky to get dinner. Ian will not get dinner.*

She and Ian planned to meet at the school. She would feed the children early, then leave Lucy to look after Rachel and Dylan. It happened to be Sean's tutoring night; so he would not be home to antagonize Lucy, who took her babysitting responsibilities seriously.

She noted her baking date on the small chalkboard in the laundry room and opened the shopping bag.

Once the colorful bingo cards were spread on the table, Helsi could not wait to use them with Dylan. The kit included a compact disk of simple songs to practice letter sounds and build retention. The bingo game was meant to be follow-up to the disk.

Scrutinizing the box, she saw that a more advanced version was available to use after mastery of this one. *Dylan loves bingo; he cannot help but love this game.* She looked forward to buying the next one. *I bet he whizzes right through his letter sounds playing this. Maybe I'll pick up a few small bingo prizes at the dollar store.*

She glanced at the kitchen clock, surprised at how late in the day it was. She took a package of boneless, skinless chicken breasts from the refrigerator and a baking pan, which she sprayed with cooking spray. She brushed the chicken with olive oil and sprinkled it with salt, pepper, basil, and a pinch of ginger.

When the preheat indicator sounded, she placed the pan in the oven and set the timer for sixty minutes. Ian should be home at 4:30. We'll eat right away so he can make his six o'clock class.

I'll pick up Sean at Drama Club about six-thirty and drop Lucy at cheerleading practice by six forty-five. She sighed heavily. *That doesn't leave much time for Letter/Sound Bingo tonight. Perhaps tomorrow.*

Helsi played the CD for Dylan at every opportunity: while driving in the car, during breakfast and bath times, and when he kept her company as she prepared dinner.

She managed to play Letter/Sound Bingo with Dylan twice that week for a full forty minutes. Though he did enjoy her attention when playing the game, he was not as excited about it as she had hoped. Occasions when he correctly matched letters to corresponding pictures impressed him little. The prizes were what really motivated him.

This saddened Helsi, who wanted him to be more excited about knowing his letter sounds than about winning those cheap little prizes. She put out of her mind, the fact that he missed three times as many sounds as he scored right.

Lucy and Robbie played the game several times with Dylan and managed to keep him interested with their enthusiasm. Of course, this had to be fed by several trips to the dollar store on Helsi's part, for more of the flimsy little prizes.

She also dismissed the fact that Rachel, during the few rounds in which she joined the game, recognized all the sounds called, even bingoing several times.

During a conference with Dylan's special-needs tutor, Helsi shed quiet tears when Mrs. Pruett described his weak skills. The fact that she was a veteran teacher, renowned for her success in getting the lowest-achieving children to learn to read, only added to Helsi's despair. *She's an expert. The buck really stops here. What will happen to Dylan if he never learns to read?*

But Mrs. Pruett, a grey-haired, kind, and wise woman with the aura of Revered Tribal Grandmother about her, made Helsi's day with breakthrough news.

"Dylan is responding well to a words-in-context approach," she said, her warm eyes penetrating Helsi's. "That means I show him two-or-three-word phrases with pictures to cue him, and he is able to sight read at a fairly consistent rate."

A wide grin took over Helsi's face and she could not stop it. She wanted to hug Mrs. Pruett. A few tiny tears seeped out for a moment; and the teacher turned to Helsi, encircling her in a soft hug. Helsi hugged back hard.

They pulled away and looked at one another, smiling. Mrs. Pruett offered a box of tissues; Helsi took a few and dabbed her eyes.

"Mind you, we still have much work to do, Mrs. Bradford. But I believe Dylan is now ready to learn sight words and master reading in that way."

She adjusted her glasses then looked again at Helsi.

"I know from his records that the sight-word approach was tried with him at an earlier time without a good response." She removed her glasses. "That is not unusual. We know in reading remediation we must try a variety of methods at different stages of a child's maturity, sometimes again and again, until we find a fit."

Helsi looked at her with concerned eyes. "What about sounding out his words, Mrs. Pruett? What do we do about that?"

"We put that on the back burner for now."

Helsi could barely contain herself. *I'm going to throw Letter/Sound Bingo in the trash as soon as I get home.*

"Most children who learn to read through sight words after not responding to phonetic methods, eventually come to understand the relationship between words and phonemes. Phonemes are tiny parts of words, each phoneme representing a particular sound in our language."

"He won't be able to learn his spelling then, will he?" Helsi said, her voice anxious.

Mrs. Pruett smiled at her a moment before speaking. "Indeed, it is during the study of word spellings that sight-word readers gradually begin to see the structure of words. Some more gradually than others, of course." She put on her glasses.

She gently touched Helsi's forearm and locked eyes with her. "We must remember that Dylan needs much practice. Practice! Practice! Practice!" She laughed lustily and Helsi joined her.

"And time." Mrs. Pruitt grew serious. "He will need as much time as you and I and his classroom teacher can give him to practice. Vocabulary drill, application, drill, application. You understand?"

"Drill! Drill! Drill!" Helsi laughed, Mrs. Pruett, too.

"That's right. The predictable thing about young children learning to read—or learning any skill, for that matter—is that they will take as much time as they need. They are not ready until they are ready." She punctuated her words with a sharp nod.

Helsi left the conference with armloads of materials: flashcards with single words; flashcards with phrases on one side, phrases plus pictures on the other; a workbook with read-along audio-cassettes; and untold amounts of hope and encouragement.

It was a brand new day for Helsi Bradford. She could not wait to tell Ian and get to work with Dylan. *I'll make out a schedule with times for each member of the family to work with him. We'll get him up a half-hour early every morning to drill.*

It was 9:15 at night. The house was quiet. Every Bradford child was sleeping. Ian sat at a small desk in the corner of the bedroom, hunched over a thick textbook. A medical dictionary lay next to him.

He pushed back his chair, raised his arms, and stretched thoroughly, moaning softly. *Why does this material have to be so darned technical? These medical terms! It's like trying to learn a foreign language, for gosh sakes.*

Ian rose and walked down to the kitchen where Helsi sat at the table with a legal pad and large-spaced desk calendar, writing intently. He took a glass from the cupboard and filled it with cold tea from a plastic pitcher in the refrigerator. Disappearing into the tiny pantry, he emerged with a bag of tortilla chips and a jar of salsa.

"Hungry, Hon?" she murmured without looking up.

"You bet. I have to fuel my brain. This terminology is about to get the best of me." He sat down at the opposite end of the table and opened the salsa. He was about to dip a chip into it.

"Get yourself a plate, Hon. Don't dip into the salsa jar. Please." He widened his eyes at his wife.

"I'm trying to teach the kids not to do that. They double dip like mad, and it's so gross."

Ian went to the cupboard. He returned with a small plate and a spoon and meticulously scooped a generous portion of salsa onto the plate. He piled chips on the plate next to it. He looked at Helsi and with feigned submission in his voice, asked, "Will this do, Your Highness?"

"Much better, My Serf. Much better." They laughed.

Helsi arranged her own plate of salsa and chips and sat down next to Ian. *This is a good time to show Ian the schedule.*

She placed the calendar next to him and showed him the first week's plan for working with Dylan, explaining that she would probably just repeat it weekly.

"But you've got me working with him Tuesday nights from 7:00 to 7:30." He tapped the calendar irritatingly with his index finger. "You know that's my study time, Helsi." He looked at her. "No way." He said with cold eyes.

His words stung. But Helsi's face revealed no emotion. "All right then." She pored over the schedule. "We'll find another time," she murmured without looking at him.

"How about Monday or Wednesday afternoon, before you go to class?"

"Helsi, you know what a rush it is to get to class on time." His intense eyes burned her face. "You know I always try to review the material right before I leave the house."

He dipped a large tortilla chip in salsa with so much force that it crumbled. As he lifted the tiny piece he was left with to his mouth, a big blob of salsa splattered the tabletop. They both looked at the red pool on the wood surface. Helsi handed him a paper napkin, and he blotted it neatly.

"It's only for a half hour, Ian, or twenty minutes. Twenty minutes twice a week would help." Helsi dipped a chip in salsa and followed it with a second one. She avoided looking at him.

"I can't do that, Hon." His eyes pleaded with her. "No. If I agree to do that, I know I will get behind and fail to live up to it. You know how rushed things are on class nights."

"Fine." Helsi pushed herself away from the table. "The rest of the family will work with Dylan then." She took her plate to the sink and rinsed it. "We'll keep you posted on his progress." She walked out of the room. Her cold words hung in the air.

What does she want from me? It's as if she has to continually throw obstacles in my path. Make me prove myself as a father every time I have to go to class. Or study.

How am I going to tell her about the cram session Chris and Joe and I plan to have in the library after Saturday morning class. She'll make a big deal of that for sure.

Ian slipped into the bedroom for his books, hearing Helsi running water in the bathroom.

Back at the kitchen table, he aligned his legal pad and pencil beside him, opened his book and began to read. Without taking his eyes from the page, he reached for a chip and dipped it. This chip, too, crumbled; and he splattered another blob. He watched the red spill seep into the dull-finish paper of the page and spread in concentric circles over the print.

Now frustrated and completely distracted, Ian looked around the room, taking deep breaths. He did not like this tension between Helsi and him. *Why can't she be more understanding? She has no idea how hard the work is for me. I'm barely keeping my head above water.*

Ian filled a glass of ice cubes from the tap. Noticing a new-looking box in the trash can, he lifted the Letter/Sound Bingo box and examined it with unseeing eyes.

What did Helsi say about that? What did she tell me Mrs. Pruett found that worked with Dylan? She was so excited for him about it.

He gave up on studying.

Pressed against his wife's stone-still body in the queen-sized bed, his mind raced. He longed to share a moment of warmth with her but lay motionless. *I'll smooth everything over in the morning.*

At breakfast Helsi was her usual cheerful self, but with a barely discernable edge. She was holding back slightly. This made it easy for Ian to avoid last-night's issue, over which his wife obviously still festered. He would make it up to her later.

They would continue in this cat-and-mouse emotional climate the rest of the week.

Ian moved to end the tension Saturday lunchtime when the house was empty of children. Sean and Lucy were at their practices, Robbie and Dylan at a scout sleepover; Rachel had left for Sabrina's birthday party at the end of the street.

He apologized for his shortness with her. She returned the apology, and they promised not to let tension get the best of them again. Helsi did not bring up the subject of the family's help-Dylan schedule.

Helsi spent Tuesday morning baking two batches of cheese squares for Conflict Managers' Night. She made them extra large and full of cheese. She arranged the squares on large platters and garnished them with small bunches of red grapes.

After the trays were thoroughly sealed with plastic wrap, she walked to Ian's desk in the bedroom. She removed the packages of adhesive-backed nametags and rolls of stickers from the side drawer. Carefully separating the nametag sheets, she placed a tiny green peace sign precisely in the upper left corner of each nametag.

The results pleased her. The twenty-three dollars she had spent to have Poore Pond Conflict Managers printed on the tags was worth it. She knew the students would love them.

When all the nametags were finished, Helsi scoured the house for a large manila envelope to recycle. She found the perfect one on Ian's desk and removed its contents. The sheets of nametags fit perfectly in the envelope, and she placed them on the table next to the cheese-square trays.

She changed from jeans and sweatshirt into freshly ironed khaki pants and a green wool cardigan. She added a wooden necklace Sean had made for her in shop class and examined the total look in the long mirror near the front door. *This will do, I guess.* She added small, wooden button earrings she had found at a craft store and grabbed her battered brown purse.

Helsi heard the loud swish of air brakes and saw a yellow bus pass the window. Robbie, Dylan, and Rachel ran in the door noisily.

The children were just finishing their hamburger patties, macaroni and cheese from a box, green peas, and applesauce when Lucy rushed in the door.

Helsi's glance at the clock was not wasted on her daughter. "I'm sorry I'm late, Mom. I stayed after to help Mr. Fink get the bulletin board finished." She took off her coat and draped it on a kitchen chair.

"Lucy, in the coat closet with that," Helsi said resolutely. "Then I need you to help Robbie wash and change clothes."

Helsi pulled the van in front of the boiler-room door.

"Come on, Robbie. Help me bring in those trays." She nodded her chin toward the back of the van. "And that large shopping bag goes too."

Energized by excitement, Robbie managed to carry two trays and the bulky shopping bag in one trip. Helsi held her breath.

The cafeteria floor looked cleaner than usual. Robbie darted across it to a group of students dressed like him in green conflict-managers' pinnies over clean white shirts and cotton pants. His mother called him back to get the envelope of nametags.

"There are three black markers in the envelope, Robbie. Make sure you put them on the table next to the nametags."

Each time another parent arrived with food, Helsi rearranged the trays on the table. She clustered all the sweets together and the savories separately. She kept adding to the stack of paper plates and napkins and wished the refreshment committee had sent home tear-offs for parents to return to school if they were coming.

Betsy had said that half the people who attend these school functions never bother to book ahead while others book but do not come. So tear-offs were meaningless. *It's just another example of how overextended everyone is nowadays.*

Families straggled in continually, and the chairs began to fill. Helsi took a deep breath and inhaled the inviting smells of oregano, cheese, and chocolate, mingled with floor wax and stale air.

She looked at her watch. Six twenty. Ian should be here any moment. He's going to be so proud of Robbie. I'm glad we did not tell him that Robbie is master of ceremonies. She busied herself straightening the stacks of napkins and paper plates.

Loud blips of electrical static pierced the air. Hope Fleming stood on the small stage, testing the microphone, as always an imposing figure in a well-cut black suit with long pencil skirt. Robbie stood next to her, holding his stapled pages of notes and exuding a bit of the principal's air of importance.

Helsi looked uneasily around the room. Ian was nowhere to be seen. *He must be on his way.*

"Hi Helsi. Where's Ian; Joe wants to sit with him?" Betsy Petersen tapped her shoulder.

"I don't think he's here yet. At least I don't see him. We drove separately." She looked down the table and waved back at a smiling Joe.

Dr. Fleming gave a short welcome speech and introduced Robbie before turning the program over to Mrs. Ricci, the music teacher. On cue, the chorus members filed in and lined themselves in rows on the risers.

The conflict managers sat in chairs to the left of the risers; Robbie took the first chair. *Robbie starts right after the chorus sings two short songs. Ian had better get here before that.*

Mrs. Ricci introduced the first song, a thank-you to parents for "always being there." Applause resounded afterward.

Stepping up to the microphone, Mrs. Ricci began, "We are very proud of this next number. Your conflict-manager sons and daughters wrote the lyrics, themselves. It was a group effort." She smiled at the audience then turned to smile at the conflict managers. Their subdued smiles reflected appropriate seriousness for officers of such responsible positions.

"And our Poore Pond Chorus fit the lyrics to the tune of a song you all know, My Country Tis of Thee." A long, loud blast of sirens from the boulevard outside obscured her words. She waited for the noises to end before repeating herself. The audience applauded noisily, some people craning their necks toward open doors into the windowed corridor. A few people slipped quietly out of the cafeteria.

"The chorus will sing it through for you once, then we want you to join us in singing it a second time."

Mrs. Ricci assumed her conductor's stance, and thirty-two young voices began:

Peace keepers we will be!
So all have liberty
At Poore Pond School!

Helsi's eyes policed the two main entrance doors, heat rising in her chest. There was no sign of Ian. She pulled a phone from her pocket and speed dialed his number, getting voice mail yet again. She shook off uneasy feelings.

She dialed their home number and spoke to Lucy. No, she had not seen nor heard from her father. "Well, tell him to call my cell phone if you hear from him, Lucy." Helsi felt sick to her stomach. *If he misses Robbie's big night, I'll—I don't know what I'll do.*

Parent voices rose with the chorus in re-singing the song, and Helsi tried to mouth words to which she had not listened.

She looked at Robbie, rolling his pages of notes with both hands, and could feel his anxiety. She thought she might burst with anger toward Ian and nervousness for Robbie. *Why is the heat up so high in here?*

The song ended and applause filled the room. Helsi speed dialed again. No Ian.

Mrs. Ricci presented Robbie, second-year conflict manager, to begin his master-of-ceremonies duties. He walked confidently to the microphone and placed his notes on the lectern. Polite applause greeted him, and Helsi's heart soared.

"Ladies and gentlemen, thank you for coming," He began, his voice a little too high. "I want to personally thank you for supporting your conflict managers." His voice lower now, "And I want to personally thank my mother and father for supporting me."

Helsi's cheeks burned with tears of joy. And rage.

Robbie introduced pairs of conflict managers who took turns explaining the ground rules of their work. Helsi could not believe how self-possessed her son seemed.

Each pair of presenters ended their explanations with a short role-play, demonstrating right-and-wrong ways to follow the rule. Helsi barely heard them, so consumed was she with anger toward Ian.

When Robbie spoke; however, she gave him rapt attention.

The program ended with Dr. Fleming listing statistics on reduced numbers of playground detentions, for a variety of offenses, since the Conflict Managers' Program had been implemented at Poore Pond. Robbie, unable to hide his delight, used a laser pointer to match Hope's numbers on a colorful student-made chart as she spoke.

The audience applauded wildly, some even whistled loudly, ignoring Hope's well-publicized ban on such behavior.

Helsi fumed. *This would have been a perfect night if only Ian had cared enough to be here.*

A ravaged Ian arrived home at 9:45 to find Helsi cleaning the remains of ice cream, chocolate sauce, and colored sprinkles off the kitchen table.

He put his arms around her waist and tried to apologize, but Helsi shrugged him off with uncharacteristic aggression.

"Not only did you miss your son's outstanding performance, you missed the family celebration afterward!" She riveted cold eyes on him. "What kind of father is that?"

She rinsed dishes in the sink and scrubbed the tabletop with great fervor, pretending not to listen to Ian's explanation.

"Just hear me out, Helsi. I had to miss Robbie's program. I had no choice."

"You were supposed to leave class early to be there, and you did not bother." She slumped into a chair. "I want to know what was so all-fired important about that blasted class that you would let down your son. And me. And the rest of the family." As if on her last breath, she whispered, "We were counting on you, Ian." She dropped her forehead and covered it dramatically with her hand.

"I never made it to class, Helsi." Ian's voice was graver than she had heard it for a long time.

Finally noticing his ragged appearance, she looked at him with wide, questioning eyes.

"I need coffee," he said calmly, his face somber.

Helsi poured him a cup from the pot she had made earlier in anticipation of his at least being a part of the celebration. He moved to the table, and she set it in front of him. She poured herself a cup and sat down across from him.

Ian stirred the coffee slowly and deliberately.

"Chief Wrangston is dead," he said, looking squarely at Helsi. He heard her quick intake of breath and continued.

"He insisted on going to the fire—there was a huge fire at the chemical plant on Fulton." He furrowed his brow at her. "I can't believe you did not hear all the sirens, Helsi. Three engines, two ambulances, and at least six patrol cars screamed right past the school."

Helsi felt chills over her entire body as she recalled the sirens' interruption while Carmen Ricci was speaking. Why didn't it dawn on me that those were Ian's sirens? That he would be involved? Her heart filled with self-loathing.

Silence and despair filled the room.

"I did hear those sirens, Ian. But that was shortly after seven. You would have already been in class by then." She needed to redeem herself for not making the inevitable connection between the sirens and Ian's work, the way wives of emergency workers always did. The way she always did.

He told her that he knew he was going to be late getting to class. Some of the equipment failed periodic tests, and Ian was one of those who had to stay and solve the problem. There was no putting it off since an emergency might happen while the equipment was down.

"We did get everything working, and I had resigned myself to the fact that I would miss class altogether. By then I knew I'd be late for the program, but I could at least get there for part of it."

He walked to the counter and brought the pot to the table, refilling both his and Helsi's cups. She pushed a potholder toward him, on which he set the hot coffeepot.

She looked at him with eager eyes.

"I had just called the college to leave a message for my instructor. I cleaned myself up to go to Robbie's program, was headed out to my car in fact when the call came in."

He described how bad the fire had been, the two major explosions in different parts of the plant. The demands were so great at the fire that even with extra firefighters from two neighboring towns, they were still shorthanded.

That's when the chief went in. He and five others were in the area of the first explosion when it happened. Two men were injured, both seriously. The chief and three firefighters, including one woman, were killed instantly.

"They didn't have a prayer, Helsi." His voice choked with emotion.

She circled the table and hugged her husband awkwardly as he sat. "Let's move to the couch," she whispered.

She cradled him in her arms for a long time. Every few minutes he would describe another incident at the fire. At one point, he sat up and sobbed uncontrollably.

A part of her ached to tell him he had missed Robbie's outstanding performance, but she knew this was not the time.

She loathed herself completely.

CHAPTER TEN—HOPE

Unable to sleep, Hope left her warm bed and dressed for school. She knew the problems she faced that day would seem somehow more solvable from her functional office than when they intruded upon the peace of her comfortable home.

The parking lot was eerily vacant when she pulled into it well before Ray's starting time. A thin coat of fresh snow covered the pavement, which had been plowed clear only a few hours earlier. Few morning lights were yet lit in neighborhood homes. Tree branches heavy with snow cast menacing shadows in the dark expanse. *The timer for the corner spotlights must be out again.*

She looked behind her uneasily as she walked from car to boiler-room door and was grateful for the dim light above it. A small wind brought the faint odor of new asphalt.

She balanced her briefcase and purse on one arm and tried to unlock the door. After three attempts, she set her things in the snow and used both hands, finally managing to turn the lock. Blocking the heavy door with her hip, she bent to pick them up and stepped inside. The door swished shut tightly.

Hope hurried to Ray's newly partitioned office, dropped her things on his desk, and quickly pressed the alarm code. The digital clock shone 5:10 in electronic red numerals. *I need to help Ray turn this cubicle into an attractive office.*

She crossed the silent lobby where Poore Pond's oversized Oscar fish swam happily in his bubbling tank. Hope welcomed the cheery noise and glow of Oscar's home.

Pressing switches, she left a trail of light behind her and turned on all lights in the outer office as well as her own. She heard the boilers kick on, heating vents emitting a surge of musty smells.

Taking file folders from her briefcase, she placed them on the table and checked the list on her desk:

7:30	*Brian re: Bluewave Stoneciper*
8:00	*Brian and Bluewave*
10:15	*PEEAC (Parents for Effective Education of Autistic Children) at Shakerag*
11:00	*Mia Drake (sub for Ali Cantrell) to pick up materials*
?	*Phone McElson-Bourney*

"First things first," Hope said aloud, pulling from her briefcase a copy of the memo she had sent Brian Glover, with a list of parental complaints against Bluewave Stonecipher.

Hope looked again at the letter she had received yesterday from Dr. Eli, regarding Martin Purdue. He agreed that the symptoms Brad and she had seen in Martin's lack of speech might possibly indicate what he called a sensory deficit. He had scheduled, with full cooperation from the Purdues, a series of multi-level tests. He promised a written report in a matter of weeks.

This meeting with PEEAC could not have come at a better time.

She quickly jotted a note to Corinne, listing teacher materials to be gathered by eleven o'clock for Mia Drake.

Her eyes moved down the list. She looked at the last item and, denying a small knot of apprehension forming in her stomach, thought there would be time for phone calls between 1:00 and 2:00 o'clock.

She returned to the Bluewave memo and jotted words in the margins.

Sounds of melodic whistling came from the hall, and she looked up at the wall clock.

"Good morning, Ray," she called, stepping out of her office.

"You're earlier than the chickens, Hope," he laughed. "Is something wrong? Or do we have an event going on that I forgot about?"

"No, nothing like that, Ray. I just have a number of appointments and meetings today." She handed him a tiny box of assorted screwdrivers she had borrowed earlier. "I had the darnedest time sleeping. My mind would not shut off."

"I know what you mean." He took the box. "Did you get your glasses fixed all right?"

"Yes, I did. And thank you. Those microscopic screwdrivers were perfect for the job. Of course, I had to find my old glasses to put on, so I could see the screws in the first place." She smiled. "Thanks. Have a good day, Ray." She slipped quietly back into her office.

Ray headed out the door.

"Oh Ray, one more thing."

He turned to see Hope leaning out her door. "The boiler-room lock is tight again, needs graphite or whatever magic you perform on it. Oh, and your office partition went up last night."

He nodded. "Me with a real office? That's something."

Her supervisor arrived on time; and he and Hope reviewed the summary of parents' complaints against substitute teacher, Bluewave Stonecipher. They were all similar and took issue with her "religious" remarks to the children.

"Thank God, Mrs. Sutton is in there a good bit of the time, keeping things on an even keel," one mother wrote, and several others echoed.

"What about her teaching skills?" Brian wanted to know.

Hope reminded him that none of the parents had complained about Bluewave's teaching.; it was her reference to the spiritual that concerned them. In fact, two mothers and one father actually praised her ability to keep the kids motivated and learning. One wrote that her son "had not been this anxious to come to school since kindergarten."

Brian skimmed down Hope's typed summary then sifted through the pile of actual notes from parents. Hope reviewed her summary and grew restless when he spent a long time reading.

Finally, Brian looked up with furrowed brow. "I just don't see how we can fault her, Hope, for things like: asking the children to take deep breaths and reach way inside themselves to do their best, or picturing themselves doing very well on their math tests, before they start." His eyes widened and he smiled.

"Or to close their eyes and be thankful for good minds and proper school books." He shrugged his shoulders and looked at the clock. "What do you think?"

"She's not actually asking them to invoke the help of a higher power. Or is she?" Hope looked into space.

Brian stared at the ceiling.

"Is she suggesting they invoke the help of a higher power, or is she asking them to look inside themselves to the higher parts of their minds?" Brian faced Hope with distant eyes.

"And giving them strategies to use to reach the—as you said, Brian—higher parts of their minds," Hope said to the ceiling. She turned toward him.

Brian, deep in thought, said nothing.

"We have eight minutes to plan our words for Bluewave, Brian." Hope broke the silence.

"How do you ask a teacher to stop doing something that is working well with the kids?" Brian asked. "Even fostering love in the class. One parent wrote," he began reading, "'She fills the classroom with love and light, which is wonderful for the children. It's just that she goes a little overboard in a spiritual, almost religious way. We're Presbyterian and we worry about cults and that sort of thing.' Did you see that one, Hope?" He waved a yellow paper at her.

"I did. I thought her words, love and light, were apt."

Hope thrust out her palms. "Perhaps we could ask her to tone down her look. She wears those long, floaty, ethereal dresses and skirts. And crystal beads. And that wild—well—natural hair." Hope colored slightly, unable to mask her mixed feelings.

She stood and inhaled intensely. "I mean, it's lovely on her; it suits her." She stepped to the window. "But that look, combined with all the deep breathing, looking inside themselves, and visualizing." She turned to face Brian.

"It's the total package, you're saying?" Brian asked, stretching his shoulders.

"Exactly." Hope dropped her chin. "She's making herself a target, perhaps more with her counter-culture dress than with the psycho-self-talk she's teaching the children to use."

"Dr. Fleming," Corinne's silken voice came over the intercom. "Ms. Stonecipher is here to see you and Dr. Glover."

Brian stood. Hope put her hand on the doorknob.

In the end, it was Bluewave, herself, who made the point that she should change the way she dressed. During their discussion, in which Hope and Brian were very frank, even sharing the parents' notes with her, she came to that conclusion.

"Perhaps the parents are put off by my dress. They don't know what to make of it." Her eyes serious, she said, "I would rather change my look than give up the self-talk, as you call it, Hope."

"Psycho-self-talk, Bluewave." She grinned at her.

"Psycho-self-talk. Actually, that's a good name for it." She smiled at Hope, then Brian. "Do you mind if I use that term with the parents?"

"You had better stick to just self-talk, Bluewave," Brian interjected. "That psycho part will send the parents over the edge." They laughed heartily.

"As I said, I'd much rather give up my style of dress than the self-talk. It's working so well with the children. They are really getting into using it, and it's working for them." Her eyes shone.

"Even David Collier. He's Mr. Reserved, so inhibited; and he's comfortable using it." Bluewave turned toward Hope.

"Remember, Hope? David was on my Math Maestros List all last week. You announced his name every morning."

"Did he come down for his ribbons?" Hope asked.

"Are you kidding?" Bluewave smiled at Brian. "He's papered his desk with them."

They were grateful for her candor, her professionalism. They were thrilled by how child-centered she seemed.

Hope instructed her to draft a letter to the parents, explaining the value of self-talk to build inner strength. Such a letter might reassure them that she was not some sort of fanatic, out to enlist their children in a pagan cult.

"Wherever did you find her, Hope?" Brian asked after Bluewave had gone.

"Just lucky." She looked, unseeing, at Brian. "When you do find those spiritual ones like Bluewave, they either create the most positive, Lion-King sort of energy in the classroom or they totally fracture it. Suck all the air out of the room and choke the kids' spirits. I guess it's all in the delivery."

"We've been blessed." Brian stood and pulled on his overcoat. "I'll see you, Hope, at the meeting on autism. Keep me posted on all this."

They shook hands briefly, and he departed, coattails flapping in the wake of his brisk step.

Hope sat next to Belva at the PEEAC Meeting, which was held in her building in the elegant Chestnut Room. Originally an office for the county superintendent, it was no longer needed since the State Education Department had changed from a county system to city and exempted-village school districts decades ago. The Chestnut Room with its dark paneling and fireplace was now a bonus meeting room.

Principals, school psychologists, and special-education supervisors listened attentively to the presenters. They were all parents of autistic children, very well versed in their subject and poised, articulate speakers, obviously from fighting so hard for their children's education.

Many administrators stared at the stone fireplace, yearning for a warm fire on this frigid winter day.

Belva, Hope, and Brian helped distribute the endless handouts provided.

"We have four diagnosed students here at Shakerag," Belva whispered when a speaker gave startling statistics. "One in every 166 children is diagnosed with autism in this country."

Martin Purdue's blank face fixed itself in Hope's mind.

The speaker, a slim, attractive mother in trendy jeans and short tweed jacket, gave comparisons of both incidence and funding rates for autism, to other childhood afflictions. Leukemia, muscular dystrophy, cystic fibrosis, and juvenile diabetes all had lower incidence and much higher funding.

"Autism is the fastest-growing, serious developmental disability in the U.S." she stated, sending another shock wave through the audience.

Superintendent Ed Amiston introduced a tall, important-looking woman in a black suit, as an agent from the State Education Department. She outlined the schools' responsibility under The Individuals with Disabilities Act of 1990, to provide a free and appropriate public education for children identified with diagnosed learning deficits. She added the fact that a year later a new version of the law extended to preschoolers who were developmentally delayed.

"More IEPs," Hope whispered to Belva, who closed her eyes and nodded.

"More crying need for classroom aides, too," Belva added.

"We are here today to provide you with necessary information on this devastating disorder, a disorder that robs young victims of their ability to communicate and sentences them to a lonely world of isolation. It robs them of their education. It prevents them from enjoying the warmth of human touch, so necessary to emotional development. It sabotages the growth of social skills. In some cases, it causes their physical abilities to regress." Her rich voice and dramatic words mesmerized the audience.

"But there are treatments, many types of documented educational treatments. The earlier the diagnosis and the earlier intervention begins, the better a victim's chances of optimizing a near-normal level of functionality."

The speaker closed with an imperious statement, calling for immediate and intensive teacher training on the types of education models that have worked with autistic children. She demanded that dates for both training and implementation be forthcoming.

The PEEAC representatives thanked, and were thanked by the participants; and they promptly left.

It was as if the very air in the room left with them.

Ed Amiston stood and announced to a roomful of drained faces, the schedule for preliminary meetings and training sessions that would follow. He urged administrators to parcel out subject information to their staff members in small bytes so as not to overload them. He sent around handouts to guide them in doing so.

Everyone filed out in silence, some dropping their armload of photocopies on autism, others stooping to help retrieve them.

Belva hurried toward echoes of lunchroom sounds.

Hope rushed to her car, anxious to make it back to Poore Pond for lunch period. She started the engine and dialed Corinne on her cellular phone. She watched her breath in the frigid air and pressed the seat-warmer button beside the cold leather seat.

"Hello, Corinne," Hope said with a sigh. "Is anything pressing?"

"Well, there is one thing, Hope. Emmylou has a suspicious-looking note, saying she is to be picked up by her uncle again." Hope could hear quotation marks around Corinne's word uncle.

"Have you reached her mother to verify it?"

"Not yet. I'm still waiting for a callback."

"Thank you, Corinne. I'm on my way." Hope steered the almost-warm Volvo out of the long parking lot.

I need a cup of tea—nothing was served at that meeting, that's unusual—and a little food. Oh Emmylou, what are you getting yourself into?

"Dr. Fleming, meet Martha Poynter," Corinne said as Hope entered the office, bringing with her, a rush of icy air. "Martha retired from Poore Pond before you came. She and I worked in federal programs together at one time."

She placed her briefcase on the floor, removed her gloves, and shook the woman's hand. Hope took in Martha's thick shock of gunmetal grey hair, warm brown eyes, and athletic frame. *What a handsome woman.*

"How are you finding retirement, Martha?" Hope asked, keeping her eyes fixed on the visitor while lifting her briefcase.

"I have not had much taste of it yet. You see, I've been teaching English in China since a few months after I retired."

"I see," said Hope. "What a noble, adventurous thing to do. You are to be commended." Hope smiled into her eyes and held her gaze, waiting for Martha's return smile. It did not come.

"Good to meet you, Martha. Corinne will sign you out." Hope said, stepping into her office. She took the packet of meeting materials from her briefcase and placed them squarely on the desk.

Emmylou's note, clipped to the pencil cup, caught her attention. She removed her coat and picked it up. This is obviously a child's manuscript, but the signature does look rather adult. Hope knew that parents sometimes dictated school notes for their older children to write, and the parents would then sign them. Was this such a case?

She grabbed the portable microphone, slipped the strap over her shoulder, and hurried to the lunchroom.

In the crowded lunchroom filled with young voices and the thick smell of cheese pizza and well-cooked green beans, Hope stood near Ray, monitoring the children as they emptied their trays and placed them on racks.

They redirected those students who left their trays askew and kept the line moving. Student helpers, their hands protected by disposable rubber gloves, pulled filled garbage bags from trashcans and replaced them with fresh ones, moving efficiently and importantly. Garbage smells rose and fell with trash rotation.

"Who is that lady, Dr. Fleming?" asked fifth-grader, Diana Collier, standing so close that Hope bumped her as she turned.

"What lady, Diana?"

"That grey-haired lady standing by my class's table," she said, stepping out and gesturing with her forearm.

"That's Mrs. Poynter, Diana. She's a retired teacher. Why are you asking?" *What is she doing in the lunchroom?*

"Well, she came to our table and asked if anybody needed help with reading or spelling." Diana explained in a low voice. "We didn't know what we were supposed to say. None of us knows her." She looked across the large room.

Hope's eyes followed Diana's to Martha Poynter who had sat down next to a boy in the class to whom she talked intently.

"Thank you, Diana. You've been a big help." Hope's brow furrowed as she moved toward Mrs. Poynter.

Alone at last with a cup of strong tea, Hope relaxed at her desk and waited for Mrs. Parks to answer the page left on her cellular phone.

At twenty minutes before dismissal, the call still had not come.

She inhaled deeply and dialed Officer Clifton's number. She exhaled thankfully when his voice came over the line. He agreed to come immediately and stake out the parking lot and the two streets feeding into it.

Hope hurried to Boris Mathews' class and removed Emmylou, instructing her to gather her things and come with her principal to be dismissed from the office.

"I'm awaiting a call back from your mother, Emmylou," Hope explained, implying that they had been in contact.

"But my Uncle Kurt is picking me up." She looked furtively toward the lobby windows. "I brought a note, Dr. Fleming. Mr. Mathews has it."

The girl turned away, "I'll go ask him for it."

"No, Emmylou. I have your note. Your teacher sent it down. But I must speak to your mother before you leave school."

"I can't be late for gymnastics; I'll get in big trouble," she pleaded. "Just let me go with Uncle Kurt. I'll explain to Mom."

Hope gently pressed the back of Emmylou's waist, guiding her toward the office.

Corinne came down the hall to say that Mrs. Parks had called in and was waiting on hold.

"May I go to the lav?" Emmylou asked anxiously. "I'll be right back."

"Use the clinic lavatory, Emmylou," Hope said firmly. She made eye contact with Corinne and knew she would monitor the child. She hurried into her office and lifted the receiver.

Mrs. Parks apologized for not answering the page. Her phone was turned off while she sat in an intense meeting. No, she had not signed the note. Emmylou was expected to come home on the bus and go to gymnastics with the car-pool driver, as usual.

The getting-ready bell sounded, Hope straining to hear.

"This is déjà vu, isn't it, Dr. Fleming? We established the last time that there is no Uncle Kurt." Mrs. Parks' voice, though calm, was edged with fear. "Emmylou has no uncles living within 500 miles of here."

In the end, Hope agreed to keep Emmylou in her office until Mrs. Parks arrived to collect her. "She can help me alphabetize practice-test booklets. She's good at that," Hope assured the mother.

The call ended just as Corinne opened Hope's door for Emmylou. The dismissal bell rang, followed by a din of high voices and stampede of young feet traveling to buses.

Emmylou's face turned ashen.

"There's a call for you on my phone, Dr. Fleming." Corinne turned her back to the child and mouthed, "Officer Clifton."

"We have a man in custody at the station. We caught him outside his car, surveying the crowd of students with binoculars. We're going to need to talk to the girl. I'll get back to you, Doctor."

Hope placed Corinne's receiver on its base and went into her office to relieve the secretary. She offered a surly Emmylou an apple and bottle of water. Lifting a tall stack of practice tests from the shelf, she placed it on the table. *That call to McElson-Bourney will just have to wait.*

Unable to stop thinking about Emmylou, Hope tossed and turned in her bed. Officer Clifton had called her at home and told her that a detective had interrogated at length, the man with the binoculars. He had no prior record, so they could not hold him longer than twenty-four hours without charges. But he had been fingerprinted, and the investigation continued.

I must close my mind and get some sleep. She took deep breaths and rolled to her side. *Thank God Mia was available to sub for Ali Cantrell. Mia is like a full-time staff member, knows just what to do and needs very little help.*

She yawned noisily and looked at the bedside clock. It was only 12:20 A.M. *Grace Singer, I'm not sure about. Her references are outstanding. She's taught fifth grade before. But I don't know if she can handle those audacious kids in Marsha Edwards' class.*

Hope leaned on her elbow and switched on the lamp. She lifted the crystal tumbler atop the monogrammed decanter and filled it with water, which she drank deeply.

Her eyes scanned the shadowy room. *I hope Grace can work well with all the parent volunteers in that class.* She took another long drink, replaced the empty tumbler, and reached for the pocket-sized book, Peace Snippets.

Settling into the pillow and drawing the covers over her chilled arms, her mind filled with visions of Frances. Her sister had given her the tiny book days after she had arrived and taken up residence in Hope's guestroom to await her death from an incurable cancer. Frances observed her comings and goings and chided Hope about her frenetic approach to life.

"You are so anal you cannot even stay away from school during what is supposed to be your summer break, Hope. What is it with you?"

Frances looked beautiful at the time. It was before the disease had shown on her face, though ravaging her internally at a rapid rate. Morning sun streamed in on her face and newly grown, coppery caplet of hair as the two of them shared a quick pot of tea before Hope's heading off for an appointment with a textbook salesperson.

"I'm terminal and I'm enjoying life more than you are these days." Frances' sardonic wit always broke her up, and they laughed lustily. "I bought you this, Sister Dear," she said pulling the book from the pocket of her peach satin robe, borrowed from Hope.

Hope ran her fingers over the cover. "Peace Snippets? What is that? Reading this will give me only snippets of peace? Not a full peace?" Her eyes danced at Frances.

"It's a start." Frances barked. "Your training wheels." She shifted her hips gingerly, her eyes giving away pain. She breathed deeply. "But before I check out, you'll be flying solo, Kid. Just leave it to Francie."

Now tears, triggered by the thought of her sister's childhood nickname, streamed from Hope's eyes. She saw the two of them as little girls, sharing a bedroom, playing together. Their salad days reeled in slow motion through her mind as she clutched the small book to her chest and eventually fell asleep.

The alarm sounded, rousing a surprised Hope, who always awakened ahead of it. Ah, Friday. Dinner tonight with Theodore.

Friday-night dinners with Theodore had become a standing date; but curiously, there were no other dates, just Friday nights.

A pattern had begun to play out each time. They would spend the first half-hour digging in mussel shells with tiny forks and discussing the foundation: new board members, the board's action, the building now being reconfigured as a shelter.

Through the seafood entrée, enhanced by goblets of room-temperature wine, George became the second topic: his growth as manager, his uncanny ability to recognize a mistake before a faulty decision had been carried out, his instinctive knowledge of physical needs the shelter should have for its particular residents.

The third topic tended to surface just before dessert. It was a detailed description of potential clients George had begun to collect. And tainting the dessert somewhat, Theodore added an assessment of overall problems to be resolved.

Hope looked forward to her time with Theodore. They seemed at ease with one another. Their common interests were many: they were both impeccable dressers, connoisseurs of fine food and literature, anchored by a code of proper manners.

And yet, behind this façade of formality, they each had an innate interest in people, a sense of connectedness to others, a sort of we're-all-in-this-together attitude. It made for a strong bond.

Hope found herself basking in a gentle radiance when in Theodore's company. The electricity generated between them told her he felt it, too. For four months, the attraction had not only endured, but had grown. In fact, lately she often had to will herself to focus on the business of the foundation, so distracted was she by the chemistry in the air.

It was a typical Friday at Poore Pond: absenteeism was up among students and staff members; the number of early-release requests rose; children's cafeteria chatter went up in volume; teachers pressed to pull students through all the week's unfinished projects and lessons.

Late in the day, Officer Clifton stopped to see Hope. Emmylou's parents had brought her to the police station the night before, and he had questioned the child at length. She admitted to occasional visits in chat rooms but vehemently denied having any sort of email relationship with a stranger, boy or man.

When asked to explain the note authorizing Uncle Kurt to pick her up after school, she claimed to have written the note herself to get back at her mother. She gave vague answers as to why she wanted to do that.

"There were many unanswered questions," the officer said. "So we confiscated Emmylou's computer. One of our forensics technicians is searching it." Officer Clifton's pager beeped and he excused himself.

When he reappeared, Hope asked, "What about the man with the binoculars? Is he still in custody?"

"He is, but not for long." He bent his arm and checked his watch. "We'll have to release him in two hours." He looked at Hope with defeat in his eyes. "Unless forensics come up with something soon."

"Can you charge him with pandering or something like that?" Hope pleaded. "Surely, it's not acceptable for a man to loiter at a school during the peak of dismissal and train binoculars on the entire student body?"

"Of course it's not." Officer Clifton pushed shut, Hope's half-closed door. In lowered voice, he explained, "Right now, he's on the books for trespassing and suspicious intent because of the binoculars. But he was smart enough to stay just off school property, so we can't really charge him with trespassing."

Heat rose in Hope's chest. "But Officer, we are talking about children here, in this culture of ours, rampant with crimes against children. Can't you hold him on the charge of suspicious intent? At least long enough to complete your search of Emmylou's computer? Please!"

He promised to do all he could, to keep her informed, and went on his way.

Anxious for a relaxing evening with Theodore, Hope tidied the office, quickly walked through the building, checking that all was in order.

She gathered her things and closed the office.

There were two notes in her inbox; so she grabbed them on her way out, tucking them into her coat pocket.

Sipping tea and opening mail at the kitchen table, Hope began to unwind. She had a whole hour until she would leave to meet Theodore. *I am glad I left the office. I need a little time alone tonight. I want to be in a weekend mode.*

She remembered the notes from her inbox and went to the coat closet to retrieve them. Spreading them side by side on the table, she saw the first was from Carol Davis:

> **The Purdues agreed to have Martin evaluated.**

That's a real breakthrough, she thought.

The second note was from music teacher, Carmen Ricci.

> **Hope, wait until you see the living nativity the children have planned for the holiday program. Titus Lal, the new student from India, wants to be baby Jesus. Hilary Butler will be Mary, and Frank Branchello is dying to be Joseph.**

> **DON'T WORRY NOW. It's only going to be a nano-second view, a quick flash in the spotlight between chorus numbers. We will show you at rehearsal Monday.**

Hope choked on the tea she had just drunk, splattering brown stains on Carmen's note. She mopped it with a napkin and tried to compose herself.

Taking the phone from the counter, she leafed through a brass rolodex for the number and dialed it. Carmen's electronic voice came through, inviting her to leave a message at the beep. "Carmen, this is Hope. Call me as soon as you get this message."

Carmen has gone too far this time. A nativity scene in a public school program? No. Not on your life.

CHAPTER ELEVEN—RAY

Ray walked through the silent school, checking classrooms for potential problems. Familiar animal smells met him in rooms with pets: gerbils, hamsters, rabbits. Switching on lights, he heard swift movements in cages. Everything seemed to be in order.

He entered the library where colorful paper mobiles swayed from the ceiling, and felt a rush of cold air. Shattered glass covered the sill beneath a far window facing the play yard. *A broken window again? That's the second one in here this winter.*

The occasional broken window was part of spring's arrival, usually caused by an errant softball, which Ray often found on site. But there was no sign of such a ball, and he wondered what caused the window to break.

Gathering the sharp shards with gloved hands, Ray noticed several small holes at the apex of some cracks. *These look like pellet-gun holes.* When all the glass had been removed and a temporary panel placed in the window frame, he knelt and ran his hands over the carpet. He collected two small, black metal pellets and put them in his pocket. He vacuumed the sills and the carpet thoroughly. He checked nearby table and shelf surfaces for stray glass.

I have to get to the hospital by 7:00. Claire had Mom practically ready to go when I left. Still, he took the time to do a thorough job on this cleanup. It was important for safety reasons, and the focus helped him deal with his uneasiness. Wanting to extend the nerve-soothing task, he methodically returned all clean-up equipment to its proper place.

Anxiety gnawed at Ray's stomach at the thought of Caroline's undergoing another six-hour treatment. Meant to strengthen her congestive heart, the first treatment had made her even weaker. But that was three months ago. She had grown strong enough to try another treatment, this time with adjustments in the medication and the rate at which it was administered. Her doctors were convinced the changes would give better results.

Ray emailed the grounds supervisor at the board office with a request for a replacement window. When he saw Hope's Volvo pull into the bare parking lot, he headed for the office, buttoning his coat as he walked. He neared her door, whistling softly so as not to startle her.

"Good morning, Ray." Hope appeared in the doorway. "How's the new office? What time are you due at the hospital?"

"I haven't had time to take it in yet. If I get there by 7:00, that will be plenty early enough." He reached a hand into his pocket. "Claire is getting Mom ready and driving her there. I said I'd check on things here and meet them later."

He handed the two metal pellets to Hope. She looked at him with puzzled eyes. "We have a broken window in the library."

"Already? It's not even baseball season." Hope examined the pellets. "What are these?" She cupped them in her hand.

"I think they are the cause of the broken window. They must be; there were no other signs. Unless I'm missing something."

"You're probably right, Ray. Is it very cold in the library? We have an eight-o'clock meeting in there. We might need the small electric heater."

"I'll set it out." Ray made no effort to leave.

"No, don't bother, Ray. I'll ask a fifth-grader to wheel it down on a cart. You have more pressing things to think about."

Noting his reluctance to leave, Hope asked, "Where's your coffee, Ray? Don't you need a cup for the road?" She took a bran muffin from a white bag and wrapped it in a napkin.

"Here, have this en route to the hospital." She emptied the other muffins from the bag, placing them on napkins, and put his muffin inside it. She handed him the bag. "Do you have your silver thermos?"

Ray nodded. "It's in the car." Still, he did not go.

"How is Heather doing, Ray?" Hope busied herself meticulously wrapping the muffins in their napkins. "You said Adelaide was working out well. Is that still the case?"

"I guess she is. I haven't talked to her in a while, but the last time I did, she said Adelaide was a big help. A workhorse."

Hope noticed his eyes did not sparkle as they normally would when Heather's name was mentioned. "You said she made vegetable soup, didn't you? Is she still cooking for them?"

Ray looked off in space. "I guess so."

It was obvious that something was troubling Ray and that it concerned Heather.

"Is everything all right, Ray?" Hope looked at him with warm eyes. "Are you and Heather still friends?"

"Yeah, sure." His eyes met hers and looked away. "I'm just worried about my mom." *We're still friends, just friends. That's all we'll ever be. That's the problem.* "Well, I'd better go now, Hope." He stepped through the doorway. "Call me if you need me."

Caroline, in hospital gown and her own fleece robe, sat on an imitation leather chair by the window. Ray, surprised that she was already settled into a room, willed himself not to feel that he had arrived late, not to feel in any way guilty. Claire arranged magazines and boxes of lozenges on the bedside table. Nurses wheeled in mobile equipment.

He hugged his mother's shoulders awkwardly.

"Hey, Claire," he murmured to his sister's back.

"Oh, hi, Ray." She smiled impersonally at her brother.

The nurses finished connecting the equipment then helped Caroline out of her robe and into the high bed. They set a pitcher of ice water next to a glass with a flexible straw.

The nursing team moved with precision, connecting her with needles and coils to the machines. They turned dials on monitor screens, adjusting red electronic numerals.

The head nurse turned to Ray and Claire. "You may as well take a break now; go for coffee. We'll stay with your mother the first hour of treatment to make sure everything is working as it should." She smiled warmly. "After the first hour, we can put you in charge of monitoring the patient and just keeping her company. Okay?"

Ray nodded and thanked them. Claire shot a few questions about liquids for Caroline and asked if the lozenges were acceptable.

"Should we go to the cafeteria, Ray?" Claire said, more of a statement than a question.

They waited by the elevator, staring at the floor. It was slow to arrive.

"Have you seen Heather lately, Ray?" Claire asked, bringing up the very subject Ray hoped she would not.

"Not for a couple weeks." Ray looked out the windows at the end of the row of elevators. A weak sun broke through the clouds.

"Davey thinks she's wanting to get back together with him." Claire's eyes sought her brother's.

Ray sighed and avoided looking at her. *Please let us not have this conversation.*

"Do you think she does, Ray? Where does that leave you?"

Ray swallowed and rubbed his temple. He was thankful to hear the elevator stopping. He looked straight ahead as a number of people got off.

Two men walked up and entered the elevator with Claire and Ray. *Thank you.* He stared at the ceiling and studied its perforated tiles.

The elevator stopped on the ground floor, and all four occupants stepped toward the door before it opened completely.

They walked the few feet to the cafeteria.

"You get the coffee, Ray; I'll get snacks. Do you want sweet or salty? Oh, I'll just get both."

Ray ordered two coffees, both with milk and lids, one with sugar. He dug in his pocket for bills. "Pay the cashier." the server said in a flat voice.

Ray placed the coffees on the counter at the cashier station and waited for Claire. He browsed through a brochure describing nutrient content of items on the house menu.

Claire appeared with a tray of cherry pie slices and nachos covered with melted cheese. Ray paid the bill and followed Claire to an out-of-the-way table in the corner.

"Is this breakfast or lunch, Claire?"

"We're in this for the long haul, Ray. Might as well chow down. Doesn't this pie look delicious?" She forked a large bite to her mouth.

"Five hours after we relieve the nurses, right?" Ray asked, making small talk. He gulped the barely warm coffee.

"Well, actually, I need to leave by 2:30." She pushed a large nacho into her mouth. "I have to finish making chicken soup. I'm having company for soup and salad tonight."

I hope she's not making chicken soup for Davey.

"Davey's coming over. He's bringing his cousin and her husband. We're going to play poker." She studied her brother's eyes.

Ray kept a straight face and said nothing.

"What do you suppose Heather thinks about Davey and me seeing each other?"

Ray looked at Claire, confusion all over his face.

"What?" She asked defiantly.

"Do you want another coffee?" He stood.

"No, but I will take ice water, if you don't mind. Thanks, Ray."

He was happy to see a line at the coffee counter.

Minutes later he returned with their drinks.

"You probably think your big sis is pretty terrible, fraternizing with Davey when Heather wants him back?" Claire cocked her head and gave him a sideways glance.

What on earth is he telling her? Davey's the one who wants to get back with Heather. He's the instigator.

Ray made a big job of pouring cream and sugar into his coffee, stirring it with concentration.

"Did you bring Mom's magazines?" He asked, looking across the cafeteria as he took a large bite of nacho.

"Of course I did, Ray. Stop trying to change the subject." Claire furrowed her brow. "We need to talk about this, Ray. We're grownups now; let's act like it." She bit sharply on a nacho.

"What do you want from me, Claire?" Ray asked, his even voice masking impatience.

"Just your thoughts, Brother Dear. I want to know if it bothers you that I'm seeing Davey?" Her eyes looked sincere, but her lips seemed to smirk. She inserted bites of pie between them.

Ray scrubbed his hands. "It does bother me, Claire. The guy is full of problems, problems you don't need; and—"

"Oh be honest," she cut him off. "You just don't want me to do anything to upset your precious Heather." She wiped the laminated tabletop with her crumpled napkin. "Does she want him or not?"

Ray flailed his wrists. "No, it was his idea—I don't know what she wants." *I've said too much. I swore I wouldn't do that.*

Claire stared at the napkin as she tore it to bits. Her voice chillingly calm, she said, "Let me get this straight. You're telling me it's Davey's idea to get back with Heather?"

"Yes, he told me so himself. That's why he quit drinking."

Ray looked at her reddening face and felt a rush of love for his sister. He wanted to protect her.

"I don't know what I'm talking about, Claire. Maybe I misunderstood the whole thing." He stood. "Anyway, this is not the time to discuss anything serious. We're too upset about Mom. Let's not pile on more upsetting stuff."

Claire excused herself to the restroom, and Ray went alone toward Caroline's room. He looked at his watch. There were fifteen minutes to kill before the nurses wanted him back.

He opened the heavy glass door for a smiling young woman in a white lab coat and followed her into the sunny courtyard. He passed a tiny-but-inviting coffee shop with its window on the courtyard. He followed the curving walkways, enjoying the green shrubbery, the leafless tall trees.

Heather can't go back with Davey; she doesn't even want to. He's the one who wants it.

Ray sat down on a cold cement bench. He thought of the sadness in Heather's phone voice when he told her he could not come between her and the father of her son. He felt ashamed because he had been, not only heartbroken by her sadness, but also thrilled by it. Now, from the distance of two weeks, he could admit that to himself. *And this thing with Claire and Davey just complicates the whole mess. Should I try to talk to him, man to man? Or talk to Heather first? I have to talk to her.*

He checked his watch and hurried to Caroline's room. He'd been in the courtyard twenty-five minutes. *Claire's really going to stick it to me now.*

But she was not in the room when he arrived. Caroline had dozed off and seemed unaware that a nurse was adjusting her tubes, tidying her covers.

"Hello, Mr. Sellers. Your mother is doing fine." She smiled at him through closed lips. "The solution is flowing properly and should not make her uncomfortable yet. She sipped a little water and may have more as often as she wants."

She walked to the door. "If you need me, press the intercom button and ask for Janet. I'll be back from time to time to check on her anyway."

She neared the monitor box. "If these wavy green lines change their even pattern, call me right away, please. And call me if your mom seems uncomfortable or upset."

Ray wondered where Claire had gone. He sat in the large chair and took a magazine from the stack she had brought for Caroline. He could not get interested in recipes and home decorating. I should have brought my folder. I could be working on the Buddy Day memo to give Hope.

He pulled from his jacket pocket, a flyer explaining what family members should and should not do while accompanying loved one's during Caroline's type of treatment. He reread it and flipped it, finding a blank page on the back. He began writing.

> **Buddies are still feeding snacks to the little kids. French-fries wrapper found under window bench! And Smarties wrappers. Also, a few Power Wrestlers trading cards found in boys' lav.**
>
> **Hope, you banned those the first day of school.**

Caroline awoke and asked for water. She smiled at Ray when he helped her drink from the straw.

"Thanks, Son." She settled back on the pillows. Her eyes scanned the room. "Where's your sister, Ray?"

"She'll be right back, Mom. She must be in the restroom or something."

"She probably went to have a smoke," Caroline said with disdain. "She's been promising to quit that nasty habit."

"She's trying to, Mom. Says she can't afford it now that she's laid off." Ray chuckled for his mother's sake.

Well, hanging out with Davey, she can just inhale his smoke second hand. He said he smokes five times more since he quit drinking. Ray felt guilty, as if his mother read his thoughts.

"Ready for one of your magazines, Mom? Or a lozenge? These berry-flavored lozenges look good."

"Maybe I will have a magazine, Ray." She took it and thanked him. Nodding toward his paper, "What are you writing there, Ray?"

"Oh, just notes. Something I have to tell Hope about."

"She works you too hard, doesn't she? You never get a let-up."

"No. No, Mom. She's pretty fair now. She's a lot more reasonable to work for than when she first came to Poore Pond. I talk to guys in other schools. I could have it worse."

"That's good, Rayley." She thumbed though the magazine with little interest. In a matter of minutes, she dozed again.

Ray arrived at Poore Pond an hour early, tired from anxiously checking on Caroline so many times in the night, but excited to have a chance to really look at his new office.

Yesterday it had seemed larger than he expected, but he knew it was just an eight-by-eight cubicle. Still, he never believed he would have a private office. He wanted to fix it up a little, make it look like a real office.

He pressed the wall switch just inside the boiler-room entrance, and lamplight streamed from the doorway of his newly partitioned office.

A brass banker's light with emerald glass shade sat on the freshly polished top of his scarred wooden desk. It shone on a leafy green plant in a terracotta pot. He plucked a small envelope from within the stems. *This is Hope's doing.*

Heart soaring, he sank into his green velour chair and rubbed the soft arms slowly. *This is what started the whole thing. This chair.* He recalled that day at the start of the school year, when Hope decided Ray should have a new office. *She walked it off right there, on the spot and said, "As the plant supervisor, you should have your own office."*

His eyes scoured the room. His dented metal filing cabinet stood under the long shelves Hope had insisted the carpenter build high on the wall to fill what she called "dead space."

The Sellers' family photograph looked down from the shelf: his ruddy-faced father, arm around a young, pretty Caroline; confident, six-year-old Rory beside a shy Ray at nine; and a teen-aged Claire, exuding attitude.

Ray chuckled. That photo was taken a few months before Rory's accident. It had been on his desk since he first came to Poore Pond. *I should put it in a new frame.*

On a shelf above the family portrait, Bucky Ames flashed his crooked smile at Ray from a silver frame. After Bucky died, Ray had bought the special matted frame for the wallet-sized school photo to make it larger and more noticeable on his desk.

Bucky was Ray's best helper and one of the most fun. He was bright with a mature but kind sense of humor. Ray had watched Bucky soldier on in the latter stages of Batten Disease. His thinking ability and vision declined, and he began to have seizures. When he could no longer participate in his beloved physical education classes, he would sit at Ray's desk during gym periods and clean tools with an oily cloth.

Bucky was still attending school a few days a week when the neurodegenerative disease claimed him at the young age of eleven. Ray had thought of the boy every day since his death.

He stood and walked around his desk. It was then that he noticed a large banner of white craft paper mounted on the white drywall. The sentence:

ENJOY YOUR NEW OFFICE, MR. SELLERS!

ran across the center in bright red tempera. Students had signed their autographs in colored marker all around the borders. Ray studied for a moment, the various handwriting styles of the children, looking for familiar names.

He walked back to his chair, feeling a cushion underfoot. Looking down, he saw a brown-and-green patterned, oval hooked rug, covering most of the worn paint on the cement floor. *Hope did this.*

He sat at his chair and opened the small envelope. He unfolded a creamy white congratulatory note, signed by Hope, Corinne, Marie, Helen, and Rosie.

A large soup can, covered with wrapping-paper decoupage, held freshly sharpened pencils; and a student-made notepad decorated with thumbprint art lay next to it.

Ray felt overwhelmed. *I'm a lucky man.*

A key turned in the lock, and Hope's over-filled briefcase thumped to the floor. Dainty footsteps crossed the room.

"Hi, Mr. Supervisor," Hope's face peered around the door. "How are things with your mom, Ray?"

"Pretty well, thanks." Ray smiled uncontrollably. "But this office! I thought I was in the wrong building, maybe the mayor's office or someplace."

"You like it then?" Hope smoothed the turned-up rug with her toe and set her large handbag on the floor.

"I'm overwhelmed, Hope. Totally."

"Well, you deserve it." She slid into the straight, wooden chair next to the desk. "So Caroline went through the treatment with no problems?"

"None at all, really. She was tired afterward even though she dozed off and on all through it." Ray, his throat dry, coughed softly and longed for coffee.

"How will you manage, Ray? Running the house, I mean." Hope looked into his eyes. "What can I do to help?"

"Oh, I think we'll do fine, Hope." He returned her gaze. "I'm used to doing it; and anyway, Claire's laid off now. She won't be able to stay away. She loves to be in charge." He chuckled and averted his eyes.

Hope stood and took her handbag. "Be sure to let me know if you need my help." She turned toward the door.

"I've been meaning to ask you, Hope." Ray stood and faced her. "What happened with those two boys I caught fighting in C-wing lav? Remember, one was short and thin; the other was big and burly. Fourth graders. I don't believe I know either of them."

"You know the smaller one, Ray. He's Rodney Cannon. He came late last year, middle of second semester." Hope sat down again, balancing the handbag on her lap.

"I don't recall. And he didn't look familiar to me. His clothes were so perfect and all. He looked like a little fashion model." Ray laughed and sat in his velour chair.

"Well, that's why you didn't recognize him, Ray. He has a new look." She looked toward the door and lowered her voice. "His mother has a new partner who likes dressing up Rodney." She leaned closer to Ray. "Buys him clothes all the time. She is quite into children's fashion."

"She?" Ray's eyes widened.

"That's right. She. And that's all I'm going to say about it." Hope stood again.

"Is that what the fight was all about?" Ray rose.

"Exactly. Ellmo Fisher, the bigger boy, is new to Poore Pond this year. He came to us from Goddard Academy. Parents are both university professors and want him to excel."

"DR. FLEMING, IF YOU'RE IN THE BUILDING, PLEASE COME TO THE OFFICE." Corinne's voice sounded on the speaker.

Hope stepped to the doorway. "So Ellmo was feeling the pressure and needed to vent. Apparently, when he found himself alone with this dapper little kid—." Hope turned up her palm and thrust her chin to the side.

"It was too much to resist?" Ray grinned.

"Exactly. They are both good boys, just dealing with frightening new situations." She smiled at him. "We'll watch for ways to help them transition. I'm off now, Ray. Have a good day."

She retrieved her briefcase by the outside door and hurried to the office.

Ray looked at the clock and decided he had time to get coffee from the teachers' lounge before they began to arrive. He made it a point to avoid teachers in small groups; he found them to be different then, teasing him more intensely than they did one-on-one. He really liked the staff and found them warm and pleasant during their individual encounters with him.

The hallways began to fill with safety-patrol students and those helping teachers carry materials from cars. Parents balancing large-scale paper sculptures climbed the stairs to Mrs. Thorpe's classroom.

Pam's robot unit. It's that time again. Ray walked gingerly with his hot coffee. He glanced at the lobby clock and knew he must hurry to the entrance doors with brooms and the mop bucket.

Is that Jeremy Baker squirming by the boiler-room door?

Ray stopped a few feet from the child and sipped his steaming coffee, so it would be less likely to splash on the boy. He could see it was Jeremy, grinning happily.

"Hey, Sport. How's it going?" Ray turned into the boiler room, startled to see Heather standing in the doorway of his new office.

"It's going great!" Jeremy said to Ray's back as he followed him.

Ray set his coffee on the workbench and went to her. She extended her hand and his fingertips brushed hers barely.

His eyes searched hers. "How are you, Heather?"

"Fine, Ray." She avoided his eyes. "I just stopped to see your new office. Jeremy could not stop talking about it." She stepped into the cubicle. Jeremy rushed to sit in the velour chair.

"Jeremy," Heather admonished.

"It's all right, Heather. Let him sit there," Ray said softly.

The boy lifted the thumbprint notepad from the desktop and waved it at his mother. She stood, studying the Sellers family portrait and did not see him.

"Did you make that pad, Jeremy?" Ray asked, working to hide his anxiety. He glanced at the clock and knew he should be in the lobby.

"My class did. We made it for you, Mr. Sellers." He laid down the pad and pointed to a red thumbprint under the R in Ray's name. "That's my thumbprint."

Ray leaned to look at it.

"Right there," Jeremy pointed.

"You mean that perfect, beautiful thumbprint right here?" Smiling widely, Ray put his finger on it.

"That's it!" Jeremy said quietly, suddenly shy.

The first bell rang, sending shards of frustration through Ray's chest.

Heather turned abruptly. "Go to class now, Jeremy." She leaned to kiss him. "Have a great day, Sweetie."

"Bye, Mr. Sellers," the boy said as he left.

"Bye, Sport."

Heather looked at Ray. "I know you're busy now, Ray, but I had to talk to you." She dropped her sad eyes. Reaching into her coat pocket, she brought out a small, flat package wrapped in shiny red paper and thrust it at him.

Ray took it from her and opened it. There was silence as he worked loose the extra layers of cellophane tape.

"Jeremy wrapped it, Ray. You know how he likes to use tape." She gave a tiny nervous laugh.

Finally, he managed to remove the paper and found a miniature double frame. Smiling faces of Heather and Jeremy looked at him from brass ovals, joined by a long hinge.

Overcome with emotion, Ray swallowed and stared at the photographs. Heather's presence filled the room.

"I have to go, Ray. I just wanted to give you something for your new office." Her voice was thick. "The photos were Jeremy's idea. Call me later if you want to." She slipped away.

Ray, his heart running over, pushed the mop bucket down the hall. Last-minute children greeted him cheerfully, uncharacteristically receiving only a nod and a wave in return.

Fiction Readers Interested in

Scheduling Author Ruth Fawcett

To Speak To Your Group

Contact Ambrosia Press

Phone 440-951-7780

Fax 440-951-0565

ambrosia03@earthlink.net

CHAPTER TWELVE—THE BRADFORDS

Ian and Dan walked through the fire station door in a daze. They crossed the parking lot in silence. Both stopped at Dan's truck.

"I'll see you around, Ian." Dan's voice was ragged.

"Yeah, Dan," Ian said, nodding.

They stood together, looking at the pavement, saying nothing, yet both reluctant to leave.

A patrol car swerved into a space next to them. It was Eric Smythe, a rookie officer. "I sure am sorry about your bad break, guys." He leaned out the window.

"Thanks," Ian and Dan muttered in unison and looked away.

Eric stepped out of the car, zipping his leather uniform jacket against the January wind. "It doesn't seem fair, does it? First, you fight the fire from hell; the next week you get your pay cut." His eager young face sought their downcast eyes.

He was patient.

"Would this have happened if Chief Wrangston were still here?" Eric broke the silence.

Dan shook his head vehemently, stepping in place in the cold.

"No way," Ian said, scrubbing his gloveless hands.

"What was the reason? What were you told?"

Dan and Ian locked eyes.

Eric waited.

"We didn't get a pay cut, Eric. We got our hours cut. There's no money," Ian said.

"No money? We just passed a city-services levy in November." Eric, incredulous, stared at the men.

"Not the city, Eric," Dan said, trying to hide his impatience. Our department, the fire department." He looked at the young patrolman, warming somewhat. "We've had a record number of big fires lately." He turned to Ian.

"Feather Ridge apartment complex in December," Ian pulled his hands from his pockets and spread them in the air. "That fire went on for days. And we had a devil of a time getting the residents to evacuate." He looked at Dan. "Remember, Dan? You had to abruptly pick up and carry that old woman and her cat."

"No kidding?" Eric said, feeling like one of the guys at last.

"We were just lucky no lives were lost in that one," Dan said, climbing into his truck and immediately starting the engine. He lowered the window. "See you guys." He drove off slowly.

"Do you think our department will be affected by the cuts?" Eric asked.

"Who knows, Eric." Ian said in a doomsday voice. "We never know. You had better have a Plan B, just in case." He headed toward his van. Eric followed beside him.

"Did Mike give any clues? Did he allude to other departments or anything?" The hint of panic in Eric's voice was familiar to Ian.

"Mike's an interim chief, Eric. He doesn't have the whole picture yet." Ian stopped at his van. "Don't worry, Eric. You're young; you don't have a family."

Ian climbed into his van. "You'll be fine, kid. See you around." Ian drove off, haunted by the forlorn face of the young patrolman.

Wait until Helsi hears this. She'll be devastated. And the kids. I won't tell her in front of the kids. They don't need to know.

He took the long way home, going down Fulton to the chemical plant. He pulled in front of the ruined complex and parked. The smell of smoldered timber filled the van, triggering horrifying visions of the night he and his fellows fought that terrible fire. The night his chief and three firefighters lost their lives. *Was the awful smell coming from his mind?*

He lowered the window to check the air and detected a fading aroma of smoke, not the heavy, pungent smell inside the van. He remained there, gazing through the open window at nothing but ashes and waste. He stared blankly at the dump trucks and bulldozers parked randomly around the site.

He watched two boys with plastic shopping bags forage through the debris. Both wore thin jackets, unzipped and flapping in the cold wind, no warm hats or gloves.

He called them over and pulled a crumpled five-dollar bill from his pocket, giving it to them along with a granola bar he found on his console. "Buy yourselves some candy, kids."

They took the bar and money without hesitation and smiled their thanks.

"You go on home now, boys, and get warm. And don't come back here. It's not safe." They nodded at Ian as he pulled into the street.

Ian thought of his own boys, warm and snug in their cozy home, of Lucy and Rachel. And Helsi. He thought of Helsi and knew everything would be okay. *I am a lucky man.*

Helsi took Ian's news like the soldier he knew she was.

"Well, at least now you'll have more time to study." She gave an imitation laugh.

For a time they laid low, sustained by quiet routine. Ian worked his six-hour days as if they were what he had always done. And Helsi was right; he did have more time to study. In fact, he had two hours a day to study, help a little more around the house, and tutor his youngest son.

The boy seemed to be making progress. Mrs. Pruett kept him supplied with new materials, and the entire family spent time with him. He could now, though faltering and straining, read a familiar five-sentence story. He showed clear signs of responding to the sight-word method, the repetition, and the ever-changing materials. Ian began to enjoy his work with Dylan.

Time was no longer a problem. The problem for Ian was his mind. All he wanted to think about were ways to generate income for the family.

He went through the motions of studying without absorbing the material.

For Helsi, it was different. Her schedule and workload had not changed although she did have the luxury of running errands without fitting them around the children. Ian was happy to meet the bus or drive them to activities during his off hours.

But like Ian, Helsi's mind worked overtime on the subject of income. She did not want Ian to drop out of his course. *I won't have that on my conscience.*

If she could just generate enough income to make up the shortage in Ian's paycheck, they could continue as before. Wasn't there something she could do while Ian was home? There must be some kind of part-time work, a few hours a day.

Helsi had followed the office-clerical track in high school and had worked as a bookkeeper at a small factory for a year. She hadn't minded the work; in fact, she rather enjoyed it. She considered it much nicer than waitressing, which she did as a student. But when an opening came up on the factory floor, she applied for it.

Her hourly wages doubled, and she continued the job through her courtship with Ian. She worked at the factory after they were married, up until one week before Sean was born.

Finally, Helsi dared to upset the comfortable peace she and Ian pretended to live. She announced that she was thinking of getting a job.

"But, Hon, how can you do that and still look after everything here?" Ian asked over after-supper coffee. The children were huddled into their parents' bedroom, watching a new DVD Sean had bought the family with his snow-shoveling earnings. Thrilled to be allowed to have popcorn and punch in that sacred room, they fell into a party manner.

"We can manage, Ian. If everyone pitches in." She refilled their cups with powdered flavored coffee and hot water. "Try this."

"I thought you didn't buy expensive treats like this, Helsi." Ian chided her as he stirred the mixture.

"It's a sample, Ian. Did you see the tiny box?" She held it up.

He sipped from the cup. "Not bad," he said and took a real drink. "I rather like it."

"Think of it as dessert, Ian." She read the box. "It's called Double Chocolate Mousse. That's dessert." They laughed.

"Pay-cut dessert?" Ian added. They laughed again.

"But, seriously, Hon." His eyes sought hers. "You're already working too hard. I hate to see you loading on more."

"Oh, Ian, other women do it." Her face assumed the I-am-woman look he had seen before.

That look had appeared when they were trying to buy this very house, and she insisted on keeping the books at the factory while the full-time person took vacation. For three weeks, Helsi had worked eight hours a day on the factory floor and two hours overtime on bookkeeping. They finally had the down payment.

That same look had kept him out of her way when she decided to lay new tile in the kitchen because the labor cost was beyond their means and the old tile, worn out completely.

And he had seen that look more recently, of course, when his wife mustered the entire family around an ambitious schedule to help Dylan learn to sight-read.

"I can do it," she said. And he knew she could.

Ian rather enjoyed mopping the kitchen floor. He had cleaned the firehouse kitchen any number of times and had developed an efficient system. He moved all the furniture to one side and then swept and mopped the bare half. By starting with the area opposite the work counters, he could scrub the sink and stove while waiting for the cleaned section to dry. He would then move everything to the sink area and clean the other half.

It felt good to help Helsi with this never-ending chore. Their large family managed to make a mess of the floor every mealtime, and wet mopping became part of nightly kitchen cleaning.

"Wish me luck, Hon," Helsi called as she tiptoed across the clean floor to the door. She wore her good black cloth coat and gold earrings. She had taken extra pains with her hair and makeup and looked quite attractive.

"You look great, Helsi, like the supervisor. They'll take one look and say you're overqualified for the factory floor." They laughed and Ian blew her a kiss.

The sound of her car backing out the drive was unusually distinct in his ears as he mopped the last area of the floor.

Realizing she might actually take a job, a small seed of despair grew in his stomach. The feeling that his life was going to change irreversibly, engulfed him.

The door scraped open and a smiling Helsi reappeared.

"I just needed to remind you to pick up Rachel early for her dentist appointment, Ian. I was down the street before I remembered we had turned in the cell phones."

"Sure thing, Hon." He managed his best smile. "Now get out of here."

Helsi laughed indulgently.

Is she looking forward to this? She seems so happy.

Pulling into the parking lot at Poore Pond School never failed to evoke memories, both pleasant and unpleasant. Ian was ashamed of his former obstinate behavior toward Dr. Fleming and the teachers.

Now his children's progress gave him great pride. The relief he felt in his ability to finally work with the school, bolstered him even more.

But today his confidence was down.

Ian checked in at the desk with Mrs.Tompkins and listened while she called Rachel's teacher on the intercom.

"Hello, Mr. Bradford," Hope said, stepping out of her office. "How's everything?"

"Oh fine, Dr. Fleming. I'm just picking up Rachel for a dentist appointment."

"May I have a quick word, Ian?" She motioned him into her office and closed the door after him.

"You must be delighted with Dylan's reading."

"Oh, we are, we are. What a turnaround! That Mrs. Pruett is something." He managed a thin smile.

"She really can unlock the mystery of how a child learns, can't she?" Hope took an envelope from her desk and handed it to Ian.

"What is this?" he asked, opening it.

"The free-and-reduced lunch application, Ian. Mrs. Bradford requested it. She said you've had your hours cut."

Discomfort covered his face. His palm pushed the air. "No, no, we don't need that. It's not that bad yet." He set the envelope on the table and stepped toward the door. *What's taking Rachel so long?*

"The lunch program is designed to help families get through financial hard times, Ian." She looked at him with warm eyes.

"No. No." He shook his head adamantly. "I'll drop out of school before I'll take charity."

"It's not charity, Ian. It's funded by taxpayers like you; there's nothing to be ashamed of."

Her eyes narrowed. "Drop out of school? You mustn't think that. That is not an option." She handed him the envelope again and reached past him to put her hand on the doorknob.

"You have your scholarship. It would be a shame to give it up. You've worked so hard." She opened the door, an intense smile forcing him to smile back.

"Here's Rachel," Corinne announced. Rachel's shy smile belied her natural boldness. She hugged her father's leg.

Ian put the envelope on the counter and took his daughter's hand. They waved goodbye and walked out the glass door.

Helsi returned from her interview, floating on a cloud of self-satisfaction and remaining aloft the entire evening.

Supervisor Russ Malone offered her afternoon work, up to twenty hours. She could pick which afternoons and stay from noon to five o'clock or from one o'clock to six.

"But that's four days a week," Ian said, furrowing his brow. "I'm gone two nights, so where do you find four free days?"

"Well," Helsi hesitated.

Ian's chest filled with dread.

"I could work ten hours a day on Saturday or Sunday, my choice." Her voice trailed off.

She breathed deeply and continued, "Ten hours on Sunday and only two afternoons." She looked at Ian, avoiding his eyes. "Or five hours on Sunday and three afternoons." She forced a brave smile.

"Geez, Hon." Ian's heart was in his mouth. "And how much would your pay be? Don't tell me that's your choice, too." He hated himself.

"Nine dollars an hour to start and ten after three months." Ian heard the disappointment behind her words.

He went to her and hugged tightly. "What did you tell this Russ?"

"I'd get back to him," she murmured, her voice liquid.

Helsi went to a few other interviews for factory jobs, but none had a schedule she could fit with her family. *I'm a capable person. I'm a hard worker, too. There has to be a part-time job for me.*

She began reading classified ads for office jobs. None were part time.

Friday Dylan awoke with a fever. Helsi called Poore Pond and asked for Mrs. Harris, the attendance secretary. An unfamiliar voice took her call, identifying herself as Mona Phelps, substitute for Marie Harris.

Friday afternoon Helsi phoned the school and asked Dr. Fleming how to go about getting on the substitute list for office work. Hope explained that she would apply at the school board office where she would be fingerprinted and take a simple written test on basic language and mathematics. After board approval, she would just wait to be called.

"But you need something you can count on, don't you, Helsi?" Hope asked. "Let me think. Oh, did you get the lunch application form I mailed to you?"

"Yes, thank you, Dr. Fleming. I filled it out this morning. Robbie will bring it in Monday."

Hope promised to check around for job openings and get back to her. Meantime, it would be a good idea to get on the sub list anyway.

Ian stayed close to Helsi all weekend, sharing the housework, even folding laundry. The entire family, except Sean, hiked in a metropark close to their house and came home to mugs of hot chocolate. After a spaghetti dinner, they played Uno and Junior Monopoly. Sean shocked everyone by joining the games. It was a lovely family weekend, and it hadn't cost an extra cent.

Sunday night after the children were in bed, the telephone rang. It was Hope Fleming and she wanted to speak to Helsi.

Hope asked Helsi if she would consider working for Heather Baker, three hours a day, three days a week, at a pay rate of $12.50 per hour. She explained that the job involved housework and laundry, some cooking, and occasional babysitting. Hope did not disclose the fact that she would be paying Helsi's salary.

Heather let Adelaide go for stealing from her. After missing a gold cross necklace her late mother had given her, she noticed it around Adelaide's neck weeks later. Heather dismissed the homeless Adelaide on the spot, calling Hope afterward.

Tuesday evening Helsi left Ian in charge and followed Hope's directions to Heather's apartment.

Heather in jeans and Jeremy in Spiderman pajamas opened the door when she knocked. They introduced themselves cordially, and Helsi waited at the kitchen table while Heather settled Jeremy into her bedroom to watch a television program. *I know I've seen her around school. She's so pretty.*

Helsi studied the cheery kitchen, noticing how clean everything looked, even the white curtains were freshly laundered and pressed.

"What grade is Jeremy in, Heather?" Helsi asked when she returned to the table.

"Fourth grade." She smiled at Helsi. "I cannot believe he's in fourth grade already."

"My Robbie is in fourth as well," Helsi smiled back. "Fourth grade is a big year. Dr. Fleming says that's when their subjects get harder and pre-puberty begins."

"That explains it. I mean, Jeremy's getting so sensitive now." She looked at Helsi and turned her palms toward the ceiling. "He complains about everything."

"I know what you mean." They laughed.

"Tell me, Heather, what will I be doing for you those three days?" Helsi began, anxious to get to business.

"Tuesdays—you did say you could work Tuesday, Thursday, and Friday, right?" Helsi nodded.

"Tuesdays are my clinical days, so I get home about the time Jeremy gets off the bus." She twirled her lovely ponytail as she spoke. "I leave work early that day to go to class and burn up the pavement rushing home."

"I could be here to meet the bus on Tuesdays, Heather. What time does it come?"

In the end, they agreed on a schedule that worked well for both mothers. Helsi would work from two o'clock to five each of the three days. On Tuesday she would cook a meal, a large enough quantity for another day's supper. Thursday she would thoroughly clean the apartment. Friday would be laundry day with a little ironing and light cleaning.

"So you are ready to start this Thursday?" Heather asked with unexpected authority.

"Yes, certainly." Helsi grew equally business-like. "You provide the cleaning supplies, do you?"

"Yes, I have them all here." She gestured toward the hall. "In that storage closet off the hall. Remember, I showed you the hamper in there."

Life in the Bradford household hummed along despite Helsi's new job at the Bakers. Ian found himself folding clothes from the dryer more and more often; he put his own stamp on the task by folding tee shirts in a different way. He became adept at dumping ingredients into a crock pot during Helsi's morning rush with the children.

Ian felt more rested from his shorter workday. But for Helsi, the opposite was true. Ian watched her scurry around the house after dinner, sorting laundry, tidying cupboards, and most annoyingly, refolding the tee shirts. He yearned for their quiet evenings on the sofa, watching television or reading.

He looked at her tired face and chose not to mention it.

"Is all this really worth it, Hon?" he boldly asked one evening when she was in full flow.

"What do you mean?" Helsi continued lining up cereal boxes in the lower cupboard.

"All this constant work; no time to relax." He saw her mouth tighten and could feel the tension forming.

"Of course it's worth it, Ian." She placed a tall cereal box on its side on the shelf and gaped at him. "That extra hundred dollars a week buys a lot of cereal." Turning back to her task, she muttered, "And full-price school lunches."

"Are you still festering about that, Helsi?

Upstairs Rachel coughed, and they both looked toward the stairway. Their eyes met for a moment, then Helsi returned to the cereal boxes.

Ian waited with uncharacteristic patience for his wife's response. A car door slammed in the driveway next door. The furnace kicked on with a low rumble.

"Are you still mad about the lunch thing, Helsi?"

"No, not mad. Just disappointed, that's all." She kept her back to him. "We qualified for reduced-price lunches, Ian, which means we could buy two weeks of lunches for what we pay now for one week."

Ian went to her. "I know it's my stubborn pride, Hon." He gently turned her shoulders toward him. "That's just how I am; I'm a proud man." He grinned boyishly.

Helsi turned away. "Well that pride is costing us money."

"I say it's worth it. You know that." His smile faded. "You can't put a price on a man's pride." He stepped away from her.

"But right now we can't afford it, Ian." She closed the cupboard forcibly, rinsed a sponge at the sink, and began furiously wiping countertops.

Ian grasped her wrist. "That's enough for tonight, Helsi. Let's go cuddle on the couch." Without letting go, he took the sponge from her hand and tossed it in the sink. Ignoring her weak resistance, he pulled her onto the sofa.

"I'm exhausted, Ian." Helsi rose. "I need to go to bed. Will you lock up?" She hurried upstairs.

Not so much as a goodnight from my wife. He stood then moved to lock doors and switch off lights. He needed to think.

Lying on the sofa, he took a deep breath and stretched his entire body. Immediately his thoughts turned to income. *If Helsi keeps working, everything will be ruined. How can I bring more money into this house?*

Ian woke early the next morning and left the house before dawn. He had barely slept from the tension invading their bed the entire night. Helsi had not softened her attitude and remained rigid and withholding when he tried to snuggle against her.

No coffee shops were open yet, so he would have to wait until he could make a pot at the firehouse.

He felt sick to his stomach. When things were not right between Helsi and him, his entire system reacted. He resented her for staying angry. It was not like her, and it was against the pact they had had all these years. *All because of a few dollars in discounts. This is crazy.*

When Ian arrived home after work, he came into a silent house. A note from Helsi lay on the kitchen table. It told him his supper, a cold plate of cheese and macaroni salad, was in the refrigerator. She had taken Rachel, Dylan, and Robbie to the Science Fair at Sean and Lucy's school and did not expect to be home before he left for class.

The lack of warmth in the note dismayed Ian. Instead of her usual, "Love you, Helsi," the note was signed simply, H.

He sat at the table with his cold supper and tried to choke it down his tense throat. His textbook propped against a cloth-covered brick doorstop, he reviewed the reading assignment.

He finished eating and rinsed the dish in the sink. He had more than half an hour before time to leave.

He walked through the rooms, feeling the weight of their emptiness.

Based on their reading assignment for the week, the class discussed the role of the physician's assistant and patient relationships. Ian related well to the topic, found it interesting; he had had no difficulty comprehending the reading.

The guest speaker, a practicing physician's assistant for seven years, engrossed the entire class in her provocative talk. She emphasized the duality of the role as she found it.

"Knowing when to step forward with authority and when to step back and defer to your physician superior is an important matter. An art really. You just have to know and accept your place."

Ian recalled his experience as a paramedic, rushing train-wreck victims to the hospital, naively expecting to be treated as an equal by emergency-room doctors.

The entire class participated in a heated discussion of equality, filling the room with adrenaline.

The speaker, Bernadine Murphy, closed her speech at break time and left everyone her card, inviting them to call or email if they had subsequent questions.

She left as well, a high energy level that continued during the break. Ian and classmate, Gene, enjoyed their own spirited discussion in the vending-machine room, moving from opinions on class subject matter to sharing parts of their personal lives.

Gene and second wife Jacque had a blended family, which included seven children: her two, his three, and their two together. Like Ian, Gene had been a paramedic with dreams of becoming a physician, reality forcing him to settle for physician's assistant.

But Gene had left his paramedic job to become a manufacturer's representative for a medical supply company. Acting as middleman, he sold to the sales companies and made a good commission.

"The company is always looking for good reps, Ian—even part-time ones," Gene said.

They exchanged phone numbers, email addresses before carrying their soda cans back to class with them.

The post-break class session continued the highly charged tone set by Bernadine Murphy, and Ian gave no thought to the dissension between Helsi and him.

In fact, he had not thought of it since class started at 4:30. On the drive home; however, it smacked him in the face.

We cannot continue this cold war. I'm not up to it. And it's destructive. We've always been good about not letting fights fester. Why, we would not even go there. All these years. Why can't we control ourselves this time?

Why is money such a hot-button issue? The lack of it is like a black plague spreading over our lives.

What must the kids think? They sense what's going on. Don't tell me they aren't bothered by the way their mother and I are avoiding each other. Don't tell me they don't see it.

Maybe I'll email Gene, see what he has to say. Something about that whole deal bothers me. But I'll see.

CHAPTER THIRTEEN—HOPE

Tears spilled down Mrs. Parks cheeks as she sat with Hope. The principal reached for a box of oversized tissues on the shelf and offered it to her.

Hope's emotions brimmed over, too; but it would not do for her to succumb to them in front of Emmylou's mother.

"Help me understand, Mrs. Parks." Hope leaned toward her. "Emmylou and this Kurt—well you said his alleged name is Curtis Jones—had exchanged twelve emails? Is that right?" She waited while Freda Parks dabbed at a fresh stream of tears.

"The police printed twelve emails sent by Jones and that many replies from Emmylou." She cast somber eyes at Hope and swallowed with difficulty. "This was the third time they had tried to meet."

"Third?" Hope touched Freda Park's forearm and with furrowed brow, continued, "Were all three planned for pickups here at school? I know of only one other and this one."

"That's the scary part, Dr. Fleming." Freda seemed to have gained control over the tear flow. Anger rose in her voice. "Before the first school-pickup attempt, this man was trying to meet my daughter at the mall. He asked Emmylou in one email where she liked to shop. She told him Cool Girls, and he said he'd meet her there to buy her—." Consumed by anger, she could not speak.

Phones rang in the outer office.

She sipped from the water bottle, then began again. "This man told my ten-year-old daughter he would meet her in Cool Girls and buy her whatever sexy outfit she wanted."

"That despicable wretch!" Hope said, her voice livid. She stood and paced the tiny office.

"Wouldn't you just like to get your hands on him?" Freda asked. She stood and faced Hope.

"However did you prevent that one?"

"Just a fluke, really." Freda fluffed her hair, thinking. "Actually, I remember the day very well. It was late August, getting close to time to go school shopping." She looked, unseeing, out the window at the courtyard, soggy with melting snow.

"Now that I think of it, Emmylou had not done her usual nagging to go for school clothes. She hadn't said one word about going." She turned enlightened eyes toward Hope.

"I guess I was too busy to notice at the time—I had just been given a big promotion and was in way over my head at work. But she had made one small suggestion about my dropping her off at the mall to buy school clothes on her own. Told me Sherri's mom said it was okay with her if the two girls went alone."

"What did you say about that?" Hope asked.

"Oh, something flippant, I guess. Like, 'that'll be the day.'" Freda looked squarely at Hope, who saw she was on the verge of tears again. "Sounds really inappropriate now, doesn't it?"

"But how could you have known?" Hope asked.

Winning out over the tears again, Freda continued. "Emmylou cried and dramatized for days about that. Just kept up the nagging, the you-treat-me-like-a-baby routine."

"And she finally accepted your no?" Hope heard sounds of student helpers arriving for the day and glanced at the clock.

"Well, her father laid down the law. He set a day for the family to go school shopping all together, make a whole day of it, have lunch and maybe even dinner out." Freda shook her head.

"Thank God he did. Emmylou knows better than to commit sacrilege by scorning family outings. Thank God."

"Dr. Fleming," Corinne's soft voice came over the intercom.

Hope turned and pressed the red button. "Yes, Mrs. Tompkins."

"Mrs. Ricci very much needs to see you before her first class. She asked me to call her if you are free before first bell."

"That's fine, Mrs. Tompkins. We are almost finished here."

Hope turned to Freda Parks. "So where is Curtis Jones? He is still in custody?"

"No," Freda cried. "The twenty-four hours were up before forensics found any evidence on Emmylou's hard drive."

Struck by the fear in her eyes, Hope chose her words carefully. "The police will pick him up, Mrs. Parks." She touched her hand. "They have his license number and car type." She rose.

Mrs. Parks took a handful of tissues from the box and stood.

Hope forced a small smile. "They could have him in custody now, as we speak." She helped Freda into her hooded storm coat.

"Thank you, Dr. Fleming, for all your help. And your kindness." She looked at Hope with child-like eyes.

Hope hugged her warmly, suppressing tears. She closed the door behind Mrs. Parks and stood frozen to the floor. A bright sun filled the courtyard, and she fixed her eyes on it.

"Shall I call Mrs. Ricci now, Hope?" Corinne's calming voice filled the room.

"Yes please, Corinne." She took the tutoring schedule prepared for Martha Poynter and saw that today she would be working with Katrina Davis' second-grade students, beginning at 9:40. *Where will she work? Let me think. The conference rooms are all full today.*

She checked the field-trip list. Brad Kushner's fourth grade would leave at 9:30 for a field trip to the health museum. Mrs. Poynter may use that room. Brad is so territorial; I'd better let him know ahead of time.

A quick knock sounded and the door opened in a rush; there stood Carmen Ricci. "Good morning, Hope! Thank you for seeing me now." Without invitation, she took the nearest chair.

"We have our fourth-grade concert nearly ready, Hope, as you know." She looked up to meet the principal's eyes. "And the kids have come up with a great idea."

Hope sat down next to her and met her gaze, unaware of the skepticism on her face.

But Carmen read it easily. "You're not still holding that nativity thing against me, are you Hope?" She forced a chuckle.

"Oh that?' She sighed. "I guess it has left me a little gun shy, Carmen, when it comes to your theatrics." Hope smoothed her skirt. "Oh don't get me wrong. It was a great idea, the nano-second flash, very theatrical."

"Thank you." Carmen laughed. "I know I should not have thrust it upon you during dress rehearsal in front of all the students. But the kids loved it, didn't they?"

"Yes they did, Carmen." Her eyes riveted to Carmen's. "It was very theatrically effective." She paused.

Carmen swallowed but did not drop her eyes.

"And it was actually good that I saw it at the performance for the student body, because it verified my decision not to allow it in the evening program for parents. It was blatant violation of separation of church and state."

"But most of the parents—"

"Carmen, we've been over all this before. We agreed to disagree more than a month ago, remember?"

Hope checked her watch just as first bell sounded. Rushing lines of students could be heard in the hallways. "Now what is this great idea for the February program?"

Carmen smiled. "Well, you know the kids wrote the play. It's about King Valentine, remember?" Hope nodded.

"Mark Pryor, the King, suggested we ask you to be Queen Valentine. The kids would be wild about it, and you know Mark." She imitated his mature speech, "I would be honored to be King to Queen Dr. Fleming."

"Queen Doctor?" They both laughed. "There's a good reason why Mark is Student Council President. He's going to run for political office one day." Hope said. "What would my role be?"

"Just minimal. Be in the royal procession at opening and closing of the play." Carmen shrugged. "And maybe one or two walk-ons in between." Hope stood and put her hand on the doorknob.

Carmen rose. "What do you think? May I tell the kids you are willing?"

"I'm willing. That is, barring any unforeseen emergencies." Hope opened the door. "I'm happy to do it." She smiled and watched a delighted Carmen depart down the hall.

Immediately following morning announcements, Hope headed to Mrs. Cantrell's classroom to see how Bluewave was managing in the transition from Mrs. Perry's third graders to this class of high-achieving first graders. The class was known for its involved, audacious parents, but none had called the office this first week of Bluewave's assignment.

In front of the room, an animated teacher led the children in calendar activities. Hope watched, fascinated by the children's total engagement in the lesson. Their ability to expand the 10th day of February in rapid time impressed the principal:

10 +0 = 10 *7 + 3 = 10*

9 + 1 = 10 *6 + 4 = 10*

8 + 2 = 10 *5 + 5 = 10, etc.*

Without missing a beat, the children progressed to higher equations:

(5 + 4) + 1 = 10 *(4 +4) + 2 = 10.*

Those unstoppable students advanced smoothly into multiplication:

(2 x 2) + 6 = 10 *(2 x 3) + 4 = 10*

Mrs. Stonecipher's appearance change was masterful. Hope admired the professional navy blazer with crested pocket, the attractive salt-and-pepper hair brushed into a neat chignon and fastened by a striking jewel-encrusted clip. She had a fleeting image of the earthy Bluewave.

She turned sharply when an under-sized child with a shock of dark hair and black-rimmed glasses volunteered his equation on yet another level:

$$(2 \times 8) + 4 \div 2 = 10.$$

The class and its leader cheered, as did Hope.

The teacher nodded to the principal and instructed the children to open their readers and turn to the assigned page.

"Read the story title and introduction and study the illustration." The teacher leaned toward the class and lowered her voice. "Use your entire brain." She framed the sides of her head with both hands, and the children imitated her. "And read very carefully. Then close your eyes and think about the words you read. After that, you will be ready to study the picture and understand what it tells you about the story we will read."

Smiling, she came to Hope.

"How chic you look, Mrs. Stonecipher."

"This is my ATP look, you know." Bluewave laughed.

"Your ATP look?" Hope smiled. "Your accommodate-the-parents look?"

"Well, that and my aim-to-please look." Her eyes scanned the children; she lifted her finger to a child raising her hand.

"It certainly is an attractive look for you, Bluewave, and a wise move on your part."

"Excuse me, please." She went to the child she had signaled and bent to speak to her.

Bluewave returned and in low voices, they chatted about the adjustment she had made to the class and the class to her.

Hope left the room followed by Mrs. Stonecipher's mesmerizing voice as she thanked the children for "using their good minds so well during Dr. Fleming's visit."

In the lobby, Martha Poynter, carrying a bulging canvas bag, greeted Hope and asked where she would be working with students. Hope gathered rosters and schedules from her office and led her to Brad Kushner's room at the end of C-wing.

"Mrs. Davis' second graders know they are to report to room C-5 at 9:40, Martha." She turned vacant, unsmiling eyes toward Hope and nodded.

"Give them a few minutes and then go to the classroom and fetch them, if necessary."

"Here they come now." Martha's face brightened in a way Hope had not seen before.

Not to worry; at least she warms to the children if not to me.

Hope hurried to her office, intent on returning McElson-Bourney's call and putting an end to their game of telephone tag.

Mr. McElson's news stunned her. Frederick Baldwin had arrived from New Zealand and filed a legal claim for his share of the estate, on the grounds of his being a blood relative of Mary's husband, his great grandfather and the very source of her wealth.

Mary Baldwin, the aristocratic, older woman who employed her during her college years, had received occasional postcards from her late husband's great grandson. Hope remembered her sharing hastily written cards from exotic locations, punctuating them with sarcastic remarks about Frederick's lack of ambition.

"Good thing he's on the other side of the world, so I don't have to watch him waste his life. Malcolm would have been appalled, I dare say."

Hope felt calm on the one hand and fear on the other. She had dedicated the entire bequest from Mary to the homeless foundation Theodore was helping George and her establish.

Mr. McElson seemed skeptical about Frederick's having a case at all.

"But we will just have to go through the legal steps to prove that to Mr. Baldwin, Hope. And it's going to take some time."

Should I cancel my date with Theodore tonight? It seems wrong to be purchasing a building for the foundation when the funding is in question.

George is meeting us there, too. What shall I tell him? If he likes this building, how will I stall the transaction?

Hope dialed Mr. McElson's number again. "How long do you think Frederick's claim will take to settle, Bernard?" she asked with feigned nonchalance. "We are ready to move on a large investment, and I am reluctant to proceed until I know the fund will be intact."

"Probably about six months, Hope. At least. Could be as long as a year." He cleared his throat. "These things can drag on, especially if the plaintiff and his attorneys have a great deal of determination."

They said polite good-byes, and Hope replaced the receiver.

In the end, she decided to go through with the meeting, hoping the building would be undesirable. *As far as I'm concerned, it is undesirable. Undesirably near PolyFlem.*

A yellow-handled dust mop seemed to be shaking itself out the side door as Hope pulled into the driveway of her Canterbury Road house. Puzzled, she hurried out the car door without gathering her things.

"Oh Adelaide," she called when she saw the large figure holding the mop. "What are you doing here today? I thought we agreed you would come Saturday morning."

"Your George brought me over today," Adelaide's speech formed unevenly through broken and missing teeth. "I finished early at the shop; and he said, 'Just knock off now, Addie.'"

Hope eased herself past Adelaide, frozen in the doorway, dust mop still poised over the step. A whiff of Adelaide's foul-smelling breath filled the air and Hope turned her face away.

"He did, did he?" *What was he thinking? We agreed that she needs to be supervised.* "I'll just get my things from the car, Adelaide. Go ahead and finish your dusting."

Hope gathered briefcase, handbag, and scarf from the front seat and carried them into the kitchen. She could hear Adelaide sliding furniture on felt-padded legs across polished oak floors.

She walked into the living room just in time to help her push the sofa back into its proper place. Fully expecting Adelaide to plow through the pile of dirt swept to the side, Hope was delighted to see her gingerly avoid it despite the clumsy men's shoes she wore. She watched her reach for the long-handled dustpan she had placed nearby and deftly sweep the dirt into it.

"What time did you arrive here, Adelaide?"

"About four hours ago, Miz Fleming." She continued dust-mopping the floor around the hearth.

"How did you get here?" Hope folded her cashmere scarf.

"Your George. He brought me." She stopped her work and looked at Hope.

She's wearing fresh makeup. And heavy lipstick, a nice mauvey rose shade, much the same shade as I wear. The makeup looked out of place on her large face, framed by unkempt shoulder-length hair, the sides clipped back like a schoolgirl's.

"I told him he had no business sending me out early, cutting my hours like that. I need my hours. I got obligations." She nodded affirmatively.

That is my lipstick shade. "So you've been here since one thirty? What all have you done in those four hours, Adelaide?" Hope tried to keep suspicion out of her voice.

"Well, let's see." She pinched her chin between thumb and forefinger, her face turning to span the rooms. "I dusted all the floors and hard furniture down here." She turned serious eyes toward Hope. "Had to go over everything twice. It was really dusty, Miz Fleming."

"Well, you have things shining now. Did you do anything upstairs, Adelaide?"

She pulled a damp cloth from her waist and bent to wipe the hearth. She spoke without looking at Hope. "Wanted to. Wanted to vacuum the carpets and all." She gave meticulous attention to wiping the edges of the marble tiles.

"What happened, Adelaide?"

"I noticed your dressing table was a sight. Bottles and jars a mess. Everything undone." She did not look at Hope.

"So you cleaned my makeup, put it all in order?"

"I did, Miz."

"Let's go upstairs so you can show me, Adelaide."

Adelaide rose and led the way, smiling and strutting like a proud child who had just tidied her room.

Heavy footsteps thumped on the stairs, and both women looked toward the bedroom door into the hallway. A grinning George in grimy work clothes sauntered into the room. Hope knew he would feel the tension in the air and tried to soften her mood for him.

He can't know how I'm resenting his Adelaide at this moment. I'm so ashamed. But she's destroyed all my lipsticks. She must have tried on layer after layer of each one, given the wads of lipstick-stained tissues in the waste can. And my new whipped makeup from Saks, it's down to nothing. Judging by her face, she used three-quarters of a jar for one application.

Hope took a deep breath and managed a weak smile. "Hello, Son. You look as if you've been doing hard labor."

George laughed. "Oh, these clothes, you mean? I have been. Had to help a customer dismantle a unit to replace one of our parts. I'm still not finished. Is everything all right, Mom?" He looked from Hope to Adelaide.

"Hey, Adelaide. How's it going? Was there enough work here to make your hours for today?" He walked over to her, and she looked up at him with wounded eyes.

"Wow, Addie, you're all made up. Don't you look beautiful!" He touched her chin gently. "Ohhh, I don't see how I can let you go out on the street looking so sensational."

Adelaide looked adoringly at him. She turned toward Hope, her face smug.

George looked from one to the other. "Is everything all right here?" He stepped toward his mother.

Look at how tenderly he treats Adelaide. I am such a wretch. I don't deserve to have a fine son like him.

She walked to George and hugged him, dirty clothes and all. He hugged her back then approached Adelaide and hugged her shoulders, trying to keep his soiled work clothes from touching her.

"We're all friends here, so hugs all around, right Addie?"

"Addie experimented with my makeup, and I'm afraid I was a bit cross with her," Hope suddenly said. Her eyes met Adelaide's and she smiled. Adelaide smiled triumphantly back.

"But you're right, George. Now that I see how lovely she looks, I forgive her. Every woman needs to feel as attractive as she can." She went to Adelaide and touched her arm. "We need all the help we can get, don't we, Adelaide?"

"Sure do, Miz Fleming. We need all the help we can get." She carried the overflowing leather waste can toward the door. "I'll just go empty this. Be right back."

Hope took a makeup case from a drawer. "George, I assume you're here to collect Adelaide. But how can you drive her downtown to the shelter, and get yourself cleaned up in time for our dinner date with Theodore?" She looked at the clock on her bedside table. "It's nearly six now, and we meet him at Joseph's at six thirty."

Theodore and Hope sat at a table near the courtyard, watching fairy lights twinkling on bare trees. The atmosphere in Joseph's elegant dining room seemed perfect; and they sat in utter contentment, relishing one another's presence.

"What time do we meet the realtor at your building, Theodore?"

"Eight-fifteen, Hope. We have plenty of time." He lifted his wineglass. "Here's to finding the perfect building to house George Fleming Foundation for the Homeless." Their glasses clicked briefly and they drank together.

Hope pondered whether to tell him now about Frederick's claim on her inheritance. She did not want to spoil the moment.

Plates of grilled salmon with dill sauce arrived, and they immersed themselves in haute cuisine and conversation about everything but the foundation.

I'm rather glad George could not join us. It's wonderful having Theodore all to myself. We can be ourselves without talking philanthropy talk. Theo and I won't spend one minute bleeding our hearts for the homeless tonight.

The glow of the lovely evening washed over Hope as she drove home. It was becoming more and more obvious that the chemistry between Theodore and her was growing stronger with each meeting. It was a feeling unfelt by her for more than a decade, and she found it exhilarating. *When I am with Theodore, everything else in my life loses importance.*

In the end, given the warm and relaxed nature of the evening, she had told him of Frederick's claim. His encouraging remarks about the size of the inheritance and the clarity of Mary Baldwin's will put her mind at ease. He saw no reason why they should not proceed with purchasing the building. She liked his positive approach.

She liked his ability to laugh as well. And they had laughed often the entire evening. In fact, he roared uncontrollably at her account of Adelaide and the makeup. He told her she had done a generous thing by inviting Adelaide to help herself to all the makeup she wanted; he was sure that gesture had helped to validate her as a woman. In his words, "the crowning touch was your giving her a Gucci makeup bag in which to carry her new potions and paint pots on the streets."

Hope completed her rounds to classrooms and headed back to the office, feeling the joy of seeing students and teachers in full flow, just as they should be in the morning.

She crossed the front lobby and was caught off guard by the sight of Martha Poynter sitting on the bench. *Martha was here yesterday. What is she doing here again today?*

Hope approached her and saw that she was copying names and telephone numbers from the master roster sheets onto index cards.

"Good morning, Mrs. Poynter. How are you today?" She sat on the bench next to her and waited for a response. None came.

"Mrs. Poynter, Martha, we weren't expecting you today." She bent her head and focused on the woman's face. Still Martha did not look at her.

She touched Martha's arm lightly and tried again. "Martha, why are you here today?"

Martha turned toward Hope with cold eyes. "Call me Mrs. Poynter, please. I'm a professional teacher." She returned to her index cards.

Heat rose in Hope's chest. She sat frozen, trying to understand the situation. *Where did she get the roster sheets? And why does she need students' telephone numbers?*

She turned and looked closely at Mrs. Poynter, watching her work, trying to read her face. The woman remained completely oblivious to Hope.

Hope's administrator mind took over, and a knot of anxiety formed in her stomach. *What if she starts calling the homes of these children she's tutoring? What if she tries to make contact with them outside school? Would she do that?*

Cafeteria workers arrived and greeted Hope as they passed.

"Hi, Mrs. Poynter," Helen, the kitchen manager, called.

Hope's antennae rose. Her face riveted on Martha's.

Helen smiled at Hope. "Mrs. Poynter, good morning." She touched her hand.

Mrs. Poynter looked up at Helen and smiled.

"Oh, hello, Ellen, what are you doing here?"

"I work here. I serve the children lunches. Remember, you took lunch from me last week." She continued smiling warmly.

"Oh, yes, I remember." Mrs. Poynter smiled. "You gave me a nice chef's salad, didn't you?"

She turned to Hope. "Ellen gave me a nice chef's salad with delicious ranch dressing." Hope nodded and felt thankful for the idea of providing complimentary lunches to scheduled volunteers.

"You could have another today, if you want." Helen began to step away. "Just come to the kitchen before the first lunch bell."

Hope rose. "Mrs. Poynter won't be having lunch here today. It's not her regular day. It's time for her to leave."

She took the woman's index cards and roster sheets from her lap and helped her to her feet, sending eye signals to Helen.

Helen watched Mrs. Poynter go willingly with Hope, then headed to the kitchen.

Corinne's eyes flickered ever so slightly at Hope's glance as she led her into the tiny office where they sat in chairs facing each other. "How did you get here today, Mrs. Poynter? Did your neighbor drop you off again?"

"My neighbor? No." Martha stared through Hope.

"How did you get here?"

"Why, I came in my car. It's right out front." She gestured toward the parking lot with her head.

"I thought you weren't driving these days, Mrs. Poynter." Hope tried to keep the concern out of her voice.

"Oh, I drive sometimes. If I have errands to run, you know. Today I'm going to the teachers' store to get flash cards for Sarah. Multiplication facts." She turned her head abruptly. "Where's my purse?"

"It's still on my desk, Mrs. Poynter," Corinne called through the open door. She rose and entered Hope's office. "Remember, you gave it to me for safekeeping." She handed the woman a black leather purse.

"I must go now." Martha stood. "Please tell Sarah Smith I will bring the flashcards to her home."

"Just bring them to school next Tuesday, Mrs. Poynter. That's your tutoring time with Sarah. Give them to her then."

"That's a long time for a child to wait." She looked squarely at Hope. "She will want to start using them."

"Volunteers don't contact students outside school. Parents do not like that. And it's against Board Policy." Hope edged toward her, delicately crowding her out the door. She walked her through the lobby and out to the parking lot.

"Have a good day, Martha. We will see you on Tuesday."

Martha waved and crossed the lot to a large, green vintage sedan. Hope watched her take a key from her purse and enter the car gracefully. She heard the ignition start and observed Martha maneuver capably out of the lot and into the street.

What am I to think? She seems perfectly normal now. But a few minutes ago, she was not acting at all lucid. Should I ring Mrs. Smith and warn her? I do not want to alarm her. But I can't have Martha violating policy.

CHAPTER FOURTEEN—RAY

Ray turned the corner onto his street, enjoying the washed-clean look of the neighborhood since all snow had entirely melted.

His heart sank when he saw Davey's black towncar in the driveway. *Not this again. Why does Claire bring him here so much? Why can't she just keep him at her place?*

When he climbed out of the van, he spotted Davey, his long legs in tight, black jeans and cowboy boots. His hand, held low, grasped a lighted cigarette. *He's obviously trying to keep the smoke away from Ma. Claire must have told him about her breathing problems.* A cloud from the dryer vent curled behind him, indicating that Claire had the washer and dryer fired up, as usual.

"How's it going, Davey?" He managed a lame smile.

"Hey, Ray," he said, turning away from him to exhale, his smoke mingling with the dryer exhaust. "I'm just helping Claire tend to her mother and all." He waved his hand for emphasis. "How's everything in the school maintenance business?"

"Oh, it's okay, I guess." Ray had his hand on the storm door.

"Jeremy still helping you, is he?" Davey took another long drag on the cigarette before tossing it in the grass and stamping it with his boot.

"Yes, yes he is. Every day. He's a good little helper." Ray opened the door. "See you later."

The smell of fried onions filled the kitchen. Claire hovered over the stove, frantically stirring a pan on too-high heat.

"What are you concocting, Claire?" Ray asked. He walked to his sister, reaching over her to switch on the vent.

"Smart-aster," she glared at her brother. "I was going to switch that on."

"I'm just helping you out." He watched her gather with bare hands, a pile of chopped red-and-yellow peppers and dump it over the onions. A rush of steam hissed and clouded above the pan.

Resisting the urge to lower the burner control, Ray said, "What are you making, Claire?"

"Stir fry, obviously. Chicken stir fry." Claire said, eyes riveted to the pan.

"I don't see the chicken. And isn't stir fry done over low heat? I mean, that's what stir fry is, isn't it?" He grinned sardonically.

Claire, stirring furiously, glared at him. "Set the table. The rice is almost ready."

"Where's Ma?" He walked down the hall to Caroline's room. She sat on the edge of the bed, steering both feet into blue terrycloth slippers.

"Hi, Ma."

"Well, hi yourself, Ray?" Your sister is making a nice stir fry for dinner. Are you hungry?"

"Not very."

"I told her to make brown rice for you." She looked gloomily at her son and whispered. "That Davey's here again. Third time in six days Claire's had him here for dinner."

"He lives ninety miles away, Mom." He moved closer and took Caroline's hand, helping her rise. 'What does he do, stay at Claire's?"

"I don't know and I don't want to know." Caroline steadied herself and took a deep breath. "God only knows what she sees in him." She dropped her chin and knit her brows. "She's doing his laundry, too."

"She's lonely, Ma." Ray guided her to the kitchen.

Tension filled the air as they ate. Claire chatted nervously, describing the hassles of collecting unemployment benefits.

Caroline tried to make polite conversation about Jeremy's helping Ray at school and what a nice boy he was. She inadvertently mentioned Heather and her good mothering, and everyone fell silent.

Davey's face and neck colored. Ray excused himself, leaving a half-eaten dinner. Claire began setting out coffee mugs and store-bought cookies.

Davey stepped outside to smoke and noticed Ray working with the driver's-side mirror on the van. He sauntered over and stood watching at Ray's back.

"Have you seen Heather lately, Ray?" He said softly.

"Once or twice, for a minute or two." Ray turned to him, hand still on the mirror. "Why do you ask?"

"Just wondered, that's all. Wondered how she's doing."

"I thought you were asking her to get back together with you, Man. Isn't that what you told me that night at her place?"

Anger rising in his chest, Ray abandoned the mirror and faced Davey squarely.

"Didn't you tell me you had quit drinking because you wanted to get back with Heather?" He did not try to stop the rage rising in his voice. "Didn't you say that to me just five minutes before you started hitting on my sister?" He found himself in the man's face and felt his fists clench at his sides.

Ray stared angrily at Davey; he stared back with blank eyes.

"Get off my case, Man," Davey finally blurted, with new energy. He thrust his face in Ray's. "What's it to you, anyway?"

He towered over Ray menacingly, but Ray did not step back. His mind's eye filled with an image of Heather quietly bringing the framed photos of Jeremy and her to his new office. He still felt her tenderness toward him that day. *I have been so dead wrong in this.*

"It's everything to me! I care about my sister and I care very much for Heather and Jeremy." His arms waved themselves harshly. "And I can't stand to see you romancing my sister while you lie to me so I'll stay away from Heather." Ray stepped back and breathed deeply.

Davey's right hand fumbled in his shirt pocket for a cigarette while his left hand brought a lighter from his pants pocket. With trembling fingers, he managed to ignite it. He inhaled deeply and exhaled slowly, looking off into the distance.

"What are you guys doing out here?" Claire called, letting the door slam behind her. She went to Davey and put her arm around his waist.

Ray went into the house.

"More coffee, Dave?" Ray asked the physical-education teacher, nodding toward a clean, new coffeemaker on a small tray table.

"Sure, Ray." He removed the lid from his styrofoam cup and held it out to him. "Just throw it in with what's left in the cup."

Ray hesitated to pour. "Well, this is just regular coffee. I don't know. Does it mix with that fancy coffee you have?" He laughed.

"Coffee is coffee, Ray." Dave laughed, too. "The only thing fancy about this coffee is the price." They giggled together like young boys.

In the end, both men agreed to several changes in Buddy Day rules. The older kids, the buddies, would not be permitted to give the primary children candy treats; only non-edible rewards, like stickers, small toys, or cool school supplies would be permitted. That would eliminate the sticky-wrappers-attracting-ants problem.

Dave mentioned the reminder note Hope had given him about the school ban on Power Wrestler trading cards and said he had already emphasized it with the buddies.

They had a brief discussion about permitting students to go to Ray's supply room for extra trash bags, paper towels, and the like, on an as-needed basis. Ray said they should get those articles from the big cart in the boiler room since cleaning substances, some toxic, were stored in the supply room.

The two men shook hands, exchanged thank-yous, and parted amiably.

Ray noticed the silence in the building and looked at his watch. It was nearly seven thirty, and he had not heard Hope arrive. He went to the outside door and scanned the parking lot. Hope's Volvo, along with Dave's truck and his van, were the only vehicles in sight.

He headed down the hall toward Hope's office but stopped. *Is it too early to call Heather? Jeremy gets the bus at 7:45. I'll wait awhile.*

He busied himself filing purchase orders.

On her way through the boiler room, Corinne poked her head into his office, "Good morning, Ray. You must really be enjoying this posh office?" She smiled warmly.

"Good morning, Corinne." He smiled back. "I am. I am." He left his chair and stood near her, folding his arms. "I might be the only head custodian around with a private office." She chuckled with him.

"We shouldn't let word get out, then. You may end up losing it. Some plant supervisors operate out of broom closets."

"Is that a fact?"

"Yes, but we'll keep yours secret. It's safe with me. Have a good day, Ray. Oh, how's your mother doing?"

"Better. She's had good results from her second treatment. Thanks for asking."

"That's wonderful." She stepped away.

He waved.

Ray hung up the phone, his heart full. He had made weekend plans with Heather and Jeremy. He hurried to Hope's office, carrying the large dust mop. Leaning it against the wall, he went to her open door. "Do you have a minute, Hope?"

"Yes, of course, Ray. Come in. Good morning."

Ray briefed her on his meeting with Dave and told her he hoped he wouldn't have to bring up Buddy Day again.

"Well, a new problem could crop up; you just never know," she said. "Meanwhile, how is everything going? Your mom's doing better, you said."

Ray nodded, hoping she would ask about Heather.

"And Heather? How are you and she doing?" Hope averted her eyes and began shuffling papers.

Ray smiled involuntarily. "We had some rough times, some misunderstandings; but everything's fine now. I'm taking Jeremy and her to the planetarium in Dalton this weekend. Kind of celebrate getting time together again."

Hope looked up at him and returned his smile. "She's been studying so hard. Helsi says that's all she ever does when she's not at work or in class."

"I don't doubt it. She told me Helsi took Jeremy home with her a few times to play with Robbie and Dylan just so she could study for a big t___." A knock on the door interrupted him.

Ray excused himself, and Hope motioned a fifth-grader into her office with his armload of handwriting workbooks.

On the way home, Ray stopped at the mall, according to plan, and selected a blue-plaid spring shirt and pre-washed chino pants. He reached impulsively for a braided leather belt and added that to his purchases. He wanted to look extra nice for the planetarium trip.

Passing through the children's department, he saw a shirt identical to his on a mannequin in the boys' section. *Jeremy and I could wear matching shirts!*

He carried the shirt to a sales clerk who helped him decide the proper size. Waiting in line at the cashier station, he enjoyed the vision in his mind's eye, of Jeremy and him in those shirts. *People will probably think I'm his father.* The thought warmed and excited him.

The customer ahead of him walked away with her purchase, and Ray stepped to the counter. *Maybe Heather won't like the idea of matching shirts.*

"May I help you," a pleasant-voiced sales clerk asked.

Maybe I'm taking too much for granted. Heather might be put off by this kind of nerve.

"Sir," the sales clerk prodded, making eye contact with buyers in line behind him.

He laid the shirt on the counter and removed his wallet from a pocket. Preoccupied as he was with doubt, he managed to pay for the purchase, put away the change, and walk away.

Driving home, he dispelled all doubtful thoughts and savored the excitement of what he had just done.

As he approached his house, he saw Claire and Davey loading laundry baskets into Davey's big sedan. He cruised right past the driveway and headed around the block.

What was I supposed to pick up at the store? He stopped at the convenience store and took his time browsing around before buying a gallon of milk and a box of donut holes. He pulled a tabloid for Caroline from the display near the register.

He drove home more slowly than usual, pulling over at a garage sale sign and perusing from the car, merchandise lined up on the driveway. Feigning interest, he stared several minutes at a lawn mower and a weed trimmer.

When he returned home, he exhaled with relief at the clear driveway. He gathered his bags and climbed the back steps, picking up a covered container of food, obviously left there by Claire.

Caroline sat at the table, finishing a plate of beef stew and sliced tomatoes. "Hi Son." She smiled widely. A pungent smell of well-cooked meat and vegetables filled the room.

Ray placed the container on the table and his bags on the counter. He put the milk in the refrigerator.

"Hi, Ma." He went to her and hugged her shoulders.

"We've got some good stew, Ray." She nodded toward the slow cooker, steaming on the countertop. "Make yourself a plate. Sit down with me."

Ray, suddenly overcome with hunger, took a large portion of stew and joined his mother at the table. He took a hearty bite and followed it with a bit of tomato and buttered bread. The rich, brown gravy tasted exceptionally luscious, and he dug in with gusto.

"Claire's cooking must be getting better, Ma. This is about the best stew I've ever had." He rose and took a second serving from the cooker.

"It's not Claire's stew, Ray. Davey made it."

Appalled, Ray looked down at his plate. He did not look at his mother.

"He put it on early this morning when they stopped here for breakfast." She chuckled. "Maybe he's trying to earn his keep."

Ray finished his tomato slices and buttered bread in silence.

"What's wrong, Ray-ly?" Caroline assumed the pitiful voice Ray loathed. "Does the stew not agree with you?"

"The stew's fine, Ma. It's the cook I can't stand." He went to his shopping bag and pulled out the box of donut holes.

"Oh, I know, Son. I'm tired of seeing that sorry face around here, too." She smiled at the box of sweet treats.

Ray poured glasses of milk for both of them and opened the box, offering it to his mother.

"I guess I can eat one or two of these little vein-cloggers, can't I?" She took one and popped it into her mouth.

Ray, on his fourth donut hole, swallowed and looked at her. "One or two won't hurt you, Ma." He hated himself for being such poor company, but he sat quietly, gorging on sweets.

"Claire will come to her senses, Ray. " Caroline broke the silence. "After Jack, she's not going to get mixed up with another cowboy."

She finished her milk and closed the donut box. Turning her shoulders toward Ray's bags, she said. "Show me what you bought, Ray."

She admired his purchases fittingly and went on at length about the matching shirts. She recalled dressing Ray, Rory, and Ray senior in father-son shirts every Labor Day when they all went to Boone Lake Amusement Park. "People always commented about how nice you looked, how it showed the family pride." Her eyes grew dreamy, and she smiled.

"I know Heather and Jeremy will get a kick out of those shirts, Ray." She stared at him until his eyes met hers. "You did the right thing."

"What do you mean, the right thing, Ma?"

"The right thing. It's about time you and Heather showed your true feelings." She braced herself on the table and rose from her chair. Taking a moment to stabilize herself, she carried the container of food to the refrigerator.

"Claire forgot to take her stew."

"How do you know our true feelings, Ma?" Ray asked, his voice serious.

"Why, anybody can see it. You and Heather look at each other with those cow eyes. Both afraid to touch but dying to."

She shuffled to him and patted his shoulders. "That kind of tension only means one thing, Ray."

"What's that, Ma?" He turned and met her gaze with innocent eyes.

"You've got the bug, and it was meant to be. That's all there is to it."

Ray smiled, and they both fell to laughing.

Jeremy sat still as a stone in the dark planetarium, his eyes glued to the changing sky. He listened intently to the narrator's liquid voice on the speaker and followed the instructions to locate the constellations and particular stars.

Ray and Heather, on the other hand, heard none of the narration, though they, too, sat in complete silence. Forearms touching, electricity coursed through their veins. Even in the blackness, those sitting near them could feel the fallout from their attraction to one another.

Ray's eyes met Heather's, even in the dark; and they smiled. She tucked her small hand into the crook of his arm, and he placed his hand on hers.

They drew their torsos closely. Constrained as they were by auditorium seats, only their thighs touched ever so slightly.

Ray felt as if his heart would burst at any moment. He had waited so long for this. After all those months of denying his feelings, he felt as if he had come home at last from a long, arduous journey.

On the ride home, Ray drove with one hand, his other locked tightly in Heather's. They sat in silence, mesmerized by the magic between them. Jeremy snored softly in the back seat.

Davey and Claire took Jeremy to an indoor amusement park in Cushing on Sunday. Ray longed to spend the day alone with Heather, but she needed to prepare for a Monday-morning assessment of her clinical practices. It was a pass or fail evaluation, one-third her grade for the course and her only uncompleted requirement.

However, with very little coaxing, she agreed to have a late lunch with him at two o'clock. They could be together until just before six, when she expected Jeremy to return home.

At precisely three minutes after two, Ray knocked on her door with take-out rib dinners, which they ate slowly, each overcome with marked shyness brought on by the profound change in their relationship.

Ray delicately tied a paper bib on her, resisting the urge to kiss the back of her pale neck. They tucked into saucy ribs, corn on the cob, and green salad. Every few moments their eyes met; and, through greasy lips, they exchanged smiles.

It was as if neither could believe their feelings had finally been unleashed, that it was safe to express them.

Ray revisited every second, the thrill of holding Heather's soft body against him as they hugged good night. A hug. Just a hug was all they had allowed themselves.

It was enough for Ray. It was everything.

He knew clearly now that their souls were inextricably joined, and this knowledge overwhelmed him. He saw the fragility in their new state of being. He did not want to upset the delicate balance. Every move he made toward Heather seemed fraught with caution.

They cleared away the remains of the meal, agreeing to forego chocolate cream pie until later.

The clock showed barely three thirty.

"I have Gone with the Wind on DVD," Heather said. "My sister Hannah gave it to me for Christmas." She looked at Ray and giggled.

"Hannah gave you that?" He giggled back at her. "All the way from Florida? It is Florida she moved to, isn't it?"

"Yes. Florida. She and Bud saw it at a cinema with a fifty-foot screen and loved it." Heather began rummaging through a shelf under the television set.

"Here it is." She handed him the box, electricity from her fingers conducting through it to his.

He kept pressing the wrong buttons on her DVD player, small twitters erupting from them at each mistake. Finally, copyright warnings filled the screen, followed by the title and menu.

He backed onto the center of the sofa, his eyes watching Heather. She sat down at the end but soon sidled over to within a foot of him.

The movie began, and their hands extended toward one another. Heather reached for a cushion and fussed overlong with it, finally gathering the courage to position it smack at Ray's side. She settled against it and into the curve of his arm. Theme music filled the room, and their hearts' dance began.

Ray glided through the halls at Poore Pond School, smiling warmly at everyone he encountered. Several early arriving teachers told him how fit and well he looked.

Hope noticed first. "You must have signed on at a gym, Ray. You look like a new man."

Ray caught a stack of folders slipping from her arms and carried them, walking alongside her.

He smiled, his face growing red. "Not exactly. I know I've been threatening to do that, but I haven't gotten around to it yet."

"Well, if just threatening to join has that effect on you, think what actually joining and working out will do." She waited while he unlocked the office doors.

She laid her briefcase on the desk and gestured to the table where he placed the folders.

"Remember, tonight is Market Time, Ray." She waited for his eye contact. "The truck should be here at four, on the dot. Paulette complained to her company about how late it came last month."

"She's a good coordinator, isn't she?" Ray asked. "She keeps the teenagers on track." Ray fussed with Hope's desk lamp, dusting it with his palm. "They get in and out of here in a flash. No loafing around, talking on cell phones either."

"Yes, she is. It was her idea, you know, to use the teens to help when so few volunteers came to unload the truck." Hope picked up pink telephone-message notes on her desk.

Ray furrowed his brow and he shook his head. “I don’t blame the parents for not wanting to unload the truck. Those boxes weigh over forty pounds each. It’s much easier for the teenagers to do all that hefting. Good for them, too.”

“And they earn hours for their community-service requirements. They need those to graduate.” She began to read the pink notes.

Ray stepped to the door. “Oh, Hope, there is one thing.”

She looked at him. “Yes?”

“Remember, I told you how the volunteers’ kids run through the school while their parents are handing out orders? They use lavatories we’ve already cleaned.”

Hope motioned for him to close the door.

“I do remember, Ray. Putting portable gates in those hallways after you cleaned the lavs did not solve the problem?”

“No, the kids figured out how to get through the gates.

“I will speak to Holly Hapwell, Ray. She’s a good PTA president; she will talk to the volunteers.” Hope reached for the telephone. “I’ll call her now. She’ll be tactful.”

“One more thing, Hope.” Ray fished in his pocket and brought out a scrap of paper. “Carol Davis asked me to tell you this. She remembered it on her way out through the boiler room, in a hurry for a meeting, so I said I would tell you.”

He looked down at his hastily scrawled note. “She said to tell you ‘Martin’s doctor wants him to be evaluated by a neurologist.’” With wrinkled forehead he raised his eyebrows at Hope. “Do you know what she’s talking about?”

“Yes, yes I do,” Hope said. “It’s good news.”

“I leave all that stuff to you and psychologist Carol,” Ray said. “I’m just the messenger.”

“And well you should,” Hope said with a grin. “Thanks, Ray.”

He stepped into the outer office, closing Hope’s door behind him. Corinne smiled at him from her desk, and he stopped to chat with her.

“Is it true that Mrs. Baker is nearly finished with her Pharmacy Assistant Course, Ray? Jeremy told me last week that his mother would be finished soon. Actually, he said, graduating. Will there be a formal graduation?”

The phone rang, and she raised an index finger at him as she answered it. He scrubbed a spot on the glass door with his finger.

Corinne replaced the receiver and looked toward Ray. “Excuse me, Ray.”

Ray folded his arms and rubbed his elbows. He could feel that unstoppable smile starting again. “I don’t know if there is any kind of graduation, Corinne. I’ll have to check that out.” His heart filled as he thought of how special it would be to watch Heather receive her certificate.

“See you later, Corinne.” He floated through the door.

I’ll get her a nice gift, something really special to show her how proud I am. It will have to be the right gift though. A ring?

CHAPTER FIFTEEN—THE BRADFORDS

Cold war at the Bradford house lasted two-and-a-half days. Helsi and Ian managed to avoid evenings in the living room, Helsi, by crowding her ironing board into the tiny laundry room or by soaking in the bathtub. Ian scheduled night meetings with Gene, then with Gene and his supervisor, both times at a truck stop outside town, designated by them.

Lawrence, Gene's boss, wanted to employ Ian on the spot. He offered him fifteen percent of each shipment's retail value.

"All you have to do is make deliveries to Argosy Medical between nine p.m. and midnight, whatever works for you." He stared at a spot above Ian's head. "Go after the kids are in bed." Lawrence's bird-like eyes darted around the coffee shop.

"Why on earth at night?" Ian's eyes sought his.

"Argosy prefers evening deliveries because the night watchman handles them. He doesn't do anything anyway." Lawrence fixed his gaze on the tabletop. "During the day, they're so backed up they'd have to hire another guy." He coughed nervously.

"Where do I get these shipments?" Having given up on catching the man's eyes, Ian aimed his at the tabletop.

"They get dropped off at your house," Gene interjected.

Ian caught Gene make fleeting eye contact with Lawrence.

Lawrence turned to Ian and stared at his forehead. "Gene is right. The shipments are dropped off at your house. We arrange to have them put right into your garage."

"What is the shipment schedule, when and on what days are they delivered?" Ian asked. He kept feeling they were not giving him the whole story.

"Oh, they can come anytime, Ian." Lawrence smiled thinly. "That's the beauty of it." He tapped the tabletop once with his thick index finger. "The shipments come to your garage." He tapped once again. "You drop them off. No timetable, no schedule. We keep things simple."

Ian shifted his hips on the worn plastic seat. "How much paperwork is involved?"

"Paperwork? There's no paperwork! I told you, we keep things simple."

"Even your pay is kept simple," Gene smiled at Ian.

"How's that?" Ian wanted to curse.

"Like the shipments you deliver, your pay is dropped off in your garage." Lawrence said in a tired voice.

"No kidding?" Ian was incredulous. "Somebody just drops off a check without my sending in time slips or any sort of record of the deliveries I've made?"

"That's right," Lawrence and Gene answered in unison.

"Boy, you guys do keep things simple," Ian replied.

In the end, he told them he would think about it and get back to them. Lawrence instructed him to go through Gene once he'd made his decision.

Ian pondered the encounter as he drove home. Nothing made sense. But two grand a month, up to five? He could not afford to turn his back on that.

He pulled into the driveway and saw all the lights on in the kitchen. His heart stopped, and he rushed into the house.

He found Helsi at the kitchen table surrounded by trays of sugar cookies, which she was decorating with colored frosting.

Relieved, he went to her and kissed her cheek. "What's all this, Babe?"

"Cookies for Dylan's class," she replied, her voice slightly tense.

"Don't tell me it's his birthday." Ian gave his all to behaving as if things had been normal between them the last few days.

"No, it's not his birthday, Ian." She did not look at him. "But it's up to him to bring a treat for the entire class when he moves up a level in reading. We agreed to it, remember?"

"How many more do you have to do?" Ian asked, sitting down across from her. "Do you want my help?"

"That would be nice," she said in a cool voice. "Wash your hands first."

He kept asking questions about technique, forcing her to respond, breaking the ice.

When he could hold it no longer, he told her about his meetings with Gene and Lawrence.

"I can't put my finger on it," he said, "but something is fishy about the whole thing. About Lawrence."

Helsi was as skeptical as he. "Why would you even consider getting involved with people like that, Ian? There has to be something illegal going on." She removed the last sheet of cookies from the oven, shuffling them with a spatula, onto a cooling rack.

"But what, Babe? What do you think? I have been wracking my brain to figure it out." He helped her transfer the finished cookies to a large plastic container. They wiped their hands on paper towels, and he led her to the sofa. She did not resist.

"I have no idea; but whatever it is, you should run the other way. Why are you wasting your time?" She settled in against his shoulder like the old days.

"I could make two thousand a month, Babe. You keep the house accounts; how many school lunches would that buy?" His eyes met hers and held.

After a few moments, her serious eyes softened. "Oh Ian," she said. "You don't have to go chasing after shady deals." She stroked his hand. "I like working for Heather. The hours are not too much. And I feel good contributing." They embraced.

Ian felt his anxiety subside. This is one time I wish she did not keep the house accounts.

He held her tightly and did not let her go until he felt the tension leave her body. With no need to speak, they switched off lights and went arm-in-arm, upstairs to bed.

In the days that followed, there were no more talks about qualifying for the lunch program and no more passive-aggressive bouts from Helsi or Ian.

But Ian had not forgotten their bitter words about money. Remembering his parents' perpetual arguments about money could still to this day, cause him anxiety. He and Helsi had vowed from the start not to allow money to come between them, and they had managed to keep that promise. Until now.

Ian sometimes talked of dropping out of school and taking a second job, so his wife could give up hers. But she had apparently worked through her martyr period and refused to allow it.

Also, Ian detected in Helsi, a certain feeling of self-satisfaction from having her own income. She began to say, "I can't afford that," or "I am going to buy that." Before, she had always used the all-important we.

Most days she went happily off to work, resuming the warm little notes and arriving home in a good mood.

Anecdotes about Jeremy and Heather began to creep into Helsi's conversation.

"You know, that Mr. Sellers from Poore Pond is really a nice man, Ian," she said one evening. He had come home early from class, elated about having earned the highest grade on an important exam.

"Who is Mr. Sellers? Did our kids have him?" Ian asked, his voice full of the joy he still felt. He tidied overflowing book bags near the back door.

"No, no, he's not a teacher; he's head custodian at the school," Helsi said. "I never paid much attention to him, just said hello and that once in awhile."

"What's changed your mind?" Ian asked, his voice mischievous. He polished the stovetop with a dishtowel.

"He takes Jeremy Baker to wrestling practice and Cub Scouts, so Heather can study. He does it quite often, too."

"Sounds like a nice guy." Ian said with slight interest. "What's Heather studying again?" He stopped polishing to listen.

"Pharmacy assistant," Helsi said, dumping unpopped kernels from plastic snack bowls into the trashcan under the sink. "She'll be finished with her coursework in another month. It's a six-month course of study." Helsi tried to mask the envy in her voice.

"Will you be out of a job then?" Ian asked, putting down his cloth and slipping off his shoes.

"No. She has three months of clinical experience to finish." Helsi washed the salt off her hands and joined Ian on the sofa. She rose again and went to turn off the kitchen lights, immediately softening the ambience in the living room.

Ian took the remote and switched on the television. The volume blasted, and he quickly pressed it down.

"Her schedule will be rough; she doesn't even have Jeremy's care worked out yet."

"You didn't agree to work more hours?" Ian looked stricken.

"No, I told her I would do what I can, though. Whatever that means." She laughed, and he joined her.

Ian awoke the next morning to loud hissing of air brakes on an enormous moving van, pulling against the curb in front of the house across the street.

Helsi was already downstairs, boxing up cookies to take to Dylan's class. She, too, heard the truck's brakes and went to the dining room, where she peered discreetly out a window from behind the curtain.

She watched as a vintage, white, once-luxury car pulled into the driveway. A tall, athletic-looking woman with a long ponytail reaching to her waist, climbed out of the car and opened the trunk. She was joined by a young girl in baseball cap and pink wind-breaker, who looked to be about six, Rachel's age.

Shortly after, an older-model Overlander pulled behind the white car. A hefty man in a bulging overcoat rushed out of the car, calling to the driver of the truck.

Upstairs Ian stepped from the shower, wrapped a towel around his waist, and walked toward the closet. Spotting the commotion across the street, he went to the window and watched. *Somebody finally leased that house. It's about time. An empty house always seems so dead, gives me the creeps.*

He saw the man in the overcoat walk from the moving van to his family. *I wonder what he does. He looks like a—let me guess—banker. He looks just like a banker. No. No. He looks more like a collections officer.*

Look at those cars. He sure likes his classic vehicles. That Overlander, it's just like the one the Queen drives around her castle in Scotland.

"Hi, Dad," Dylan called from the doorway.

"Good morning, Son. Come in here." Ian smiled at Dylan and scrubbed his chest.

"Mom says you're taking me to school today." Dylan said as a wide smile spread across his face. "I have cookies to bring."

"Oh, that's right. Cookies. Happy birthday, Dylan." Tucking his shirt into his trousers, Ian turned to the boy. "Oh, wait a minute. You already had your birthday."

'Dad, Dad, stop it," Dylan laughed. "You know it's not my birthday."

Ian began brushing his hair. "Well then why are we taking those extra-special cookies your mother made to school today? Tell me; tell me." He turned and applied the brush to the cowlick at Dylan's forehead.

"I went up a reading level." He smiled sheepishly and dropped his eyes.

Ian made him repeat it before hugging him lustily. He grabbed him under the arms and swung him around. They both laughed joyfully.

Dylan tried to fix his face into a business-like expression. "We have to go now, Dad. Mom says. Robbie has a Conflict Managers' meeting before school."

Sean and Lucy's bus swooshed to a stop, three houses down the street. "There's the middle-school bus, Dad. We have to go." Dylan hurried downstairs. Ian grabbed his wallet and followed him.

Helsi stood at the door with three sealed plastic boxes stacked on her arm.

Ian took the cookies and bent to kiss her. "I got a look at the new neighbors," he teased.

"You're such a busybody, Ian." She laughed. "So did I."

She waved to Dylan and Robbie in the backseat.

"Pizza and fruit salad for dinner," she called to Ian. "We're celebrating Dylan's success!"

"I'll pick up donuts," he shouted from the moving car.

It was Dylan's night. The pizza dinner was his favorite, and the greasy donuts were a rare and delicious indulgence for the entire family. He read aloud, pages from the last book on his completed level. Everyone applauded his fluency and cheered when Ian announced that Dylan was now in level three!

Helsi shared a form letter from the teacher, announcing that he had been accepted into Computer Club. Everyone cheered even more loudly, and Dylan smiled sheepishly.

The family was on its second round of donuts when the doorbell sounded sharply.

Helsi grabbed a paper napkin, wiping chocolate frosting from her fingers as she hurried to the door.

She immediately recognized the callers, the new family across the street.

"We're the Meadow family. From across the street?" The stout man, now wearing a casual jacket, explained forcefully. "We just wanted to introduce ourselves since we'll be neighbors."

"Nice to meet you," Helsi said warmly. "I'm Helsi Bradford. Come in. Come in and have a donut with us."

They entered single file and waited for Helsi to lead them. Ian instantly stood and extended his hand. "I'm Ian Bradford," he said pleasantly. I didn't catch your first name."

Mr. Meadow introduced his wife and daughter to Ian.

Ian introduced Phyllis, Herb, and their daughter, Mercedes, to the children, who assumed shy demeanors and asked to be excused. Sean fought an embarrassed reaction and mumbled something about homework. "Good to meet you," he muttered without eye contact and slid out of the room. Only Lucy and Rachel remained.

After the new family had gone home and the children were tucked into bed, Helsi invited Ian to share the last donut with her. She poured hot water into cups with spoonfuls of flavored instant coffee powder and stirred them thoroughly.

"What did you think of the Meadow family, Ian?" Helsi asked.

"I don't know what to think," Ian said. "They seem nice enough." He stared into the distance. "Mercedes—what kind of name is that for a young girl—seems like a great kid. All those health problems and everything; yet, she acts like a happy kid."

"She does. And she and Rachel hit it off, didn't they? At least it looked that way." Her eyes met Ian's and held. "But there was just something about her; I can't put my finger on it."

"I felt that, too, Hon. Sort of a, not fear, not fear." He shook his head. "I don't know. How old is she anyway?"

"No, not fear. She laughed so much with Lucy and Rachel. She's eight-and-a-half. She doesn't look it, does she?" Helsi glanced at the ceiling. "But some sort of hesitation, a kind of holding back." She looked at Ian. "Well, you know how our kids are." She put her hand on his arm. "They're more open, you know. They say what they feel." Her eyes squinted at him.

"Guarded. Mercedes is kind of guarded, wouldn't you say?" Ian asked.

"That's it exactly, Ian. Guarded. You've got it." They laughed with delight at this fresh example of their being of like mind.

"Oh, I forgot to tell you, Ian. That Lawrence guy called this morning. Right after you left the house. He said he was really hoping you'd come to work for him."

"No kidding? I haven't seen Gene for weeks. He hasn't been in class." Ian stared into space. *I guess I should have called right away and turned it down. Two thousand a week. Minimum. Gosh.*

"You're not still thinking of doing that are you, Ian?"

Helsi's earnest voice broke his thoughts.

"Doing what, Hon?" Ian's eyes met hers.

"Working for them. Getting involved with the likes of them." Contempt filled her eyes.

"Don't be ridiculous." Ian said, his voice lacking conviction. *I guess I don't want to close the door yet. Who knows what may happen. My hours are cut now; I could be laid off altogether. And Helsi's little job wouldn't carry us one week.* "I'll call him, Helsi."

"Just put an end to it. Tell them you have no interest in their job. Tell them the whole thing smells." She grimaced and nodded her head emphatically.

"I'll handle it, Helsi." Ian said curtly.

"Phyllis said this will be her first experience going to school," Helsi said, pointedly changing the subject.

"Who's Phyllis?" Ian asked, still absorbed in thought.

"Phyllis Meadow." Helsi waved her hand in front of his eyes. "Remember, we were just talking about the family? About Mercedes. Phyllis said the girl has been home-schooled until now. This will be her first time going to regular school. She's a third grader. She doesn't look it, does she?"

"Is that a fact?" Ian said, willing himself to pay attention. "She looks about six, like Rachel." He inhaled deeply and exhaled slowly. "What exactly does home-schooled mean? I know the kid learns at home. But who teaches her?"

"I don't know much about it either. I think it's usually the parent who teaches her. To be honest, I thought about looking into it for Dylan." She grinned with closed mouth.

"You didn't!" He patted her knee. "Knowing you, you'd pull it off. You'd have all of us teaching Dylan. We wouldn't dare miss a lesson either, would we?"

They laughed together.

Monday afternoon Jeremy Baker came home with Helsi when she finished her shift at five o'clock. Heather, immersed in the process of designing a goals-and-objectives plan for her upcoming clinical work at an actual pharmacy, needed help.

It had rained all day, so Jeremy had not been able to play outside. Poore Pond School had indoor recess as well. The boy, restless and needing an energy release, had pestered his mother to take him to Kids' Play. But she faced a deadline for the written plan and had to refuse him.

Helsi saw how it troubled her to put her studies ahead of her son, so she suggested he come to her house for dinner and playtime with her children. She would bring him home by seven-thirty. Jeremy was thrilled. He optimistically brought along his new baseball mitt in case the weather broke.

But the Bradford children were not at home. Ian had left a note, telling Helsi he'd taken the younger ones for pizza and to the city recreation center to swim and shoot baskets. Sean was at a track meeting. Lucy was at a briefing for student candidates for the National Honor Society. Both she and Jeremy were disappointed.

They ate their dinner of boxed macaroni-and-cheese with turkey frankfurters and fresh fruit, both aware of a void without the children. Helsi managed to maintain a kind of conversation that was little more than her questioning Jeremy and his responding politely.

Noticing that the sky had cleared, she suggested Jeremy go outside and use the backboard Ian had dragged into the yard a few days ago.

Socking the ball against his new mitt, then throwing it against the backboard and catching it when it bounced back delighted Jeremy. He loved the sound of the ball hitting the leather mitt. Using the tips Ray had taught him, he practiced controlling his pitch.

Helsi kept checking on him from her ironing board set up near the front window.

She saw Phyllis Meadow come out her front door with a broom and begin sweeping debris from her wide front walk. Eight-year-old Mercedes bounced a large ball on the driveway. Her red jacket stood out as she bobbed around after the ball. Helsi saw that she was quite skilled, dribbling rhythmically and turning abruptly.

Ian called to make sure Helsi had found his note. He, too, was sorry they'd missed Jeremy. "He could have come with us if I'd known. But the kids are having the time of their lives."

"What about Sean and Lucy? Do they have rides home?" Helsi asked. Ian gave her the names of other parents who would bring them home.

When she resumed her place at the ironing board, Helsi noticed the red jacket standing next to Jeremy. He and Mercedes were talking. Helsi watched as he gave her a turn with his ball and mitt while he bounced her large ball on the Bradford's driveway.

Helsi ironed on, wondering how Heather was doing with her work. *Single mothers have a hard time. I'm just beginning to understand how hard. I never realized.*

She glanced out the window and saw Jeremy and Mercedes immersed in taking turns pitching the ball. They both wore mitts. *Mercedes must have run home to get hers.* She looked around for Phyllis and saw her through the open overhead door, sweeping the garage floor with the zeal of groundskeepers sweeping a baseball field after a rain delay.

Helsi heard twelve chimes from the clock near the front door. The clock face showed six-forty-five. She finished the last piece and put away the ironing board. Opening the front door, she called to the children. From the corner of her eye, she saw Phyllis hurrying across the street. She went outside to meet her.

They exchanged greetings and made small talk. Phyllis was anxious to bring Mercedes home. She told Helsi the girl would miss school tomorrow to have tests at the hospital.

"She's been having bouts of diarrhea and vomiting," Phyllis explained. "So the doctor wants to do tests."

"Could it be just a case of flu?" Helsi asked, worrying to herself that she may have exposed Jeremy to a contagious condition.

"No, they've ruled that out."

Jeremy and Mercedes walked over to them, and Phyllis put her hands on her daughter's shoulders. Behind Mercedes' back, she put her finger to her lips.

"Mercedes Honey," She turned her daughter's shoulders to face her. "Why don't you go on home and start running your bath. Mommy will be right there." Turning toward Jeremy, the child said an embarrassed good-bye and ran home.

Jeremy ran to get the ball she'd forgotten and began bouncing it.

Phyllis immediately resumed talking. "She's had these bouts off and on for months now. They may be related to her father's trips out of town because there seems to be a pattern of flare-ups then. Doctors say it may be psychological, but they want to rule out anything physiological first."

Helsi expressed her concern and offered to help however she could. They spoke a bit longer. Jeremy brought the ball to Helsi, and she explained his presence to Phyllis.

She hurried across the street, promising to let Helsi know the outcome of the tests.

What a friendly and open woman she is. It will be fun having a girlfriend right across the street.

Helsi returned Jeremy to his mother, or rather to Ray Sellers, who answered the door.

"Hello, Mrs. Bradford," Ray said.

"Hi, Ray. Please. Call me Helsi." Ray nodded, grinning.

"Hi Sport," Ray said to the boy. "Maybe I'm just in time to help you with your homework." He smiled warmly at Jeremy.

"Where's Mom?" Jeremy called, looking around the apartment.

"She's studying at your desk, Jeremy." Ray caught him on the shoulder as he started down the hall. "She needs to work another hour or so, Sport. Get out your homework. I'll help you at the kitchen table."

"Heather is really working hard, isn't she?" Helsi said.

"Yes. Yes, she is," Ray said, picking up a hammer and other tools from the floor.

Helsi noticed new, raw-wood chair rail on three walls in the eating area. "This chair rail looks great, Ray." She stroked it with her fingers. "Did you do it yourself? In just a few hours?"

"Yes, I did." He rubbed a spot with a small square of sandpaper. "Heather is crazy about chair rails. She hasn't stopped talking about them since we took Jeremy to Jefferson Farm." He brushed away the sawdust with his hand.

Jeremy carried his book bag to the table.

"You must have had it pre-measured and everything." Helsi said.

"That's right. I cut it in my garage and brought it over ready to mount. It didn't take long at all."

Helsi edged toward the door. "Good-bye, Jeremy." Jeremy waved from the table.

"Jeremy," Ray looked at the boy and nodded toward Helsi.

He went to Helsi and extended his small hand. "Thank you, Mrs. Bradford, for taking me to your house."

She shook his hand vigorously. "You're welcome, Jeremy. We'll do it again, but we'll make sure the kids will be home."

Ray watched her descend the long outside stairway. She waved from her car.

Helsi pulled into the open garage beside Ian's van just as he slammed its back door. He smiled and helped her out of the car.

"Is everything all right?" she asked, feeling tension from Ian.

"Sure, Hon." He kissed her gently. 'The kids are getting ready for bed. They're worn out."

"Did Sean get home? Lucy?" Helsi put her arm around Ian's waist and walked into the house.

"Yes. Everybody's accounted for." He stopped in the kitchen, rubbed an elbow and looked away. "Actually, you're just in time, Helsi. I should drop off some things at the firehouse. They need to be back there tonight for the late shift."

"You'll be right back?" she asked, one ear cocked toward shouting-and-running noises upstairs.

"Right back." Ian gave her a quick hug and left.

Helsi rushed upstairs. "You'd better be ready for bed, not wasting time getting at each other!" she called.

Ian drove with one hand, a square of paper held in the other. He kept rereading the directions, trying to watch the road at the same time.

The warehouse, tall and dark, loomed ahead, right past the junction, as the directions indicated. He followed the driveway around to the rear of the building where a single bare bulb cast dim light over a wide industrial door.

He checked the note again for the night watchman's name.

Wally. Wally will unload your car, the note read. There'll be union problems if you unload or even help. Just buzz the button at the service door.

Ian climbed out of the van and pressed the buzzer long and hard. He heard no signs of life. Shuffling his feet, he looked at his watch: 9:07. He waited three minutes then buzzed again.

A fierce-sounding dog barked repeatedly. The barking grew closer and closer. Ian stepped back from the door.

Half the wide double door scraped open, loudly slamming into its frame. A large dog with mean eyes and brindled gray hair raised his nose at Ian and barked ferociously.

Ian stepped further away.

"Quiet, Ripper!"

Ian looked squarely at the man, noticing his large, bulky body, his flaccid face and untrimmed mustache. "Wally?" his tense voice called over the racket.

The man extended his closed hand toward Ripper, instantly silencing him. "Yeah, I'm Wally," he said, his tone insolent.

Beside him, Ripper whined and pranced. Again Wally aimed his closed hand at the dog. Ian saw the small device he held and looked at Ripper's thick collar. He could see the metal sensor embedded in the black leather and understood that Wally had zapped the dog with a current of electricity.

"You've got to be Ian." Wally said, his dark eyes softening somewhat. Ian nodded and they shook hands awkwardly.

"What do you have for me? How many boxes?" He looked toward the van.

"Just two. But they're heavy. Must weigh about eighty pounds each."

Ian led him to the back of the van and opened the doors. He looked around. Wally had vanished. He looked for Ripper but did not see him. His chest tightened with fear that the dog was lurking in the dark very near him.

Ian started to grip a box, then recalled the written instructions. Sensing a presence, Ian turned to see Wally coming silently toward him behind a rubber-tired dolly.

Feeling like a sluggard, he stood by as Wally, heaving noisily, transferred the boxes to the dolly.

"That's it, then," Wally said curtly and walked away. Ripper came out of the darkness and, without a glance toward Ian, followed his master.

Ian slammed shut the van doors and rushed into the driver's seat. He backed up to turn around and shifted into forward gear. He looked back at the heavy doors, now closed, and saw no sign of Wally or Ripper. The dim light was now dark.

Well, that was pretty simple. Except for Ripper. But he'll get used to me. This is a piece of cake. Ian ignored a small knot of fear growing in his stomach and sped down the narrow road toward the highway.

CHAPTER SIXTEEN—HOPE

Hope, still exhausted from the weekend, struggled to turn her key in the lock of the boiler-room door. Suddenly, it opened on its own, and a smiling Ray faced her. She was struck by how fit he looked. His eyes were clearer than usual, and his skin glowed.

"Good morning, Ray. You look as if you just won the lottery. Is there something you want to tell me?" Giggling childishly, he held the door open for her.

She lifted her briefcase and tote bag from the ground and walked past him. "I did not see your van. Did you park in the back?"

"No, my van's not here. Heather has it." He closed the door tightly and took Hope's bag and briefcase from her.

"Heather has it." She repeated his words, trying to discern their real meaning. She walked alongside him in thoughtful silence.

"Her car is in for repairs, so she drove me to work." He seemed to emit each word with a caress.

There is obviously more going on here than the sharing of a vehicle. "And it seemed a better idea than your driving her to class—or to her internship; she's in the throes of that now, isn't she?" Hope looked at his profile, seeing no clues.

They reached the outer office, and Ray managed to open the heavy glass door with his elbow, holding it with his hip. He followed her into her office and set her things on the table.

"Well, yes." His eyes widened. "Heather has her last class this morning. She meets her supervisor at the pharmacy this afternoon for orientation." His sentence ended with an excited squeak.

"Already?" Hope dropped into her desk chair and motioned for Ray to sit at the table. "I just cannot believe it. The time has gone so quickly." They sat in silence, basking in the joy of Heather's accomplishment. Hope visualized her young protégé behind a pharmacy window, looking very much the professional in a white lab coat. Oh, if only George's foundation business were as straightforward as Heather's path to pharmacy assistant.

Corinne appeared at the door and greeted them cheerfully.

"Where's your van, Ray? I thought you were ill when I didn't see it." She stepped toward her station and placed her purse and lunch on the counter.

She returned to the doorway. "I did not know where to park." She laughed. "You know I always line my car up next to your van." They laughed together.

"Mrs. Baker is using Ray's van today, Corinne." Hope offered before Ray could speak. Their female eyes met knowingly.

Ray stood and rubbed his elbows. "Yeah, she meets her pharmacist today." Suddenly shy, he avoided looking at either woman. "Her internship starts this week."

"That's wonderful! I am so happy for Mrs. Baker. I know how hard she's worked." Corinne said, rushing to the ringing phone.

Safety patrol students entered the building noisily, and Ray went off down the hall.

Hope pulled papers from her inbox.

Corinne hurried into Hope's office, apprehension on her face. "I saw Mrs. Poynter's car pull in, Dr. Fleming. She's not scheduled for today, you know." She slipped out again and reappeared in seconds. "She's bringing a huge bag, almost bigger than she is."

Both women exited the office and rushed to the front door. Corinne held it open for Martha Poynter. Hope met her and took the bag from her arms.

"Good morning, Mrs. Poynter," they said in near unison.

"I have to see Jerry and Philip. I brought these clothes for them." She headed toward third-grade hall.

"But Mrs. Poynter," Corinne called.

Hope put the bag down and hurried after her. "Mrs. Poynter."

Mrs. Poynter continued walking.

"Mrs. Poynter." Hope tried again. "Martha." Getting no response, she passed her quickly and stood before her. Martha stopped short, turning to circumvent the principal.

Hope quickly slipped her arm around the woman's waist and reversed her direction. "Let's have a nice cup of tea, Martha, and we will talk about the things you brought for Jerry and Philip." She walked at a brisk pace, and Martha kept in step. She could feel surprising energy in Mrs. Poynter's compact body.

"Tell me, Mrs. Poynter. Why do you think the boys are in need of clothing?" They were crossing the lobby now. "Have you noticed that they were poorly dressed?"

Corinne held open the glass door; Hope ushered Martha through the outer office, into her own small one. She pulled out a chair and guided her into it.

"Now, let's see about a cup of tea." Hope said to herself as much as to Martha Poynter.

"I'll get that," Corinne said from her desk. "It won't take a minute." She dashed to the kitchen.

Martha's eyes darted around the office. "That bag of clothes." She looked at Hope, hovering near her. "Where did you put it?"

Hope sat in a chair opposite Martha. "Corinne put it in her office, Mrs. Poynter. It will be fine there."

"We must take them to Jerry and Philip." She stood abruptly. "They're expecting them. They are such nice boys." She stared imploringly at Hope.

Corinne came in, carrying two mugs of tea and sugar packets on a red plastic cafeteria tray. Large food-service cookies in cellophane bags lay next to thin, institutional paper napkins. She arranged a mug and cookies in front of Martha's chair and directed her to sit down.

Hope took the other mug. "Do you take sugar, Mrs. Poynter?

Corinne turned to leave, and Hope thanked her, passing her a folded note.

"I thank you, too, Mrs. Tompkins," Martha echoed.

"They sat drinking tea in silence for a few moments, Hope's mind racing. *I wonder if Corinne has reached Martha's daughter. Amelia, I believe, was the name I saw on her emergency form.* She looked at her desk phone and saw Corinne's lighted extension button.

Hope inhaled deeply and exhaled slowly. "Mrs. Poynter, how many years did you teach here at Poore Pond?"

"Me? Here at Poore Pond?" Mrs. Poynter set down her mug. "Oh, a long time." She stared out the window.

"Were you here when Keith Broski was principal?"

"Broski? Mr. Broski? Yes." She took a sip of tea, swallowed, and continued. "I was here before that. I taught under Mildred Franklin before Broski came."

"So you were here when the cafeteria was renovated, is that right?" Hope noted how lucid Mrs. Poynter seemed now.

"Cafeteria?" Martha's mouth turned down dramatically. "They kept promising us they'd build a cafeteria. They never did. We had to eat lunch in our classrooms."

Hope, overcome with disappointment, fell silent.

"She's in there with Dr. Fleming," Hope heard Corinne say. *Please, Lord, let this be Amelia.* Hope stood.

An attractive young matron with glossy chestnut hair appeared. She introduced herself and shook Hope's hand.

In the end, Amelia took her mother home, promising to send her husband and son to pick up the car later in the day.

Hope, saddened from the ordeal, sat at her desk in a stupor. She looked forward to lunch time and seeing the children. *I need a dose of normality before tonight.*

Theodore collected Hope at five-fifteen sharp, just as she knew he would. Looking polished in good black wool trousers and well-tailored camel-hair blazer, he looked admiringly at Hope. She had changed into dark tweed pants and soft natural leather jacket, a rich velour scarf looped at her neck.

They stood in her warm foyer, admiring one another's dress.

"You are looking smashing, Dr. Hope." He smiled.

"As are you, Sir Theodore." She returned the smile.

"Are you as up for this training session as I am, Theo?" He smiled and took the door key from her outstretched hand.

He opened the door to a rush of invigorating cold air, which sent them hurrying to his still-idling car.

Hope settled into warmed leather seats, feeling cocooned and content. Soft string music whispered from the rear speakers.

Engulfed in delicious sensory surroundings, they drove in silence. Theodore traveled slowly in dusky light, down clean-swept, late-March streets, preserving the moment.

He's obviously no more anxious than I to help train the four employees at the shelter. George, I'm sure, is either already there or racing to get there.

"What time is George meeting us, Hope?" Theodore broke the silence, turning to smile at her.

"Well, he told us six, but I'd bet the farm that he is already there. Digging in with gusto." They laughed.

"He really does get off on helping those poor unfortunates, doesn't he? I admire that about him, don't you, Hope?"

Hope leaned forward to press off the seat-warmer button. "I do. I really do, Theodore. He seems to understand them. I suppose that comes from living among them for four years." She sat back again.

"Was it that long?"

Hope nodded.

"Four years in the streets." He shook his head slowly. "Can you imagine what he must have endured?"

"I cannot bear to think about it, Theo. It's too painful."

They rang the bell at the front entrance and were greeted by none other than Adelaide—her face fully made up—carrying a wet mop. She directed them around the wall of the lobby, away from freshly cleaned terrazzo tiles.

Theodore and Hope stifled grins and exchanged knowing glances as they proceeded down the corridor. They heard voices from the common room. Sounds of tables being dragged across the floor and a microphone being tested spilled out the double doors.

"Here they are!" George called happily as they entered. He nodded to a trim-figured, mustached man at the other end of the table they carried; abruptly they placed it on the floor.

"Mom, Theo, you remember A.J. Case. From the second interview? He's our new resident shrink." George said cheerfully.

Oozing charm, A. J. beamed his dazzling smile, made more so by the dark mustache, first at Hope, then Theodore. They shook hands thoroughly as Hope sensed figures approaching from the opposite end of the room.

George linked arms with a striking, classic-faced young woman with sleek black hair, swept off her face and secured in the back by a wide, antique-silver clip. Hope, trying to determine her age, took in the youthful, fit body and flawless skin.

"This is Brooke," he announced, stepping near them. "Brooke is our social worker." His cheerfulness matched that he had given to introducing A.J., and it gave Hope no clues.

There is the tiniest hint of attraction between them, though. She tried not to stare although she wanted to study Brooke completely.

She graciously shook hands with Hope and Theo, engaging them in a spirited account of her gratitude for the opportunity to work with the new shelter and her admiration for their making it possible.

Hope detected maturity in Brooke's outlook and mentally tallied the number of years it would have taken to experience all that she described in the career chronology Theo managed to elicit. She must be at least thirty-five. A sense of watchfulness filled her mother's heart as George led Brooke away to a stack of photocopies on the front table.

A tall, sturdy, take-charge-type woman with steel-grey hair and a formidable manner introduced herself before George could get to it. "I'm Grace Jones," she said, thrusting her hand toward Theo. "I remember you, Mr. Keller, from the interviews." She looked at Hope, and he introduced them.

"Yes, Grace, I remember you well." He looked at Hope. "Grace has the most outstanding credentials. Just the sort of experience a new shelter needs in its residents' manager." He scrubbed his hands and continued. "Why, she has held every position from chambermaid to intake officer to floor manager. And she comes highly recommended."

"That's right," Grace said matter-of-factly. "And you forgot to say that I started at the bottom. Rock bottom." Her eyes held his resolutely.

Hope could feel Theo's discomfort.

"I started out as a vagrant." She looked at Hope. "I needed the services of a shelter—for some time—and I'm not ashamed to admit it." Grace locked eyes with Hope.

Breaking the moment, George approached and put one hand on Hope's shoulder, the other on Theodore's. "We're getting started now. Take a seat at the speakers' table in front."

He touched Grace's arm gently. "You sit at the table with A.J. and Brooke, Grace."

Looking around the room, George asked, "Where's Milan? Has anybody seen him?" His face full of concern, he left the room.

Hope and Theodore flipped through the handout packets on the table while Brooke and Grace chatted softly. A.J. sat alone, quietly watching the others, occasionally staring into space before jotting words on a pad of paper.

Milan, face set in a mix of defiance and humility, entered the room ahead of George. George gestured toward the chair next to A.J., and he moved into it with aplomb. From the front table, Hope's eyes searched his face; and he stared her down. She coughed silently into her fist and looked away. *I wonder what his story is. Those dark eyes, they're piercing.*

He was medium height with large, well-padded frame. His facial skin had the red cast of a drinker. *I'd say he's in his early fifties. Or younger maybe. He's definitely had a hard-knock life; that can age a person. But still, there's a dignity about him. I am sure he's intelligent; George would not have a manager who wasn't.*

The sound of George's introduction broke her thoughts.

"Folks, we need to start now." He stood then to get their attention and sent a warm smile to each person, one at a time.

"Has anyone seen Father Elijah?" He scoured their faces. "He wasn't sure he could make it, but he'll be here regularly once we start the full schedule."

"We have much to cover. But first, let's go around the room and introduce ourselves. Tell your full name, your position here, your philosophy toward homeless people, and anything else you want to tell us about yourself." He looked from one to the next, squinting his eyes.

"You know me, so we'll hear from Grace, Milan, Brooke,

A.J., Hope, in that order." He ignored the smile Hope sent. "Theodore, you're last." He grinned at him. "That's one of two power positions, Theo. First and last." His words brought polite chuckles, but light tension hung in the air. "Take as much time as you need." He took his seat and looked at Grace.

She rose, proudly drawing up to her full six-foot, three-inches. "My name is Grace Ellen Jones, and I've been around shelters all my life. I learned about shelters from my mother. She whored and drugged her way through her young years and ended up staying in shelters after she had a kid: me." She stabbed her chest emphatically with the five fingers of her right hand, then paused for effect, making fierce eye contact with everyone in the room.

"I've cleaned up after a gazillion poor souls who are guests in shelters, and they all have one thing in common." Again, she paused for effect and locked eyes with each person in turn. "They all smell." Another pause.

"They don't put anything over on Grace." She moved her head exaggeratedly from side to side. "I've seen and heard it all." Eyes widened, she shook her head up and down, raising an index finger.

All eyes riveted on Grace, awaiting her next shocker.

"As I said, I've cleaned up after them. Elmer Dannerly made me intake officer, and then I had to decide who was qualified to be a guest at the shelter." With pursed lips, she mocked the word. "I was so good at qualifying, our numbers shot up."

Laughter broke out, surprising Grace, who bestowed a rare smile.

"Then they made me floor manager. That's when I really came to understand the poor wretches." Enjoying the attention, she paced the center aisle between the tables.

George and Hope made eye contact, as did Brooke and Theo. A. J. scribbled notes. Milan squinted at Grace.

Turning abruptly, she shouted, "They'll manipulate you! They'd rather lie to you than tell the truth." She spat the words.

"They go out of their way to lie to you when it would be much easier to just tell the truth." Her voice softened. She stared ahead of herself, into space.

"But they're all God's children, and they've been dealt a cruel hand." Her voice choked. "They deserve our help." With downcast eyes, Grace hurried to her seat.

Silence filled the cavernous room. It was minutes before anyone spoke.

"Well, Milan," George called gently. "It's just your luck to be next." He looked at Grace. "She's a tough act to follow, Buddy."

Hope sat on the edge of her chair, anxious to hear his story.

Milan remained seated and in a monotone voice, gave a banal account of having worked in maintenance all his life. He'd had his own cleaning company for a short time, he said, "making money hand over fist until his partner stole him blind."

Obviously uncomfortable, he shrugged his shoulders and looked at George. "You heard it all in the interview, George, you and Mr. Keller." He looked at Theo.

"That's right, Milan," George said gently. He stood and faced the group. "Milan worked for twelve years as maintenance manager for Heartwood Rehabilitation Center. He comes to us with a high-performance record there."

I wonder why he left. Why didn't George say, 'He comes to us well recommended'? Hope pondered, looking at Theo.

George asked Milan his philosophy toward homeless people. He elicited a curt, "They need a break."

After the others gave introductions, George outlined the meeting agenda. They would cover the entire organization of the shelter. From dormitory arrangements to daily schedules of meals, showers, prayer services, laundry-room, to rules. One important rule required all able-bodied residents, except mothers with infants and pre-school children, to leave the shelter early every week-day morning.

Hope was taken aback when George said that. *I never really thought about children staying here. Did we discuss that when George and I met all those times with Theo? I don't remember any talk of children.*

The first half of the meeting faltered tiresomely as staff members called out their random opinions on every point George, Hope, and Theo presented, seriously disrupting the flow of ideas.

Unable to bear it a moment longer, Hope stood abruptly. Riveting her eyes on the small group, she saw them as children being unruly in the library or lunchroom.

"All right, Ladies and Gentlemen," she began, unsmiling and in her most commanding voice. "We are not going to proceed with this meeting until we establish ground rules." She walked to the end of the table where Grace and Brooke sat, an empty chair between them. Neither woman looked at her.

"This free-for-all will not continue." She stared unmercifully. "Only one person speaks at a time. The speaker will finish his or her entire presentation before anyone gives opinions." She paused for effect, making eye contact with all, glancing back to meet George and Theodore's gazes.

She turned again to the four staff members and squared her shoulders. "And opinions will be invited only from those raising their hands and waiting for permission to speak."

She moved to the next table where A.J. and Milan sat with downcast eyes. *How very like the children they all are.*

"Either you respect the speaker's floor time and follow rules of human decency, or you will be excused." Again she paused, studying their faces. "Let me remind you: this is a mandatory orientation."

Nose in the air, she swept regally back to her table, tension and heat from incensed bodies raining down on her.

George quickly distributed notepads with pencils before seamlessly moving into the next topic.

In the end, the meeting took more than three hours. But they covered all the essentials, even managing to role-play a few scenarios. George had them typed neatly on index cards, which he spread on the table and let people choose.

Milan gave a surprisingly good role-play of himself as residents' manager, chastising George as a resident, hoarding bags of goods and crowding them around his bunk.

Grace praised him for being right on with his depiction.

The staff members, tired and drawn, all left at the same time, calling, "See you Monday," to George.

Hope, bone-tired herself, asked George how he thought the meeting went.

"It went okay, Mother," was all he could manage, his voice full of exhaustion.

The three of them said hasty good-byes and hurried to their cars. Theodore and Hope, lost in private thoughts, drove home in silence.

Besieged by recall of the meeting, Hope prepared for bed. She suddenly realized that the tone of the meeting had fluctuated between her directorial approach and George's more cooperative one. She had a nagging feeling that this element had confused the new staff members and lessened the effectiveness of the meeting. She regretted the fact that George and Theo had not discussed this with her. They must have opinions on the meeting.

Staring at the mirror through ghost-like eyes peeking out of a cream-slathered face, she pondered. *George called me Mother tonight when we were finishing up after the meeting.* Her heart sank as she recalled how he had always referred to her that way when the situation between them was serious.

Denying the thought, her mind moved to other aspects of the evening. The one that stood out was George's talk of accommodating children at the shelter. Homeless children? Parents unable to give their children a proper home—or any home at all? What could be worse for a child? What could be worse for a parent?

For Hope, sleep was a long time coming.

Everyone at Poore Pond had a part in the Friday-afternoon Peace Assembly to invigorate the No-Bullying Campaign. The school hummed with preparation activities. Small groups of students worked on posters in hallway corners. Chorus rehearsals sent familiar melodies echoing through the building. Students had written anti-bullying lyrics to favorite tunes, including It's a Small World and The Gambler. Parents decorated front and rear lobbies in school colors, the reddest reds and the brightest whites they could find. Classroom teachers led even the youngest students in practicing their original skits.

Hope, sleep-deprived and feeling she had let George down, drew energy from the enthusiasm permeating the building and was grateful for it.

Corinne brought her the file of a new third grader from Champion City, who had been home-schooled until now. "You will want to look over her health records, Dr. Fleming. She has a thick medical file."

She put the file aside, headed off to tour the rooms, and found each class project more impressive than the one before.

Bluewave Stonecipher's first graders created soft anti-bullying messages; such as:

Hearts Full of Love Have No Room for Bullying

Love Stops Bullies

Learn to Love Yourself and You Will Never Be a Bully .

Fourth- and fifth-grade classes produced more pointed messages:

Bullies, Just Stop It!

Bullies Are Cowards

Stamp Out Bullying; Report it Every Time.

Brad Kushner's students proudly showed her their class collage. They had artfully arranged photographs of the smiling faces of every class member and inserted captions beneath. The captions expressed their views on bullying and bullies.

One introspective student's caption read: "I have been tempted to bully a few times, but I always think of my cousin and stop myself. In fourth grade a playground bully slammed him to the ground and injured his spinal cord. Now he's in a wheelchair for life."

The caption beneath the friendly face of a girl read, "Girls are the worst bullies. They pretend to be your friend and then say mean things to you, personal things about the way you look or your clothes or your family.

They spread mean things on email. My mother says, Those girls are not your friends."

"These are very real comments, aren't they? Did the children write them on their own?"

"Oh yes," Brad said, his voice emphatic. "Can't you tell? They are all so different and very much to the point."

Hope nodded, then quietly asked Mr. Kushner to show her Martin Purdue's project and, walking with him to a long table at the back of the room, was pleasantly surprised. Martin sat intently applying rubber cement to the backs of cut-outs, which he carefully arranged around an enlarged photograph of his own unsmiling face. The cutouts included a child-like drawing of a heart broken in half, a small boy with his arm in a cast, a little girl crying alone, even a cat with a bandaged foreleg.

They left an oblivious Martin and walked to the door.

"That's a powerful message, isn't it, Brad?" she whispered, her voice thick with emotion.

He nodded and said, "Martin surprises me again and again." He turned to look around the room.

"You're getting through to him then?" she asked. "You see promise of progress?"

"No question about that." He nodded to a student mouthing a request to go to the bathroom. "You know, once Martin was diagnosed with Pervasive Developmental Disorder and we wrote all those behavioral strategies into the IEP, there has been growth—small steps—but still growth" His eyes scoped the room again and fixed on a girl waving her arms wildly.

"Excuse me, Dr. Fleming," he stepped toward the girl.

He returned to Hope within minutes. "Sarah is such a perfectionist." He smiled proudly. "She noticed a misspelled word on her finished poster and grew frantic. I showed her how to put a clean, white label over it and paint the corrected word on that."

Hope grinned and shook her head with admiration. "What were you saying about Martin's progress, Brad?" She cupped an elbow in her hand and gave her full attention.

"Rewards. Martin responds to rewards, like high fives, handshakes, sometimes bear hugs." His voice rose with excitement. "Simple things like that." He glanced toward Martin's table.

He lowered his voice and continued. "Eye contact. He makes eye contact with me at least one or two times a day now." He took a breath. "We're working on getting him to make it with his classmates." He frowned thoughtfully. "I think the rewards will have to come from them, though, for that to work."

A student office page stopped at the open door and looked at Hope. "Come in, Carrie," she said gently.

Carrie politely told her there was a man named George in the office, and he needed to see her right away.

Hope thanked Brad and rushed down the corridor. Librarian John Knowles, face full of excitement, stopped her in the hall with an armload of bibliotherapy books on bullying.

Waving him away, she said, "I'm needed in the office, Mr. Knowles, but I'll come back as soon as I can. I want to see those books." His face fell, but he smiled and nodded.

She sailed into her office and abruptly closed the door.

"What brings you here, George?" she asked, her voice full of dread. She glanced at the clock. "Why aren't you at work?"

"I have to talk to you, Mother. Please, sit down."

Hope, her heart trembling, took the chair opposite him.

"A guy named Frederick Baldwin came to see me at PolyFlem just an hour ago." He looked at his watch. "About 9:30." His troubled eyes locked Hope's.

She willed herself to stay steady. "Whatever about, George?" she murmured, her voice too casual.

"He said the foundation had been formed with illegal funds," George leaned forward and scrubbed his hands. "He told me he was going to shut the place down before it ever opened."

"He didn't! That little gangster!" Heat rose in Hope's chest. "Don't you worry, George, he can't do that. He is powerless." She spat the words, exuding anger that masked the fear in her heart.

CHAPTER SEVENTEEN—RAY

Ray heard running water and dishes clinking and rushed, shirtless, into the kitchen. "Ma, what are you doing up at this hour?" he called as Claire came out of the pantry.

"Oh, it's you, Claire. Well, what are you doing up at this hour?"

'Who the heck can sleep with your mucking back and forth from the bedroom to the bathroom? It's the middle of the night, still dark out." She combed dark, straggly hair over her forehead with spread fingers and tied her robe belt.

"Well, I'm not used to having anyone sleeping in your room. Ma's at the other end of the hall. She never hears anything anyway."

He heard the drip coffeemaker sputtering and looked toward the counter. "You made coffee. So nice of you, Sis," he chided, knowing she loathed being called that. He stepped to the cupboard for a cup.

"For gosh sakes, Ray, put on a shirt. If there's one thing I can't stand, it's sitting at a table with a shirtless man." She glowered at him. "Davey does that all the time, drives me crazy," she called to his back as he went to the bedroom.

He returned, buttoning his blue work shirt, leaving it untucked. He filled a coffee mug and carried it to the table.

"What's for breakfast?" He smiled teasingly.

"Cereal. It's in the cupboard. You live here; you know that." She gulped coffee.

Ray dropped bread into the toaster. "Do you want toast?"

He waited without pushing down the toast lever.

"Maybe I will have a piece. Something hot sounds better than cold cereal."

They sat together munching toast, both missing the hot breakfasts Caroline always made for them their entire lives, so long as they lived in the house. That all stopped last year when she took sick.

"So Davey drives you crazy, does he?" Ray looked at his sister.

"Yes, sometimes he does." She frowned at Ray, who noticed that the lines in her forehead seemed deeper. "Not all the time, though, like you do."

"Knock it off, Claire." He said, his face burning with impatience. "We're not kids anymore. It's about time we stopped this stupid bickering. Anyway, you know how it upsets Ma."

He rose and brought the coffee carafe to the table, refilling both their mugs.

Claire stared at the steam rising from her coffee and cradled her hands around the mug. With softening eyes, she looked at her brother.

"You're right, Ray. It is time we behaved like adults." She took a quick sip of the scalding coffee and immediately put down the mug. "It's just that, well, I don't know where my life is going. I feel like a ship without a rudder." She averted her eyes.

"I know what you mean, Claire." He patted her arm. "But you're tough. You'll get through this." He looked tenderly at her.

"If I could just get another job." She stood and carried her dishes to the sink. "I need to be around normal people again." Her fingers massaged her forehead.

"You will; you'll get another job. With your experience? It's only a matter of time." He looked at the clock on the stove.

"I have to go." He carried his dishes to the sink and began wiping the table.

"I'll get that, Ray," she said, taking the dishcloth from his hand.

"Okay, thanks, Claire." They locked eyes and hugged awkwardly. "Maybe hanging out with Davey is depressing you. He's not really your type, is he?"

"No, no, I guess he's not. He's just someone to be with, that's all." She avoided looking at Ray and took the butter dish to the refrigerator. "At least he's generous with his money, buys me nice dinners and things."

"You mean, unlike Jack, your ex? He spent money on you, too, didn't he?" He giggled sardonically. "Only it was money he didn't have."

Claire stared at her brother. "You know, Ray, I exaggerated that whole thing. A lot." She turned on hot water and rinsed the cloth. "I realize it now." She began wiping the table, then stopped and looked at Ray.

"I spent money, too. More than Jack did. I went crazy charging things." She began wiping again. "Actually, Jack needed a better car, needed it badly. His old beater was constantly breaking down." She sat in a chair and looked forlornly at him.

"I had a new car. But he couldn't get one because I ran our credit into the ground." She stared into space. "It wasn't fair."

"We should stop dragging Jack's name through the mud, then." Ray said, utterly serious. His eyes sought hers. She met his gaze but said nothing.

"Well, I'm off to work. Are you going to be all right today?" He turned the door knob.

"Oh, I guess." She rolled her eyes with resignation. "Maybe I'll get on the phone and try to book a few interviews from those ads in the paper. Mom has her doctor's appointment this afternoon, so there's no time to go knocking on doors. Anyway, I hate going in cold, asking about openings; it makes me feel like a clueless, green, high-school kid." She waved her brother on.

Ray pulled into the drive at Poore Pond and saw that the school sign had been changed. It read:

HELP STOP BULLYING!

NEVER BE A BULLY - ALWAYS REPORT A BULLY

He recalled the campaign and mentally reviewed everything he had to do before this afternoon's assembly:

- *Put up flats in the multi-purpose room right after lunch clean-up today (Ask Corinne to send student helpers).*
- *See that Rosie puts large garbage bags in all the classrooms on her shift tonight.*
- *Write out an announcement with the rules for eating lunch in the classrooms on Friday.*
- *Help supervise the kids hanging posters on the flats.*
- *Roll the piano into the room.*
- *Set up the microphone system.*

He felt a little resentful. All these extra activities just drained time away from his regular duties. It was easier for Rosie on night shift. She didn't have to work around the lunch schedule or all the students.

Maybe I should go back on nights. But he knew he would miss the kids too much.

He pulled into a parking space and hurried through the boiler-room door to his office.

Thoughts of Claire and her struggles filled his mind.

He placed a lunch bag on the desk, his eyes immediately darting to the photographs of Heather and Jeremy in their tiny frames. Just last week, he had moved them from the shelf, closer to his line of vision. It was right after the planetarium visit.

I do have a chance with Heather now. I need to make a move, or I could lose her—to Davey.

He looked at the clock and saw there was time to hunt down the portable microphone system before helping with student arrivals. If he finished some tasks for the assembly this morning, he could stay in the multi-purpose room in the afternoon to help Carmen and the other teachers set up and run the program.

He headed first to the upstairs storage room next to Vicki Perry's class since her children used the microphones often.

If Claire dumps Davey and we're not officially engaged yet, he's going to go after Heather. Heck, he might even go after her if we are engaged.

He opened the door to choking, stuffy air in the storage room and switched on the exhaust fan. He looked everywhere, moving a puppet theatre and several flattened refrigerator cartons, managing to kick up more dust and finding no microphone. Coughing fitfully, he hurried out, closing the door tightly. *I should change the filter on that exhaust fan.*

He headed to fifth-grade wing, remembering that Annie Klements used the system for a Presidents' Day project.

Maybe I should buy a ring now, today. No. Heather should choose her own ring.

He found no microphone in the fifth-grade workroom.

Suddenly he recalled the parent-group meeting last week. There had been a guest speaker who used the microphone. He hurried down the hall to their private closet.

Whoa! Am I jumping the gun here? I haven't even asked Heather if she wants to marry me.

Ray could barely open the closet door; the microphone case was blocking it. He squeezed through the small opening and lifted the heavy case.

What if she turns me down cold? What if she opts to go back with Davey? Didn't she say one time that she probably should go back, for Jeremy's sake? So he'd have a father.

Back in his office, he sat at his desk to draft the memorandum of procedures for eating lunch in the classrooms. He searched in the lower-right file drawer for an old memo from a few years ago. Former principal, Keith Broski, had held Sports-Day assemblies to break up the long winter months of indoor recesses. The kids ate lunch in their classrooms with no problems.

He would make a few changes to that memo to allow for the first-grade classes that had been added, and he'd have it done.

He found the faded memo and began to review it. The part about student trash collectors made him think of Jeremy. His eyes turned to the photo faces. He could feel the warmth of Heather's shoulder against his as he looked at her face. *No, she cares for me now, whether she wants to or not. Mom's right. "We've got the bug and that's all there is to it."*

Chuckling to himself, he wrote changes on the memo and laid it where he would remember to put it on Corinne's desk .

Air brakes on buses whooshed outside; footsteps sounded in the corridors, and young voices filled the air. Ray put on his windbreaker and grabbed his gloves, stuffing them into the pockets.

The cool March morning invigorated him. He noticed a safety patroller at the crosswalk, struggling with a signal flag, torn loose from its pole. He hurried to relieve the boy so he could get a new one from the boiler room.

Ray took a deep breath and straightened his shoulders. The bustle of arriving students and the brisk air enlivened him. His senses were keen. He felt ready for anything.

Jeremy climbed off his bus and sheepishly handed Ray a folded note. "Hey Sport! How's it going?" They shook hands routinely.

"Great, Ray." He tightened his grip on Ray's hand but did not meet his eyes. "Mom says she's going to give me an allowance when she gets her pharmacy job." He pulled his hand away to adjust his book-bag strap. "She's going to give me chores to do, you know, to earn it."

"You're a big boy now, Jeremy. " Ray grinned at him. "I think you're ready for more responsibility." He waited in vain for Jeremy's gaze.

The first bell sounded; Jeremy, looking past him, waved and hurried to the door.

Ray unfolded the note with joyful anticipation. Heather's familiar, child-like handwriting made his heart skip a beat. He smiled at the tiny heart after his name.

But her written words stunned him. They told him that he would not need to take Jeremy to the Scout Banquet Sunday afternoon because Davey was in town and would take the boy. He wanted to see his son get his badges and awards.

The guy is starting already. He must know things have changed for Heather and me, so he's making a move. Heat filled Ray's chest, traveling up his neck and into his face. He jumped at the sound of a honking bus horn. Exchanging angry looks with the driver, he stepped out of the crosswalk, onto the curb.

He had no idea how he made it through the morning overwrought as he was by Davey's suddenly acting like a father.

Before and during the assembly, he was so flooded with demands from Carmen and the teachers, he gave no thought to the matter. They needed extension cords; they needed the larger risers for the choir; they needed the staple guns refilled.

Hope came in just before the assembly began and instructed Ray to wheel in the small truck of folding chairs in case a few parents dropped in. And they did; more than a few. About eighteen arrived, including a grandparent trailing an oxygen tank on wheels.

He managed to catch a few anti-bullying skits; and when a group of students presented their dramatization of non-physical types of bullying, Ray's thoughts returned to Davey. *He knows exactly what he's doing here, trying to get to me. Why, he is a bully, himself. He's using Jeremy to bully me.*

Ray glanced at the clock; Carmen was running overtime with this assembly. He needed a minimum half hour before dismissal to get the room torn down while the students were here to help. Then Rosie could wet mop it on her shift.

He began quietly folding empty chairs and gingerly loading them on the truck, all the while listening to the program and relating every point on bullying to Davey.

He felt a tug at his shoulder and turned to see Hope.

"Claire called, Ray. The doctor ordered your mother right into the hospital from his office," she whispered above the din.

He followed her through the open doors.

"You must leave at once, Ray."

"But I need to tear down," he said, his voice unnatural.

"Don't bother with that." She shook her head and furrowed her brow. "Rosie will just have to do it—I'll try to get a sub. You go on; your family needs you."

As he drove to the hospital, his mind raced. He worried what could be the emergency with Caroline. *I wish Claire had asked to talk to me.*

That Davey better not show up at the hospital; that's all I need to put me over the edge.

It's a good thing Heather and I don't have plans for tonight.

Maybe it's not a good thing. Maybe Davey will be over there trying to make time with her. I guess it would be better if he came to the hospital with Claire.

But he's the last person Ma will want to see.

He thought of what Rosie would say about having to tear down the assembly; she was sure to use his name in vain. But he knew her attitude would improve when she heard about Caroline. She would understand and outdo herself getting done more than her share of the work.

In the end, the doctor told Ray that Caroline had a dangerous level of fluid in her lungs and would remain in the hospital for as long as it took to bring it down.

"But I thought those treatments she's had were supposed to prevent fluid."

"They lessen the chances of fluid accumulating, Ray, but don't always prevent it entirely."

The doctor studied Caroline's chart. "It's been two months since her last treatment. Her first one was four months before that."

He patted Ray's shoulder. "Let me look at all aspects, all her tests, and all possibilities."

Ray did not miss the uncertainty in his eyes though his voice and words gave hope.

"We will keep her comfortable in the hospital, keep treating the fluid retention and bringing it down. I will talk with you and your sister on Monday and lay out all our options." He offered his hand and Ray shook it.

"Your mother's a fighter. That's the best thing she has going for her." He stepped away. "I will call you early Monday morning."

Brother and sister left their mother sleeping peacefully and walked silently through the hospital and out to the parking lot.

They stopped at emergency-room parking, and Claire gestured toward it with tilted head. "My car's over there, Ray. I'll see you in a little bit."

"I'll see you at home, then, Claire. I'll put on the coffee."

Ray hoped they would talk over coffee and she would tell him she had dumped Davey.

"Don't make it for me; I'm meeting Davey. I'll be home later." Digging in her purse for car keys, she avoided his eyes.

"Where?" His heart sank with fear. Surely she's not meeting him at Heather's apartment.

"He's at a motel over on Ford Street, came to town for Jeremy's Boy Scout Banquet Monday night. Hey, are you still going to that, Ray?"

Ray muttered a vague response and waved, turning on his heel toward the visitors' parking lot.

He left the hospital and headed toward Heather's place on Pearl Street. He checked his watch. 8:20. *Jeremy's probably in bed by now, but Heather should be up.*

It had been a mistake to stop. Heather was in pajamas, her face scrubbed of makeup and hair tied back with a sock. She clearly did not want Ray to see her that way and avoided looking at him. He ached to hug her, captivated as he was by the chemistry flowing between them.

Jeremy overheard and came cautiously down the hall in rumpled pajamas.

"Oh, it's you Mr. Sellers!" His face broke into a wide smile. He ran to Ray, who knelt to return the eager hug. His eyes met hers over the boy's back, and they exchanged emotional smiles.

Ray stood and Jeremy stepped back, suddenly serious. "Dad's taking me to the banquet, Ray." His eyes clouded. I'd rather—." He looked at his mother's finger crossed at her lips and fell silent.

Seconds later Jeremy broke the awkward silence, "But you could come, too, Ray." He avoided looking at Heather. "We have to go early, so you could pick up Mom and come later when it starts."

Ray stiffened. His chest froze.

"We'll have to see, Jeremy." She took his hand.

It's getting late; you need to be in bed now." She walked him to his room.

"Good night, Mr. Sellers," he called over his shoulder.

"Good night yourself, Sport," Ray said, his voice artificial. He stepped into the kitchen.

Minutes later excitement filled his body; he turned as Heather padded down the hall and straight into his arms. They held tightly then kissed lingeringly.

He took her hand and led her to the sofa.

Now, ask her now. He tightened his grip on her fingers and reached with his left hand for her right. They sat silently with both hands locked together, electrical charges coursing through their bodies.

Ask her. There'll never be a more perfect moment.

But he did not ask her.

Claire arrived home while Ray, trying to settle his nerves, sat drinking hot chocolate at the kitchen table.

She cheerfully declined his offer to make her a nice cup of chocolate with marshmallow, but her good humor set him on edge again. He lost all hope that she had broken up with Davey, knowing she would have taken her wrath out on him with cutting words.

"I'm off to bed, Ray. Good night."

"Good night, Claire. I checked voice mail. There were no messages from the doctor." He watched her walk away. "I guess no news is good news."

"Oh," she stopped and turned. "Davey says you're welcome to ride to Jeremy's banquet with him Monday night." She resumed her steps. "That was nice of him, don't you think?"

CHAPTER EIGHTEEN—THE BRADFORDS

Jeremy came home with Helsi all three work days in one week. Heather's internship at the pharmacy made heavy demands on her. She stayed overtime nearly an hour every day to double check her work, so intensely she felt the responsibility.

Helsi agreed to change her shift, starting and stopping a half hour later. She and Heather hoped the additional half hour would cover the lateness and still have Helsi on duty when Jeremy arrived home from school at two-fifty. But in a matter of days, the extra half hour stretched to forty-five or fifty minutes.

The new shift threw everything off at home. Ian, in an effort to start a dinner of some sort, put potatoes in the oven or on the stove in a pan of water. If Helsi had planned pasta or rice, the potatoes went into the refrigerator for another day. But she tried to work them into the menu if at all possible, so he would not be offended.

Everything seemed to offend Ian lately.

He was excelling in his classes, but he complained bitterly about the workload. Two of his coworkers were laid off; and he went on for days about that, expecting his notice at any moment. He had a short fuse with the children, berating them as he never had before when they were playing normally about the house. Helsi tried to talk to him on several occasions; but he discounted her concern, saying she was irritable from overwork and just looking for reasons to pick on him.

Instead of helping tidy up the kitchen the way he once did, he kept taking drives to the firehouse after the kids were in bed. Helsi missed their evenings together on the sofa, but she told herself that he needed to commiserate with the guys about all the job upheavals in the department. She wanted to be understanding.

So Jeremy played with the Bradford children while Helsi tried to keep their dinner hour on normal time. Jeremy would eat with them, play awhile after dinner until she drove him home.

That was another thing. Ian refused to help her out by driving the boy home occasionally, so incensed was he by Heather's imposing extra child care on his wife.

"Are you getting paid for the time he's here?" He asked. "Not to mention for giving him dinner every night."

Helsi began to wonder what happened to the old Ian.

It all came to a head when she ran into Myra Abernathy in the grocery store. Her husband, Dick, was one of Ian's laid-off colleagues.

"I can't thank you and Ian enough, Helsi, for lending us the money for our house payment. When Dick's lay-off came, we were already stretched to the limit. My hours were cut six months ago." She touched Helsi's hand and looked at her with worried eyes.

All Helsi could manage was a barely audible, "I know how it is, Myra." *What is she talking about? Ian lent them money? Where did he get it?*

She listened without hearing to Myra's account of the second job she would start next week and how everything was sure to fall apart at home.

"But we'll be able to pay you back in a matter of weeks, Helsi." Myra said with conviction.

"Good to see you, Myra. I have a ton of shopping to do." Helsi hurried off.

Ian lent Dick money? Enough for a house payment? What is going on here? And why didn't he tell me?

Helsi could barely follow her grocery list, so preoccupied was she with Myra's news. She scanned the list for things she could put off buying, picked up the essentials, and hurried to the self-checkout stations.

Once she arrived home, there was just enough time to put away the groceries, eat a bit of lunch, and leave for Heather's place.

She kept rehearsing mentally how she would broach the subject of the loan with Ian. She certainly understood his willingness to help a friend through a tough time, but how could they afford to do that? They were struggling with money, themselves.

Heather arrived home at 5:20; and Helsi, eager to get to the bottom of Ian's loan to Dick Abernathy, left the apartment immediately.

Ian had the phone to his ear when Helsi entered the kitchen. She tried to make eye contact, but he turned away and walked into the laundry room.

Is this a secret conversation? Illicit money deals? She saw Ian's potatoes boiling on the stove and decided to make salmon patties and fried potatoes. *I'll just tell him I ran into Myra today and wait for him to come clean.* She probed the potatoes with a fork and turned off the burner, carrying the pan to the sink where she drained it. She pulled out a colander and dumped the steaming potatoes into it.

Stepping to the pantry, she strained to hear Ian's conversation, just a few feet around the corner.

"Well, where does that leave me?" She heard him say in a voice full of anger. "You guys didn't give me the whole story going in, did you? You misled me!"

Helsi, overcome with anxiety, took two cans of salmon off the shelf. Her hands trembled as she placed one on the electric can opener, welcoming the grinding sound as if it could drown out her thoughts. *Gene. I bet it's that Gene from class. Ian did get mixed up with them. I knew it. I knew it.*

Feeling utterly sick, she sat down at the table. Engulfed by fear, she laid her head on the cool wood. She heard distant shouts of Robbie and Dylan from the backyard.

Ian walked in and placed the cordless phone on its base. Lucy ran down from upstairs, "Mom, are you all right?"

She rushed to her mother, bending to embrace her.

Helsi lifted her head. She tried to hide the panic she knew must show on her face and looked at Lucy. "I just feel a little sick, that's all."

Ian came to her. "What's the matter, Hon? What symptoms are you having?" He lifted her wrist and felt for a pulse. She welcomed his touch and forgot for a moment, the ominous news she wanted from him, yet dreaded to hear.

A rush of commotion from the front door sent Ian and Lucy running into the living room. Helsi stood and steadied herself for a moment before following them.

Robbie, with grave face, held the door open for Phyllis Meadow, carrying a limp Mercedes in her arms. Dylan stood outside on the step, paralyzed with fear.

Ian immediately swung into action. "Lay her on the sofa, Phyllis." He ran to the van for his emergency kit. Helsi took a cushion and placed it flat, guiding Mercede's head onto it as Phyllis carefully laid her on the sofa. The child's body and soiled pajamas reeked.

"What happened, Phyllis?" Helsi asked.

Ian rushed in and began to work on the girl, questioning her mother as he moved. "How long has she been out?"

"Only minutes, Ian."

"What triggered it?"

"She's been having rampant diarrhea and vomiting and was stuck on the toilet with an unending flow. I was sitting on the tub, holding a basin in her lap because she was expelling at both ends." Helsi admired the woman's remarkable calm.

Ian looked warmly at Helsi. "Call 9-1-1, Hon."

Lucy ran to the phone and dialed.

"Lucy," Helsi said, "take your brothers and Rachel—where is Rachel?"

"She's at Sophie's, Mom. Remember, Mrs. Baldridge invited her to go to Sophie's riding lesson after school. She's eating dinner at their house, too."

"That's right. I remember now. Lucy, take Dylan and Robbie into the kitchen and give them cheese sandwiches and a tangerine. They must be starving."

"What about dinner, Mom?" Lucy asked.

"Lucy, do as your mother told you," Ian instructed. "You see we're dealing with an emergency here."

"But, Dad," Lucy said. And she offered to make her famous dinner from home-economics class, the only meal she could manage completely on her own: fried potatoes with green pepper and scrambled eggs, sliced tomato on the side. It was a family favorite.

"Great, Lucy," Ian said.

"Your father's boiled potatoes are in the sink, Sweetie," Helsi added. "Use those."

Phyllis never left her daughter's side; she kept checking Mercedes' breathing by placing fingers under her nose.

Ian noted on a chart, the child's blood pressure, pulse, color, and size of her pupils. He lifted her limbs one at a time.

Helsi left the room and returned with a basin of warm water, clean washcloth and towel. She had a fresh pair of Rachel's pajamas over her arm.

Ian knew she meant to sponge bathe the child.

"Better not disturb her, Helsi." Ian looked into his wife's eyes. "Leave it to the hospital staff." He checked his watch. "The ambulance should be here any minute."

Flashing red lights washed across the windows, creating a strobe-lamp effect. Wailing sirens pierced the air. Ian ran outside.

Mercedes moaned and began shaking, striking fear in Helsi's heart. Her mother looked into her face and patted both cheeks tenderly. The child grew still once again. *It's good that Phyllis is calm. I'm a wreck. That poor child.*

Two paramedics familiar to Helsi followed Ian into the house, carrying a gurney. They laid it on the floor alongside the sofa, positioned the straps, and turned to Mercedes.

"How does she look to you, Gentlemen?" Phyllis asked, rising from the sofa.

"Are you the mother?" one of them asked.

"Yes, yes I am. I'm Phyllis Meadow, and this is my eight-year-old daughter, Mercedes. How do you think she looks?"

"It's hard to tell, Mrs. Meadow," the other said. "But Ian checked her out, as you know. He's one of us, so we won't go through it all again." He and Ian made fleeting eye contact.

"Well, I'm grateful to have a team of three medical experts looking after my daughter.

"We're just paramedics, Ma'am."

"Still, you have experience with emergencies. You must have seen cases like this before?"

"Ian says her vital signs are stable. Has she shown any signs of consciousness in the last few minutes?"

"No, she hasn't," Phyllis murmured.

"Phyllis," Helsi said. "Just as the ambulance arrived, she moaned and stirred, remember?" She looked squarely at Phyllis, who did not respond.

Helsi looked from Ian to his two colleagues. "The child moaned sharply, then began to shake." She looked at Phyllis with earnest eyes, but Phyllis's face remained fixed on her daughter. "It lasted only a moment. It was right before you came through that door."

Ian shot his wife a look that seemed to say, "It's all right, Hon." Helsi, perplexed, looked away.

Ian rode along in the ambulance, leaving Helsi to look after the family.

Lucy had everyone seated at the table, eating and conversing like adults. Sean arrived from track and joined them. The children seemed to be in a celebratory mood from the change in routine. They seemed to enjoy having Lucy take over their mother's role.

"Sit down, Mom. I'll bring your plate." Lucy fussed.

Helsi sat at the table. "Just bring me a tiny bit."

"You have to eat," Lucy said, echoing her mother. She brought a plate with sliced tomatoes artfully arranged around the potato mixture and buttered bread on the side.

"This looks lovely, Dear," Helsi said. She took a few bites and put down her fork. "I seem to have no appetite. I'm sorry, Lucy."

Lucy urged her to lie down, insisting she would clear the dinner and get the children to bed.

Helsi filled a glass with ice water and started upstairs. She heard Rachel bound in the front door and Lucy call a thank you to Mrs. Baldridge in the driveway.

She rolled over sleepily when Ian crawled into bed. "How is Mercedes?" she asked in a barely audible voice.

"She's stabilized. Apparently she was so dehydrated from the diarrhea and vomiting that her system shut down." He spooned himself against her. "How are you feeling?"

"I'm okay," she said wanting desperately to stay asleep.

"Did you know the Meadows lost a child to SIDS? Before Mercedes was born?"

Helsi did not respond.

That family has had so many bad breaks. We have five healthy kids. We're so blessed. Ian pushed his problems with Argosy out of his mind, vowing to dissociate himself from that dark deal as soon as possible. *I'll have to come clean with Helsi, too. I've been a jerk about this whole mess.*

Bright morning light flooded through the windows, and Helsi woke with a start. She looked at the clock, wondering why the alarm had failed.

She slipped into a worn, pink terrycloth robe and knotted the belt. Opening the door, she stopped to ponder why on earth it was closed. The family always slept with open bedroom doors.

Descending the stairs, the awful news from yesterday, both Ian's mysterious money deals and Mercedes' emergency, filled her mind. Thankfully, the happy din of the children eating breakfast and preparing to get their buses forestalled the painful thoughts.

Rachel and Dylan ran to hug her. "Are you all right now, Mom?" Rachel chirped.

"Yes, I'm fine, Sweetie." She could feel Ian's eyes watching her but did not return his gaze.

"You're not sick now?" Dylan asked, his small voice tinged with dread.

"Sit down, Hon. Sit down." Ian took her by the elbow and steered her to the table. Her place, all set with steaming oatmeal, a small ramekin of sliced bananas and grapes, and a mug of coffee, comforted her.

"Ian," she met his gaze. "You did all this? What time did you get up? Why didn't you wake me?"

"The bus is coming!" Robbie called from the front step. Dylan and Rachel ran to their book bags and zipped them hurriedly. Helsi rose to help get the children into their jackets but stopped short when Ian thrust his palm at her.

"No, Babe. I'll do this. You eat."

She sat back down and stirred cream and sugar into the coffee, blowing on it before taking a sip. She took a spoonful of fruit. *This fruit cup looks like Lucy's work.* Realizing how famished she felt, she quickly finished every piece.

"Bye, Mom! Bye, Mom!" the children screeched above the bus engine. She called good-byes to them, managing only a whisper as tears began to spill down her cheeks, astounding her completely.

She noticed a folded paper under her fork and lifted it. A crayon drawing of hearts, flowers, and a brilliant sun face covered the front. Inside, the signatures of all five children, each one distinct and beautifully uneven, filled the space beneath a carefully inscribed message: We love you Mom.

Across the bottom, Ian, in his straight manuscript, had printed: "Count me in, too, Hon. Your loving Ian."

Tears began to flow again, floods of tears. She dug into her pocket for tissues and mopped her eyes frantically. *I won't have Ian see me blubbering like this. How can I confront him looking like a weakling? What's keeping him anyway?*

She rose and went to the door. He was talking to Herb Meadow in his driveway. *I wonder how Mercedes is doing this morning? Herb must have been called back from the road for his daughter.*

Not wanting to face either of the issues harrying her, she returned to her breakfast. She took the oatmeal, now cooled, to the microwave. She needed a potholder to carry it to the table where she added a large chunk of butter and rich, brown sugar.

She concentrated on the divine taste, imagining each oat flake as a separate entity, savoring the caramel-like sweetness. She added a little milk from the small pitcher. Another Lucy touch. She focused on the effect the milk had on the taste of the oatmeal.

Ian opened the door, abruptly ending her escape orgy. She felt her stomach tighten.

"Oh good, you're eating," Ian said. He poured coffee for himself and brought it to the table. "I was just talking to Herb Meadow."

"How's Mercedes this morning?" Helsi asked between spoonfuls of oatmeal.

"He hasn't seen her yet; he said he just finished a two-hour drive to get here." He poured milk into his coffee and stirred. "But Phyllis told him she was stabilized."

"What was that you were telling me last night, Ian? I was half asleep." Helsi met his gaze.

"About what?" He grinned.

"About Herb and Phyllis losing a child to SIDS?"

"Oh that. Yes, She told me while we waited at the emergency room, that two years before Mercedes was born, they lost a baby boy, three-months old, to SIDS."

"That must have been devastating for them." Helsi pushed her oatmeal bowl aside and drank from the coffee mug. "I wonder if Herb traveled in his work then?"

"I don't know. We didn't talk about that." He looked at the clock. "I need to go, Hon." He rose and took his windbreaker from the rack by the door.

Helsi stood, taking his silver thermos from the counter. She waited while he slipped into his jacket, then handed him the thermos and accepted his brief hug.

"Ian, we need to talk. There are some issues I—."

"We'll talk tonight, Hon." He set down the thermos and hugged her properly. They kissed. "I'll be home late; I have to make up the hour I lost this morning."

"But today is Wednesday, Ian. You have class tonight. Won't you be studying before you go?" Helsi willed from her voice, the exasperation she felt.

"It's spring break, remember. It starts today, so I won't have class for two weeks." He blew her a kiss and rushed through the door.

She tidied the kitchen and, feeling her old energy, went upstairs to shower and dress.

By ten o'clock, she had mopped the kitchen floor, scoured both upstairs bathrooms, and folded and put away two loads of laundry.

The physical work calmed her nerves. Seeing the house clean with everything in its proper place made her feel in control again, as if everything were right with the world. Working about the house enabled her to put aside for a time, the serious issues tearing at her.

Cleaning Heather's little doll-house apartment gives me similar satisfaction. Putting things in order, making them nice for Jeremy and her. It's a good feeling, and it's not really very hard work. Maybe I should do more of it, take some of the pressure off Ian, at least until he finishes his courses.

She switched on the television and began dusting the living room. A Miracle Maids commercial ran repeatedly in the background. It played twice successively and came on again in a matter of minutes. At the end of each commercial, a strident voice invited viewers to call for information on employment opportunities. The third time through, Helsi took notice.

Covering the entire downstairs, dusting, vacuuming, and scrubbing, she pondered the idea of getting more cleaning jobs.

At noon, she placed the vacuum cleaner at the foot of the stairs, glancing out the front window as she coiled the cord. Phyllis's big, white car pulled into the driveway. Helsi moved closer to the window and watched her help Mercedes through the front door. The child appeared to move normally up the steps.

I wonder how she is, what was wrong with her. I should call Phyllis.

Herb's bulky Overlander pulled around Phyllis's car and into the garage as the overhead door rose. The door closed.

I'll wait until they settle in, then I'll call them.

She made a small green salad and scattered shredded cheddar cheese on top. She placed several saltines and the butter dish on the table along with a glass of milk.

Before sitting down to eat, she surfed through television channels, settling on a women's talk show.

Women entrepreneurs were the focus of the show. Three guests presented their small, home-based businesses: one sold lovely, special-order cakes; another wrote free-lance advertising copy; a third ran an office-cleaning service.

Office cleaning service. I should think about that.

Helsi finished the salad and all the saltines, forgetting to butter them, so engrossed was she in the show. Her mind raced with ideas. During a commercial break, she went to the cookie jar and took one large, oatmeal-chocolate-chip cookie.

She sat down and reached for the half-banana in the fruit bowl, eating it along with the cookie.

The show resumed. Drinking milk, she watched intently as the office-cleaning woman described her work.

No, offices are too impersonal. I like to clean homes. Homes are living spaces. Offices are just, well, where people have to go to pay for their homes. They can't wait to leave the office. They look forward to going home to nest. Their nests would be more inviting because of me.

A pleasant-looking bank officer began talking about small-business loans underwritten by the federal government for women and minorities. Loan qualifiers were entitled to advice and assistance in setting up their businesses. Interest rates were below market the first five years. "Ongoing advice is available from SCORE, Senior Corps of Retired Executives. They are experienced business people who provide counseling for entrepreneurs."

How do you go about getting such a loan?

"Just call for an appointment and bring your business plan, including start-up costs, to our offices. You can go to our website or call the 800 number on the screen for a free business-plan guide," the banker explained, as if hearing Helsi's thoughts.

Helsi dug in the fruit bowl for a crayon and jotted the number and SCORE on her napkin.

She cleared away the remains of lunch, dried her hands, and dialed the phone.

"Hi, Phyllis, how is Mercedes?" she asked.

"Well, she's doing fine now. They tested her drug levels, did a urine toxicology screening, even gave her an ECG. The only thing they could find was the possibility of acetaminophen poisoning. They found trace-levels of that, which the pediatrician where we used to live prescribed for Mercedes' headaches; and I gave her, strictly following the daily limits set by the doctor, not just on the label but by the doctor." She took a breath.

"Mercedes suffers from headaches?" Helsi managed to interject.

"Frequent headaches, Helsi," Phyllis said with emphasis.

"I've suffered with headaches for years, sick headaches; so I know what Mercedes is going through. That's why I never leave her side or sleep when she is ill. I know what it means to feel desperately sick and in severe pain." She took a breath. "I've been there."

"Will she go to school tomorrow?" Helsi asked. You know, it's school-photo day?"

"It is? Well, she will want to be in school for that. The emergency-room doctor left it up to me. He said that I have such good instincts and obviously give my daughter the best possible care, so I should know when she's able to handle school. He said he's seen so few mothers as devoted to their children as I am. He even asked me if I was a trained nurse. Actually, I did go through nurses' training. I just never practiced. Well, I practiced for a short time. Then I got married, and Herb wouldn't let me work. When I became pregnant with Madeline, of course, I would not have dreamed of working."

"Madeline?" Helsi asked gently, concluding that she must have been the SIDS victim. *No, wait, Ian said a boy.*

"Yes. Madeline was our first child." Her voice lowered and thickened.

"We lost Madeline when she was only fifteen months old," her voice began to choke.

"Phyllis, you don't have to talk about all this now. I understand," Helsi said tenderly.

"No, no, it's all right. I consider you and Ian our friends. We lost little Madeline to a rare disease that gave her convulsions. I knew how to stop the convulsions and was always able to do that in a matter of minutes after they started." She grew silent.

"I'm glad Mercedes is better, Phyllis. I'll call you later." Helsi wanted to escape this morbid disclosure.

"The last convulsion Madeline had was the very worst one. It was so bad I couldn't stop it. God knows I tried. It killed her. The doctors said I had done everything humanly possible to save her. I guess God just wanted to bring his angel home. And she was an angel." Her voice faltered. "You never saw such an angelic child."

"Good-bye, Phyllis. I'll call you tomorrow." Helsi quickly hung up the phone.

She carried the vacuum cleaner upstairs and cleaned all the bedrooms relentlessly, so unnerved was she by Phyllis' outburst.

After an hour of exerting herself more than was necessary, her mind turned to the earlier idea of forming a cleaning business.

She fantasized about it all afternoon and while she prepared a large pan of lasagna for dinner.

She heard Ian pull in the drive and was about to call the children to the table when she saw the grave look on his face.

"Sit down, Helsi." He led her to the sofa. "I'm in big trouble," his voice broke with emotion.

See What Other Readers Say About

Honor Me Honor You

Visit
http://honormehonoryou.wordpress.com

Have Something to Say Yourself?

Post Your Comments

CHAPTER NINETEEN—HOPE

"Come in, Mrs. Meadow," Hope said as Corinne held open the glass door of the outer office.

Phyllis Meadow extended her hand, and they shared a cordial handshake.

"Please excuse my appearance, Dr. Fleming," she unzipped her black nylon active-wear jacket, smoothing the waistline of the matching pants. She finger-combed a thick, blonde ponytail.

"I had to see you, but I have only a moment. Herb is with Mercedes now and has to get to an appointment." She swept her eyes over Hope's impeccably tailored off-green suit and matching Italian pumps.

"I don't usually go out in public this way, but I had no time to dress and still allow Herb to keep his appointment." She followed Hope into her office and seated herself in the chair toward which Hope gestured.

"Are you here in regard to the letter I sent you about Mercedes' attendance?" *You enrolled her six weeks ago, and she's been absent more than she's been in school, for heaven's sake.* She took a chair opposite Phyllis.

"Yes, that's right," Phyllis murmured. She began rooting in her handbag. "I wanted you to be aware of the problems Mercedes faces every day. Health problems." She unfolded a thick set of papers, handing them to Hope.

The principal began reading but stopped when she noted the address of the clinic on the letterhead. "These documents are from a doctor in Champion City, aren't they?"

"They are," Phyllis said. "I just have not found a doctor for her here yet." She furrowed her brow. "Mercedes has been sick so much since we moved, I have not had time."

"Then who's been treating her?" Hope managed to keep a neutral face.

"Emergency room. We've taken her to ER every time."

"And ER does not issue reports to schools, I know." Hope said, looking into Mrs. Meadow's eyes. "Do you have their yellow sheets with going home instructions, though?" She flipped through the packet.

"I don't know where I put them, Dr. Fleming. I'll send them in with Mercedes." She stood and zipped her jacket.

"Thank you for your time. I must go to my daughter now." She rushed through the door.

We never really discussed why Mercedes is absent now. She didn't go into the child's specific problems. I hope these papers will tell me something. She began earnestly reading.

After school, Hope hurried home to meet Theo and George, who were coming to Canterbury Road to discuss shelter clients.

They were due at five, and she needed time to set the table. *I hope the chicken tortilla stew in the slow cooker is all right. I have nothing else to feed them.*

The stew tasted fine to Hope; the experimental spices she had tried this time enhanced the flavor. She pulled crusty, whole-grain rolls from the freezer and spread them on a cookie sheet.

George loaded his bowl with toppings of shredded cheese and crumbled tortilla chips, devouring it and taking a second helping.

"This is really great, Mom," he said, happily eating.

Theodore, too, indulged in extra toppings and ate hungrily but artfully in that refined way he had.

In the end, they ate the pieces of cut-up fruit, intended as salad, for dessert instead. They laughed heartily when George brought the aerosol can of whipped cream from the refrigerator and sprayed it—without bothering to ask—over everybody's fruit bowl.

All three ate the voluminous cream and fruit with gusto.

"Okay, Mom, Theodore, let's talk about our clients," he said before the dessert course was finished.

He put down his spoon. "We have seventeen clients now, counting Adelaide."

"Adelaide's such high maintenance; she counts as two," Theodore interjected, his eyes twinkling.

Everyone seconded that.

"Well, eighteen, if you put it that way, Theo," George said good naturedly. "But, seriously, fifteen of those seventeen are in therapy with A.J."

He looked across the table into their eyes. "I'm talking extensive therapy, two-to-three sessions per week, not counting group.

Hope's eyes met Theodore's, and she smiled through closed lips. "Does that surprise you, George?" She turned toward him. "Those intake interviews I sat in on were real eye-openers."

She rose from the table. "Who wants coffee?" She gathered fruit bowls and carried them to the sink.

Theodore nodded for coffee.

George raised his hand. "But Mother, those people always act a little strange when they're in a normal situation." He gestured with spread hands. "I mean, homeless people are unaccustomed to standard social graces. Their code on the street is different." He stepped to the refrigerator with the can of whipped cream and exchanged it for a carton of fat-free half-and-half.

His mother came up behind him with a tiny china cream pitcher, which she handed to George. "I understand, George. But everyone, to a person, gave odd answers to very basic questions. It was hard to believe that they had ever been in a normal situation."

"Well, they're uneasy, embarrassed about their failures."

He shook his head rapidly. "Not failures, they don't often see them as failures. But they know others are judging them by their lack of material goods." He looked at Theodore. "You can see that, can't you, Theo? They know most people do not understand the freedom of living on the street. It's the freedom they value."

"Freedom from responsibility?" Hope asked.

"Well, yes, that and freedom from having to conform." George's gentle voice belied the exasperation covering his face.

"Some of them have had accomplished lives, I believe." Theodore looked at George, then Hope. "It seems to me that Elvin had his own CPA firm. And Dorothy managed a restaurant at one time. Is that right, George?"

"That is right, Theo. And Roscoe, though he doesn't look it, was a hairdresser for years, in an upscale shop. He even had his manager's license." George and Theo exchanged smiles.

"Roscoe's not that burly guy with the grey pony tail down his back, is he?" Hope asked.

"Yes, that's the one," George said. "Roscoe and Dorothy are the only two of our clients not seeing A.J."

"And they probably should be seeing him. Is that the case?" Hope asked.

"Well, we are already using forty percent of the psychological-services budget for fifteen people," Theodore said. "If we reach capacity of sixty people, each one will need to be evaluated, not to mention the fact that many are likely to need A.J."

"We'll just have to cut back on services. Reduce their time with A.J. by one half." Hope announced.

"We can't do that, Mother!" George cried, drawing to his feet. "Those that need service need it more than anything else we can do for them."

George, scrubbing his hands fiercely, walked to the window. He stood, staring into the darkness for several minutes.

Theodore's eyes met Hope's, concern on both their faces.

"Let's take another long look at the budget," he said, rising and stepping to George's side.

"If we have to dip into the principal, we should do it, Theo. What would be the harm?" George asked with child-like innocence.

"Out of the question, George!" Theo retorted, shocking Hope with his use of an incomplete sentence.

That's a first. I don't think I've ever heard Theo use an incomplete sentence. She stared at him in disbelief.

"Why can't we, just this once, Theo?" George laid a hand on his forearm. "The Board would understand."

Theo stepped back to his chair and sat down. George followed, looking squarely at him with earnest eyes.

"This money has been put in trust to form a foundation." Theo took a deep breath. "If the foundation is to have long life, only the interest may be touched. The principal must remain invested. It's the cardinal rule for foundations. And it's written into the bylaws for every legitimate foundation, including yours." He glanced at Hope, appreciating the admiration on her face.

George stared as if frozen.

"We'll look at the budget, Son," Hope said tenderly.

But despair remained on his face and drew all energy from his young body.

The meeting ended. Hope tenaciously elicited from each of them, a promise that he would scour copies of the budget and bring ideas to another meeting next week. She would do the same.

George could not get out of the house fast enough. He grabbed his jacket and rushed out, carrying it. He walked right past the plastic container of leftover stew his mother had set on the counter for him.

But Theo stayed awhile and shared a glass of wine with Hope.

Sitting side by side on the sofa, they savored the warmth of the wine and began to relax. They sighed deeply, their heads falling against the back of the cushy sofa.

"George was devastated, wasn't he?" Hope looked at Theo.

"He cares too much for his own good," Theo said tenderly, taking Hope's empty glass and leaning forward to refill it from the bottle on the English tea table.

He leaned back and handed her the glass, properly half full. "Has he always been such a bleeding heart?"

"Thank you, Theo." She took the glass and sipped it luxuriously. "Always. Always. From the time he started first grade, he wanted to watch the news. He worried about the environment. He worried about world hunger. I forbade him to watch the news, so he began to read the newspaper." She thrust her hands, palms up, at him.

"He worried about animals. Stray dogs and cats, animals in the news that were in trouble: sea animals in oil slicks, abandoned animals during hurricanes and floods, and so on and so forth."

"Did he bring in articles about animals for current-event days? I went to school with a kid like that?" Theo chuckled.

"Oh, of course. And he still has not forgiven me for never letting him have a dog." She looked away. "I should have given him a dog. He had no siblings; he needed a pet to love and to love him back." She turned toward Theo.

Noticing tears glistening on her cheeks, he moved toward her, putting his arm around her shoulder. "Don't bother yourself about that, Hope. George is a wonderful young man." He felt her body trembling and put his other arm around her, drawing her against him.

"I don't deserve such a fine son, Theo." Her voice was thin.

"Of course you do, Hope." He brushed her tears away with his index finger.

"No, I don't. I wasn't a very good mother." She shook her head rapidly. "It's okay. "I've come to terms with it now."

They sat holding each other for some time.

Hope, greeting early bus riders, noticed many children arriving in bright spring jackets. Giddy from the warmer weather, they smiled and laughed uncontrollably.

Of course, several jacketless boys and one girl caught her attention. It's only forty-eight degrees today! What are they doing?

She looked for bulging book bags and insisted they take their jackets out and wear them while waiting in line for the bell.

"And jackets will be required for recess today, children."

"But it's hot," the smallish Frankie Egan complained.

After morning announcements, Hope began classroom rounds. Sun flowed through the tall windows, warming the building and energizing everyone.

She headed first to Pamela Thorpe's third-grade room to see Mercedes Meadow, finally back in school. The teacher greeted her with a smile and a nod to the class. "Good morning, Dr. Fleming," the children called in unison.

"Good morning, Children," Hope returned.

"Would you like to stay and watch opening activities, Dr. Fleming?" Mrs. Thorpe asked. "The students have checked our weather instruments and will give a forecast for recess today."

Hope enjoyed the exercise and admired the students' use of both Fahrenheit and Celsius temperature scales. She observed closely when Mercedes compared today's temperatures to those of the previous two days. *That child is unusually poised for her age. Her color looks great; she seems energetic as well.*

She noted Mercedes' ability to fit herself back into lessons after so many absences. *One would never know she has health problems.*

As she finished rounds and throughout the day, the mystery of Mercedes' health problems niggled at Hope.

A more delightful thought; however, tempered every issue that arose for Hope. The vivid memory of Theo's wonderful attention last night soothed and warmed her at every turn. It gave life new sparkle. It minimized all problems.

She received a late-afternoon telephone call from an associate of McElson-Bourney Law Firm, remaining calm and unafraid by their startling news.

The caller told her that Frederick Baldwin had won a complete audit of his step-grandmother's financial papers.

Hope walked into the mild April air and inhaled deeply. She could feel a spring in her step as she crossed the parking lot to her car. Her mind was on the dinner date she had with Theo at six o'clock. Her heart was light. Nothing else mattered.

Shall I wear my taupe silk pantsuit? Or the red cashmere sweater and slacks with that new animal-print scarf Belva gave me?

She waved at Brad Kushner and Lou Ann Newhouse, waiting for her Volvo to pull into the street. Lou Ann mouthed words, so she lowered her window and stopped the car.

"I have your note, Dr. Fleming," Lou Ann said, smiling. "Do you want to see me first thing tomorrow morning? My class has P.E. first period, you know."

"That will be fine, Lou Ann," Hope said.

"Do you mind telling me what it's in regard to, Hope?" Lou Ann asked, glancing at Brad, who waved and hurried to his car.

"It's a concern Ms. Cutler brought to my attention."

Lou Ann's face relaxed at her words.

I'd just as soon not go into it now; but she is certainly entitled to know the reason for our meeting, if not the specific issue.

"If it were any other parent, I would insist we discuss it right this minute," Lou Ann said. "But Ms. Cutler? She's the most rational parent I know."

"Why not get in my car and I'll give you a quick overview, Lou Ann?" Hope blurted, suddenly uncomfortable with the turn of events. "Then we can both think about it overnight and be ready to discuss our response in the morning."

The teacher opened the passenger door and sat down next to Hope, who pulled into a parking space.

As she switched off the engine, she looked over at Lou Ann and smiled warmly.

Buying time, she turned the engine back on and pressed the button to raise the window. She again turned off the ignition key.

Lou Ann's all-American face and neat brown hair with smart, asymmetrical cut emphasized her large brown eyes winningly. They completely disarmed Hope.

She did not want to tell the teacher what Ms. Cutler had said. She preferred to talk about her outstanding ability to motivate her students, about the wonderful climate for learning she created in her classroom, about her strong public-relations skills.

Lou Ann riveted those beautiful, expectant brown eyes on Hope.

"Ms. Cutler had nothing but positive remarks about your presentation at the parents' workshop on bullying, Lou Ann." Hope kept her voice even, feeling her serious face taking over.

Lou Ann sat quietly, listening intently.

"She praised your teaching and the way you run the classroom, as she has on a number of occasions." Hope shifted her hips on the leather seat and glanced out the window at a small dog sniffing car tires.

"But when Terry told her that you had punished him by making him stand outside at the classroom window in full view of all the other children, she was taken aback."

Hope turned toward Lou Ann. "You did not do that, did you, Lou Ann?"

The teacher sighed and exhaled, her shoulders slumping as if the expelled air came from them instead of her lungs. She stared out the window for minutes.

"Terry's a good kid," Lou Ann began, her voice edgy. "But sometimes he obsesses on things and gets way off-task. He causes a lot of other students to go off-task, too."

She looked at Hope before continuing then looked away.

"That day he had been running to the window every few seconds, watching builders on the lot next door. They were pouring cement. He kept taking other children with him."

"Then you did make him stand outside the classroom?" Hope asked in a flat voice.

"I tried other things first, Hope, strategies that sometimes work with Terry. I warned him several times. I put his name on the board. I put him in time out." She thrust her palms up and looked at Hope with misty eyes.

Shaking her head slowly, she explained, "I thought it would be a way to let him watch the builders. He was so enthralled by what they were doing." She paused, looking helplessly at Hope.

"But I had to make him think it was a punishment. And the other kids, I knew they had to see it as a consequence for his disruptive behavior." She stared ahead at nothing.

They sat in deafening silence for what seemed to Hope like minutes. She glanced through the steering wheel at the clock. It showed 5:15.

Robin Cutler had said she "hoped it wasn't a case of teacher bullying, but it certainly sounded like it."

Hope, lost in thought, finally concluded that this did not seem, from the account she'd just heard, like a case of teacher bullying. She knew that Lou Ann Newhouse was the last teacher on the staff who would be capable of bullying a student.

She touched Lou Ann's arm. "Shall we just let the world turn and face this tomorrow with clear minds?"

"Will you meet me before school, Dr. Fleming? I know I won't be worth anything until this is settled." Lou Ann asked, looking toward Hope, but avoiding her eyes.

"Of course. I'll be in my office by seven-thirty." Hope watched her open the door and wave faintly. She watched her walk slowly to her car, looking worn-out, completely drained.

Hope barely had time to shower and change after telephoning Theo and asking if he'd mind eating in by the fire tonight. He agreed readily, promising to bring take-out dinners from Chef Giovanni.

She chose emerald green velvet lounge pants and matching shirt with antique buttons, opting for tapestry slippers instead of high-heeled black mules.

She hurried downstairs and lit the gas logs in the family room. She removed a lamp from the pedestal table near the sofa and positioned the table before the fireplace.

Moving quickly in flat-heeled slippers, she covered the table with a white Irish-linen cloth. She placed a pair of crystal candlesticks and two place settings of china on the cloth.

Unable to find fresh candles, she had to make do with used ones, glancing at the kitchen clock as she trimmed off uneven globs of wax at the sink.

The doorbell rang just as she placed the candles into the candlesticks, and she swept graciously to the door to see Theo.

Everything will be all right if I can just have a few hours with Theo.

CHAPTER TWENTY—RAY

"I'm off to work now, Claire. Ma's sleeping like a baby," Ray whispered from the open bedroom door." He stepped to the night stand, placing the baby monitor on it.

"Okay, Ray," said Claire, her voice sleepy. "Will you be home for dinner?"

"Yes, but don't bother making anything. I'll pick up pizza."

"You won't have to. Davey's coming over to make a pot of his special chili," she said.

"Davey?" Ray said, indignation slipping into his voice. "I thought he went back to Breezewood." He moved toward the door.

"He stayed a little longer to spend more time with Jeremy. He said he had so much fun at the scout meeting, he realized what he's missing."

"Ma can't eat chili; you know that, Claire," Ray said, no longer whispering.

"We can make her something else, Eggbeater sandwich or soup. She's not picky." She rolled over and faced the wall.

Ma won't feel like eating at all with Davey here. Ray walked to the door. "Call me at work if you need me."

"But pick up shredded cheddar cheese, will you? Davey likes that on his chili." She called after him. "Bye, Ray."

Ray found notes from three teachers in his box: Brad Kushner, Boris Mathews, Desiree Osmond, all asking him to make sure their rooms were cleaned. *How I wish Marty had not been laid off last August.* We need him..

I'll give them a quick once-over as soon as I dust and vacuum Hope's office. He glanced at his watch: 6:15. *Hope will be here by seven thirty, if not before.*

The wheels of the cleaning cart squealed against the terrazzo floors, their sound echoing through empty corridors.

He breathed with relief to find the office dark. *I don't know why Hope has to have her office freshly cleaned every morning. I've never noticed her having any kind of asthma symptoms.*

He managed to finish the office and make his way to B-wing before he heard Hope's French heels tapping down the hall. The heels tapped their way to room B-four, obviously following the cleaning cart and lighted room.

"Good morning, Ray," Hope called from the door. "How is Caroline doing?

"Good morning, Hope," Ray said, walking toward her.

She pulled a plastic container from a bag and handed it to him. "It's chicken noodle soup, homemade with sodium-free, low-fat broth and lean, trimmed chicken. It's just the thing for a restricted diet like your mother's."

Ray thanked her and, anxious to finish the classrooms, grabbed a dust cloth.

"What is her latest prognosis, Ray?" Hope asked, concern filling her eyes.

"Well, the doctors said there was nothing more they could do for her in the hospital." He began dusting the heating vent meticulously. "They told us to take her home and keep her calm. We're not to let her get upset or do any physical work." He turned toward Hope.

"So she's to have complete rest and a low-fat, low-sodium diet?" She dug in her bag and placed a small tray of rolls on the counter. "These are low sodium, too; and they're made with beans in place of fat."

Ray furrowed his brow. "Beans?"

"Sounds strange, doesn't it? But they are not bad."

She gathered her things. "I leave you to your work now. You obviously heard from Brad and Boris. And Desiree."

Ray completed Brad and Desiree's rooms before they arrived and was just finishing the third when Boris came into his classroom, balancing two boxes of library books about the Civil War. Ray helped him carry in another, larger box from the car before hurrying back to his office.

Although he had resolved not to call her there, he dialed Heather's number at the pharmacy. He recognized her voice at once, delighting in the professional way she said, "Pharmacy, Ms. Baker speaking."

She agreed to meet him for an early dinner at Berrigan's, near the recreation center where Jeremy had swim class.

"But I will have to leave right at 6:30 to pick up Jeremy. I want to get him in bed on time, so I can study these drug inventory sheets."

"When does he have his dinner?" Ray asked.

After she told him that Helsi Bradford fed him before she dropped him off to swim, he remembered their routine.

"Has he-uh, been-uh spending more time with his father?"

"I have to go now, Ray," she half whispered. "Thank you for the invitation. You're my rock."

Shoot! Now I can't stay after to catch Rosie. Well, I'll just have to rework the schedule and leave her a copy to look over. This one, for sure, isn't working.

Ray reached for the draft of the work schedule he had started for Rosie and tried to think of new ways to get essential cleaning done with half their former night crew.

What areas could we do every other night and still meet health-department code? Not lavatories, not the servery.

Maybe the teachers' lounge. But they'd have a fit.

Hope's office? I could use that time in the morning to clean a classroom. He sipped his coffee, now cooled, and grimaced at the bitter taste. *No, she'd never stand for it.*

He rubbed his temples. *There has to be a way to do this.*

A soft knock came from his open door; he looked up to see fifth-grader, Emmylou Parks, wearing a grave face.

"Good morning, Emily," he said. "What can I do for you this fine morning?"

"It's Emmylou, Mr. Sellers." She stepped toward his desk. "May I ask you something?"

"Sure, Emmylou. Sit down." He gestured toward the chair facing his. He immediately recalled having helped Hope and Boris Mathews watch to make sure she boarded the bus after school. *It was last year, in the fall. She was talking to some sexual predator on the internet. I wonder what happened to him?*

"Mr. Sellers," she said, eyes on her hands, folded in her lap.

"What's on your mind, Emmylou?" Ray smiled hard at the child, forcing a slight grin from her. Air brakes whooshed outside as buses began to arrive.

"I was wondering. My dog Ringer died last night—he was hit by a car." Her eyes remained downcast. We found him in the street this morning."

"I'm very sorry to hear that," Ray said softly, leaning toward her.

"We were wondering if we could bury Ringer in the school memorial garden." Her eyes met his. "All the kids here know him. He used to follow us around the neighborhood. Everybody wanted to pet him; they loved him so much. They knew he loved them."

"I don't know, Emmy. We'll have to check on that." His brow furrowed.

"Ringer went to all the little league games. Every summer. He got excited every time a Poore Pond kid was up to bat." she said earnestly. "You might say he's the Poore Pond School official dog." Her large, liquid eyes compelled him to grant her this wish.

"Official, huh?" Ray asked, thinking of the child's close call with the internet predator, yearning to give her whatever she asked. He stared into space. *This means a lot to her. But our memorial garden is to honor people. We can't start with kids' pets.*

"Mr. Sellers." She waited. "Mr. Sellers." Finally he turned to her. "Please, I need an answer right away. Ringer has to be buried today."

"I know he does." He rose and the child instantly stood.

"I'll get back to you by lunchtime." He reached for his windbreaker and slipped into it.

"Thank you, Mr. Sellers. I knew you would help."

He watched her walk away and his heart fell.

He responded automatically to waves and greetings from children as he walked down the hall and out the door. *How can I help Emmylou make Ringer's burial special? We can't put him in the memorial garden. We could plant something for him though.*

The brisk air and exuberant children forming their class lines broke his thoughts. Their smiles, hellos, and high-fives cheered him. He enjoyed their clean fresh look when they arrived in the morning. They were rested and eager for the day, just as the adults seemed to be.

Two students on litter duty showed him half-filled plastic bags of discarded paper, soiled cups, and the like.

"Thank you, Litter Patrol," he said. "You're early today. I'll see that you get pay raises." They laughed and headed for the trash bin.

A student page came to tell Dr. Fleming she was needed in the office. Ray waved to her and took her place monitoring the sidewalk along the bus lane, reminding students to stay inside the yellow safety line a foot from the curb.

"Good morning, Mr. Sellers," a small-but-loud voice called from behind him. He turned to see Dylan Bradford, followed by Helsi.

"Good morning, Dylan, Mrs. Bradford." He turned and grinned at them.

"Good morning, Mr. Sellers."

"You go on, Dylan. I want to speak to Mr. Sellers." She waved her son away.

They spoke at length, Ray trying to comprehend what she was telling him while keeping an eye out for the safety of students working their way around cars and buses.

Helsi told him how concerned she was about Jeremy. He seemed upset and anxious lately. She had finally managed to draw out of him, the reason for his unhappiness.

Ray did not like hearing her account although he had been sensing such feelings in the boy for a few weeks.

Jeremy had confided to Helsi that he feared his parents might get back together and move him to Breezewood. "He does not want to leave his school or his friends or his apartment."

"But especially, he does not want to leave you, Mr. Sellers," she said, searching his face.

The first bell rang and still they talked. The discussion continued amidst pockets of students, hurrying through the door before second bell.

Helsi delighted Ray by telling him how happy Jeremy had been that Ray had gone to the scout banquet after all.

"Anyone could see it meant as much to the boy to have you there as to have his own father," she said. "He was afraid you would not go if Davey went."

Pretending not to notice the emotion in Ray's face, Helsi continued, "Jeremy said 'you and Davey try to be friends, but you can never be friends because you both love his mother.'" She shook her head. "He is one perceptive child, isn't he?"

They both looked around at the silent schoolyard. Thanking each other for their help, they departed, Helsi to the parking lot, Ray to his duties inside the school.

Ray, his heart full, walked to his office. He found a pink phone-message note on his desk.

> **Claire phoned. Your Aunt Peggy arrives from Florida tonight. She and Davey will meet her plane about 6:30 and see you at home.**

He was excited about seeing his favorite Aunt Peggy. She had moved to Florida four months ago and had not come for a visit even once. She lands at 6:30; my dinner with Heather ends at 6:30. That'll work. He wrote a quick note and left the room.

Hope stood in the rear lobby, talking with the parent-group president, Holly Hapwell. Not wanting to interrupt, he slipped her a note, asking her to let him know when he could have a word. He would be in the equipment room, changing a blade on the large mower.

Not ten minutes later, she joined him there. He brushed off a worn wooden stool with a clean shopcloth, inviting her to sit down then seated himself on a low, metal drum. He had not noticed until now, quite a few grass clippings clumped on the floor and felt embarrassed. *I really need to give this room a good cleaning.*

She chuckled when Ray told her about Emmylou's request.

"But that child has been through a rough patch, and now she's lost her dog." Hope said, suddenly serious.

"Well, we can't start burying pets in the memorial garden, can we? It's for people's memorial plants, isn't it?"

"Probably." She rubbed her chin and looked at the floor.

"But let's think about this."

"We don't have a lot of time." Ray said. "Emmylou reminded me that Ringer has to be buried today." He nodded emphatically. "She's right. There has to be another way to give that dog a special resting place."

They agreed that each would mull it over and touch base just before lunch. Hope stood and made her way around boxes and chests to the door.

"Oh, one more thing, Hope," Ray called, stepping toward her. "What about that guy on the internet, the one stalking Emmylou? Where is he now?"

"I'm glad to tell you he is incarcerated. At the state prison in Johnsville. Officer Clifton told me they set a trap for him on the internet; they had his email address from Emmylou's computer."

She waved at a student passing in the hall and turned her face to Ray, finger crossing her lips.

"You mean they emailed him, pretending to be the girl?" Ray asked, his eyes skeptical, voice lowered.

"I believe what they did was wait for him to email her again and sent a reply as if they were Emmylou." She whispered and stepped back into the room. "Officer Clifton promised us a written report, but he needed Mrs. Parks to sign permission. Nothing has come in yet."

Ray stopped at home long enough to shower, change, and check on Caroline, avoiding Claire and Davey in the kitchen as best he could.

Caroline stretched on her bed, half sitting, half lying, against a thick cushion with arms. Ray sat in the bedside chair to chat about Aunt Peggy's visit. She was clearly excited to see her sister and was wearing new blue silk pajamas with matching bed jacket, sent by Hope and her staff. The azure silk gave her face a needed bit of color.

"My baby sister is the best medicine you could give me," she said with emotion, patting Ray's hand.

He told her about Emmylou and Ringer. After dismissal, he had taken Emmylou and a few friends on a long walk behind the fence, near the pond at the other side of school property.

Mrs. Parks met them there with the beloved Ringer, resting on styrofoam in a clean microwave-oven box, lined with a purple-flowered towel. Ray had built a crude wooden cross from garden stakes, and the mother had brought Emmylou's white-leather Bible and a few wilting, purple crocuses from the garden.

The devoted group of mourners held a proper ceremony, young voices reading scripture; adult voices joining them for the Lord's Prayer. Two boys from Emmylou's class acted as pallbearers, helping Ray lower the cardboard casket into the hole they had helped dig earlier. Each person poured a shovelful of soil on the box, and Ray drove the cross into the ground above Ringer's head. Emmylou, with great reverence, scattered purple crocuses atop the grave.

"I wish you could have seen those kids, Ma." Ray grinned with pride. "You would think they were burying a saint, they took it so seriously."

"It sounds so special, Rayley. And they couldn't have done it without you." She beamed at him.

"Well, there was no way we could have put Ringer in the memorial garden." His eyes widened mischievously. "But it was tempting to go ahead and bury him there and watch the fireworks when everyone heard about it." They laughed heartily, sending Caroline into a fit of coughing.

Ray gave her water to drink and promised he would be home by seven to see his aunt.

The dinner with Heather did not go the way Ray hoped it would. Both she and he arrived later than planned, ending up with less than an hour to spend together.

Ray saw when she arrived that she was tense and looked tired. He told funny stories, including the Emmylou-Ringer one, to help her relax; and she did calm down a bit.

But after only two or three bites of her favorite sizzling- skillet dinner, she felt ill and could eat no more. Ray ordered a cup of hot tea, which she quietly sipped, withdrawing into herself.

He worried that her new career would be too stressful for her; it was quite a big jump in responsibility from her usual minimum-wage jobs.

The evening ended too soon. Ray felt cheated out of the emotional sustenance he had come to expect from Heather. He told himself that she would be under less stress once the internship was finished. Then they could get back to the way they were.

Arm-in-arm, they walked to her car. He kissed her gently but meaningfully and opened the door.

"You take care of yourself now, Heather." He took her elbow, easing her gently into the driver's seat.

She looked up at him. "All I need is a good night's sleep. I'll be fine." But the defeat in her voice worried him.

Ray pulled into the street, fighting to keep from heading to Heather's apartment to help with Jeremy, so she could rest.

He knew he had to get home to Caroline, so Mrs. Birney, their neighbor, could leave. He looked forward to seeing Aunt Peggy but knew that Davey's presence would put a pall over everything. He was glad he did not have to eat his chili.

At 7:30 Ray heated a can of chicken noodle soup and made cheese toast for Caroline. She preferred to have it in her room, so he served it on the hospital tray Claire had rented. He joined her with a cup of coffee, tuning her television set to their favorite game show.

"I wonder what's keeping them," she said during the commercial.

"Maybe the flight was late. Or traffic. You know how the airport is, Ma." Ray, dreading to see Davey, fought his own escalating tension.

They heard a car engine outside, followed by the door opening, footsteps down the hall.

Aunt Peggy lit up the room with her bright smile and hugs for Caroline and Ray. She looked tanned and fit as she crawled upon the bed and stretched out next to her sister. They locked hands.

Claire came in, wearing a false smile and troubled eyes. She poked Ray's shoulder and asked him how his dinner date had gone. She sat on his knee playfully, enjoying the little family reunion.

"Where's Davey?" Ray asked suddenly.

"Oh he went home," Claire said flippantly, avoiding Aunt Peggy's eyes turned on her.

Relief flooded over Ray, though he burned with curiosity.

They savored one another's company, laughing and talking until Caroline pushed her tray table away from the bed and announced that she was tired. Claire helped her mother to the bathroom and into a nightgown. She insisted on saving the blue silk pajamas for her waking hours.

Ray and Aunt Peggy moved to the kitchen. She accepted his offer of a bowl of Davey's chili, and Ray insisted she let him serve her. He helped himself to a square of Claire's pineapple cake and glass of milk, joining his aunt at the table.

"So Davey made this? She asked.

"He sure did," Ray said, loading the words with innuendo.

"It's really good!" Aunt Peggy said, surprise in her voice.

"You met him. What did you think, Aunt Peggy?" Ray asked.

"Well, he seemed like an okay guy at first." Her eyes met Ray's. "But I don't think much of him after the crude remarks he made in the car." She stared into her chili bowl.

"What did he say?" Ray asked, feeling guilty about half enjoying her words.

Aunt Peggy kept silent for a moment. "I'll let Claire tell you, Ray."

They fell into a discussion of Caroline's health, trying to work up to full realization of the fact that she was seriously ill.

Claire came in and joined them at the table with a cup of coffee.

"Okay, Claire, let's have it. Why didn't Davey come back with you?"

Claire looked from Ray to Aunt ~~Patsy~~ Peggy. "You didn't tell him?"

"It's not my place, Claire." The aunt said soberly. "You tell your brother."

"What kind of crude remark did he make?" Ray asked.

Claire explained the conversation in the car. She and Aunt Peggy had discussed Caroline's illness and her poor prognosis. Claire quoted the doctor who said there was nothing further the hospital could do for her. The only thing left was to take her home and keep her comfortable for as long as she has with us.

She looked at Aunt Peggy's trembling lip and moved to a chair next to her, putting an arm around her shoulder.

"So what remark did Davey make?" Ray asked, brimming with impatience.

Claire turned to face her brother squarely. "Aunt Peggy and I were trying to be practical, get our emotions into check, figuring out what you and I would do if Ma dies."

She began to pick up with her fingertips, bits of shredded cheese from the bowl on the table. "I said 'you and Heather would probably get married and live in the house. That's what Ma would want; she's said so a million times.'"

She looked at her aunt. "I said maybe I'd rent Heather's apartment, assuming, of course, that I had a job by then."

"That's when he said it," Aunt Peggy said, voice raised.

Ray looked at Claire expectantly. "What did he say, for gosh sakes?"

Claire began slowly. "Look on the bright side, Claire. You and your brother will get the house free and clear when your mom dies. You'd get a niece piece of cash if you sold it outright. And let me give you some advice. Don't you move out first. Ray could keep it all to himself, saying you abandoned it."

Ray's eyes squinted. He looked at Claire. He turned to Aunt Peggy. "He really said that?" He swallowed. "Is that all he said?"

The two women exchanged looks.

"Tell him, Claire."

Ray looked at Claire. She began in a careful voice. "Davey said 'Anyway, Heather'll never marry Ray. She's just using him until she gets her education.'"

They saw Ray's wounded eyes and immediately regretted telling him the second part of Davey's remarks.

Ray accepted another cup of coffee from his sister although his nerves were bristling from too much caffeine.

Aunt Peggy and Claire excused themselves to change into pajamas, asking Ray to meet them in the living room with his coffee.

Does Davey know something I don't know? Heather didn't treat me right tonight. Are they making plans together?

He went to the sink and threw the coffee down the drain, rinsing his mug. He filled the teakettle with water and put it on the stove to heat. Pouring powdered hot chocolate into the mug, he rooted in the pantry for marshmallows.

Suddenly, he felt sick to his stomach. He turned off the burner and went straight to his room where he crawled into bed.

The alarm blared, and Ray woke with a start. He reached for the off button, sat on his elbows, and looked around the dark room. He thought of last night's conversation and sank back into the pillows. *Davey thinks Heather is just using me. Well, how would he know?*

He thought of the tense dinner with her the night before and wondered if she had given Davey that impression.

Then he recalled the night he left the hospital after visiting Caroline and stopped at Heather's place. Though he was angry and disappointed to hear that Davey planned to go to the scout banquet, Jeremy's sincere suggestion that Ray take his mother to the banquet, had made up for it. But the best part came after the boy went to bed.

He could feel the warmth of her body in his arms now. They had sat very still for some time, just holding each other tightly, letting their love flow between and through them. *Why didn't I ask her to marry me that night? I love her and I know she loves me back.*

Armed with new courage, he resolved to call Davey on those crude remarks the very next time Claire brought him over. *I think Davey sees that Heather and I really love each other, and he can't stand it. He's trying whatever he can to break us up.*

Ray climbed out of bed and into the shower. He could hear the phone ring, knowing it was Hope and she would try again.

He dressed quickly and gathered his keys and wallet from the dresser top. He nearly collided with Aunt Peggy coming from the bathroom.

"What are you doing up so early, Aunt Peggy?" he asked, returning her hug.

"Well, who can sleep with that phone ringing before dawn?" she laughed.

"That was Hope. She probably had directions for me to do some kind of necessary job first thing this morning." He rolled his eyes at his aunt. "She'll call back."

"No, Ray. I answered it. It was not your boss." Her eyes widened. "It was Heather. She wants you to call her before she leaves the house at seven forty-five." She shook her head and smiled through closed lips. "When are you going to marry that girl?"

Before removing his windbreaker, Ray dialed Heather's number from his office phone. It rang twice.

"Hello. Ray?" Her voice set his heart pounding.

"Heather, hi." He swallowed. "You called me? What's going on?" Suddenly warm, he struggled out of his jacket, phone propped under his chin.

"Ray, I just wanted to—I felt bad about ruining our dinner the other night."

"Don't give it a thought, Heather. We were both tired and stressed. It wasn't your fault."

"You know it was. You're just being nice, Ray." She called to Jeremy that his bus was coming. "Excuse me, Ray."

"Aw, Heather. You know you're excused. Anyway, let's have a special dinner when you finish your internship. Just the two of us."

"Ray, we don't have to wait until then. I'm making you a home-cooked dinner tonight. Be at my place at 6:30."

Aunt Peggy is making her cheese meatloaf tonight. But I would rather go to Heather's apartment.

"Ray." She waited. "Are you there?"

"Yes, I'm here."

"Don't you want to come?" Her voice fell.

"Yes, I want to come, Heather. It's just that my Aunt Peggy is in town, and she's making dinner at our house tonight."

"That's all right, Ray. We can do it another time," she said, her voice low and thin. "I have to go."

"No, wait. You come have dinner with us. Aunt Peggy wants to see you."

"Will Davey be there with your sister?"

"I doubt it. No. No. I think they broke up or something."

"I'll pick you up at 6:00, your place. Jeremy, too."

"Maybe you'd better ask your family first, Ray."

"They want you to come, Heather. I told you Aunt Peggy wants to see you. She's here for only a few days."

"Just warn them first, Ray."

"Heather, they want what I want. Mom says I'm like half a pair of scissors without you." The words shocked him.

"Oh, Ray." He could hear her breathing rapidly. "That's just how I feel when we're apart. Like half a pair of scissors."

He chuckled with delight. She joined him, laughing through their goodbyes.

Ray's trembling hand crashed the phone into its base. An unstoppable smile spread across his face. He wanted to shout for joy. He thrust his fist in the air. "Yes!" he shouted.

"What are you celebrating, Ray?" Hope's voice startled him; he had not heard the door. Turning to face her, he tried to put on a business-like face. The smile would not erase.

"Let me guess," she beamed at him. "You asked Heather to marry you and she accepted?"

How does she know this is about Heather? I always thought she was psychic.

He explained to Hope that he wanted to ask Heather but had not gotten around to it yet.

I should give her a ring tonight. In front of Aunt Peggy, the whole family. We need to make it official.

In the end, Hope insisted he leave work at two o'clock and buy a ring. She wrote the name of her jeweler on a square of paper, suggesting he use her name to get a better deal.

"I'll call and tell him you are coming in, and he's to take good care of you." She folded the paper and handed it to him. "He and I go back a long way. He'll give you a good discount."

She stood, staring at him for a moment before hugging him awkwardly. "Go for it, Ray. You deserve some happiness."

Speechless, he watched her walk out the door.

CHAPTER TWENTY-ONE—THE BRADFORDS

Ian and Helsi slipped through the side door of the county courthouse. They were met by a tall, lanky man in a cowhide jacket.

"Hi, Jake," Ian said, shaking his hand.

Jake shook Helsi's hand, covering it with his other one. "Don't you worry, Ms. Bradford. Everything will work out okay." He looked into her eyes. "Ian made only three deliveries and received just two cash payments. They can't get him on much for that."

Helsi stared at him.

"Let's go then." Jake started down the wide corridor. "The deposition starts in ten minutes."

Ian held his wife's hand as they followed him. He could feel her tension.

Jake went ahead into a small conference room and came out carrying a heavy wooden armchair. He placed it a few feet from the door and motioned to Helsi to sit in it.

She and Ian hugged; he helped her into the chair. They could hear low voices coming from the room.

"We shouldn't be long, Ms. Bradford. It's pretty cut and dried." He gestured toward an open door across the hall. "There are vending machines in there, cokes and snacks, if you need something before your deposition starts after Ian's." He glanced at Ian. "There will be a short break between them."

The two men entered the conference room and closed the door.

Helsi, feeling chilled, closed the lapels of her thin blazer over the scoop neck of her sweater. At the same time, the musty air seemed to take away her breath.

She began square breathing, a technique Sean had learned from his coach and taught the entire family. She inhaled for a count of five, held her breath for a count of five, exhaled for a count of five, paused for a count of five. Then she repeated the process.

Craving a hot drink, she rose and followed refrigeration sounds to the small room across the hall. Only cold drinks were available. Her eyes scoured the snack machine. *Something salty sounds good.* She dug in her purse for coins, dropping them into the slot and selecting shoestring potatoes.

She tore at the package and popped a few of the dry sticks into her mouth. The too-salty taste startled her. Moving back to the drinks machine, she fed a dollar bill into it and pressed the tab for bottled water.

Handbag swinging on one arm and both hands occupied with the snack pack, she meandered down the corridor past the room where Ian was in deposition. She strained to hear, but no sounds came from behind the thick wooden door.

Portrait photographs of city officials watched her from their neat rows on the wall. She stopped and read names and dates of service for each, recognizing faces of more recent mayors. Mildred Farris, the only woman in the group, caught her attention.

She remembered Mrs. Farris' two terms in office and the way she had fought to bring daycare centers into public schools for children of teachers and other school employees. Though unable to realize this goal, Mrs. Farris had won over Helsi and many of her friends, serving as a courageous role model for women.

I will start that cleaning service. I will.

She allowed her mind to shift back to the horror of Ian's illegal deed. *I have to now. If Ian goes to prison, it falls on me to earn an income we can live on. No more piddling little jobs helping Jeremy and Heather.*

She looked again at the clock on the wall. Its hands seemed to stand still. *I should have brought a book or a magazine.*

What if Ian goes to prison? She tried to envision their family life. *What would we tell the children?*

A television commercial she had seen before she knew of Ian's misdeeds flashed through her mind. An artist had created a line of humorous greeting cards to send to people in prisons.

"Talk about a small market." *What did I know?* "And what could possibly be funny about being in prison?" she had scoffed.

Feeling sick to her stomach, she pulled the bottle from her purse and gulped water.

The sound of a door opening drew her back toward her chair. The knot of anxiety in her stomach ballooned to her chest. She stuffed the bottle into her purse, crumpled the half-empty bag into her blazer pocket, and dusted salt from her hands.

She walked briskly, gathering herself.

Jake came out first, his face unreadable. He saw Helsi and smiled with his eyes only.

Ian, white-faced and shaken, came out next, followed by several other men in dark suits. He stopped, dazed, as if rooted in their path. Taking no notice of her, they walked around him and headed briskly down the corridor.

Helsi froze. *Jake was wrong. They must have really grilled Ian. Oh no.* Tears stung her eyes and tried to spill out. She blotted them with her fingertips and moved to her husband.

Jake motioned for them to follow him, leading the way to a tiny waiting room. "You stay here, Ian, until we call your wife. It should be in about twenty minutes." He gestured toward a vented door. "That's a toilet in there. A coffee maker's against the wall."

He walked away then turned at the door. Helsi noticed the high heels on his cowboy boots. "I'll come back to get you, Ms. Bradford, when they're ready to start."

He looked toward Ian. "Just try to relax, Buddy. Have a cup of coffee. We'll work things out." He left, closing the door behind him.

Helsi tried to get Ian to tell her what had transpired, but he would not answer her questions. He just shook his head at each one as if she spoke a foreign language.

His vacant eyes frightened her. She sat down on a hard wooden bench and motioned for him to join her.

He shrugged his shoulder and stepped away. He began to pace the room. Helsi watched him pass by the coffee machine.

"Ian, please. Tell me what happened."

Still he paced, moving as if his body were switched into slow motion.

"How bad is it, Ian?" She was desperate now.

He stopped suddenly and stared at her. "I most certainly will lose my job, Helsi." He swallowed. "And I'll never work as a paramedic again. Not ever." His face crumpled into tears.

She went to him and eased him down to the bench. She poured two cups of coffee from the stained pot in the corner. Handing one to Ian, she sat beside him and took a big drink. *Bad coffee never tasted so good.*

They sat in silence, sipping the hot brew as if their very lives depended on getting stagnant coffee down their throats.

"Ian, talk to me," Helsi's eyes sought his. *Whatever it is, I want to know all about it. We have to face it, no matter how horrible it is.*

"I could go to prison, Helsi." His turned, his eyes boring into her face. "For six years. Six years." His chin shook.

"I thought Jake said they'd go easy on you, that you were such small potatoes."

"Well, he's going to plea bargain on that basis, I guess." Ian buried his face in his hands.

Helsi stared at him, incredulous. *Who is this simpering man? Where is my brave Ian?*

"Ian. Ian, stop that." She pulled at his hands on his face.

He shrugged her off with his elbows.

She stood. "Ian Bradford, stop all that whining. You're not like that." She raised her voice. "You're a Bradford, for heaven's sake! You don't whimper in the corner. You fix things."

The sound of the door opening caught their attention. Jake sauntered in, looking his relaxed self again.

"They're ready for you, Ms. Bradford." Helsi started toward the waste can. "Oh, take the coffee with you if you want."

Helsi tossed it into the can, squared her shoulders, and walked through the door ahead of Jake.

The deposition took barely thirty minutes. She could testify only regarding those nights Ian spent away from home and the news from Myra Abernathy about Ian's lending Dick money for their house payment.

She had not questioned his whereabouts on the nights he said he spent at the station when he was really delivering to the warehouse. She had been oblivious to strange boxes delivered to their garage.

It troubled her to think she had admitted warning Ian not to get involved with Gene, that the scheme sounded suspect to her. When the attorneys kept going back to that point, she realized it was probably key evidence that would work against Ian. Regret filled her heart.

But she refused to be intimidated by the proceedings, remaining calm throughout. She surprised herself with her poise. She had learned from Ian, how to be strong during crises. She would stay strong now for him.

I just wish I could trust Jake more. I'm not sure he's the lawyer for us.

Helsi offered to drive home; but, to her relief, Ian insisted that he would. Though she was primed to talk things over, they rode in silence.

Ian spent an hour at his desk, preparing for class.

Helsi had dinner in the slow cooker. Since they had skipped lunch, they sat down together before the children came home and enjoyed sausage and sauerkraut with potato dumplings.

Ian seemed more like himself, and they talked a bit about his case. He suggested they may need a better attorney, relieving Helsi. She became preoccupied with ways to find another.

They shared a lingering hug before he left for campus.

"Go and enjoy your class tonight, Ian. Let it take your mind off this other problem."

"You're right, Hon. I need to think about something I've done right instead of that attack of idiocy I had."

The minute he was out the door, she was on the computer, searching for attorney-referral sources.

The ringing telephone interrupted her. She answered it and heard Jake's down-home speech.

"Is Ian there, Ms. Bradford?" he asked.

"No, Mr. Uella. He's gone to class."

"Well, you just tell him to call me. I've got to give him a few things about the plea bargain."

"Does it look good for Ian, Mr. Uella?" Helsi asked.

"Call me Jake. You might say that. Bye, Ms. Bradford."

She heard the dial tone.

Ian arrived home to a quiet house.

Helsi, freshly showered and wearing her cotton-seersucker, summer robe, sat on the sofa. A square plate of cheddar-cheese spread, wheat crackers, and apple wedges waited on the small coffee table. Two half-filled wineglasses stood beside the plate.

He hugged her gently. Instantly reassured by his calm manner, she gave him Jake's message.

Taking the cordless phone into the laundry room, he fished in his pockets for the attorney's card.

I hope Ian feels like talking. I really need to understand what's going on. She spread cheese thickly on a cracker and ate it in one bite.

The low hum of his conversation drifted into the room, but she heard no actual words. It seemed as if he had been talking to Jake for a long time. She lifted a glass and sipped the chilled white wine.

"Plea bargaining! Charge bargaining! Sentence bargaining!"

Ian's voice boomed through the house. "What the—Jake? Sort it all out for me, dammit."

Helsi rose, still holding the wineglass, and slid quietly to the laundry-room door. Ian's back was turned toward her, and she watched him flex his tense shoulders as he listened to his lawyer.

All day she had managed to keep the knot of anxiety in her stomach from growing, but now it began to expand rapidly. She refilled her glass from the bottle on the counter and fairly ran to the sofa.

I won't let that dark mood cover me again. I won't.

Ian replaced the phone on its base and washed his hands at the sink.

"Come sit, Ian." Helsi said, her soft, even voice belying the turmoil inside her.

He sat on the sofa and unlaced his shoes. He slipped his feet out of them and lined them neatly under the table.

"Have some," she offered, gesturing toward the food.

I probably should not bring up the hearing.

He ate two crackers loaded with cheese, then sank back into the sofa and drank the wine.

Helsi watched the silent television set, its sound muted. Ian stared into space. Neither spoke.

"Jake says I could plead no contest and do a plea bargain, probably get three-years probation, 500 hours community service," Ian blurted, suddenly looking at her.

Please, God. She sought his eyes.

"But they might throw the book at me and give me ten years plus a big fine." He nearly shouted, still not looking at her.

Helsi's eyes darted toward the stairs. Putting a finger to her mouth, she shushed her husband.

Her heart sinking, she asked, "What were all those bargainings you were yelling about on the phone?"

"I don't know. It's so much gobbledy gook," Ian said, utter exhaustion filling his voice and lowering it.

"You're home now, Ian. Just relax." She lifted his legs onto the sofa, placed a pillow at the arm, and eased his shoulders down until his head rested on it. "There."

"Mama," Rachel's small voice cried from the top of the stairs.

Helsi clipped up the stairs and led the child back to her bed. She tucked her in and sat beside her, stroking her small hand to calm her restlessness.

The room felt warm and safe in the rosy glow of Rachel's pink night light. She wanted to crawl into bed next to her daughter and sleep and sleep and sleep. Until this terrible ordeal was settled.

Sensing a presence, Helsi awoke, straining her eyes in the dark to see the figure standing over the bed.

"What are you doing, Hon? Sleeping with Rachel?"

"Oh, Ian. It's you." She looked at her daughter sleeping soundly next to her.

"I slept on the sofa all night. I'm stiff as a board." Ian stretched in the dark room.

"What time is it?" Helsi asked.

"Five-oh-five," Ian said, laughing softly.

They descended the stairs and had cereal and coffee together, adults only.

Helsi told Ian that Robbie had made third honors, earning a place on the "Cs or Cooler" half-term honors list.

"His teacher says he has a chance of making the "Bs or Better" list at the end of term. But he has to work very hard."

Ian smiled widely and poured another bowl of cornflakes.

Helsi saw the last Bradford child out to the bus and began clearing away breakfast dishes. Keeping physically busy was her way of dealing with fear.

I wonder if the new chief will give Ian a break and let him keep his job. She squirted detergent into the sink and ran hot water over it, creating a rising tide of foam.

He hasn't known Ian very long. Maybe it's not up to him.

Glancing out the window, she noticed a police car in front of Meadow's house across the street. The garage door was open, and both Phyllis and Herb's cars were there.

I hope nothing's wrong with Mercedes again.

Drying her hands, she brought the cordless phone to the window and was about to dial their number when she saw two officers come out the front door, Phyllis Meadow between them. They helped her into the rear seat of the police cruiser, then climbed into the front seats and drove out the drive.

Oh my word. What's happened? Poor Phyllis.

Fighting an urge to call Herb, she threw herself into tidying the kitchen, making mental plans to scrub the floor on hands and knees.

Supper that night became an unexpected celebration. Sean had outdone himself at the school's last track meet for the year, following three consecutive meets where his achievement in the shot put had grown stronger and stronger.

"Are we talking about lettering in ninth-grade track, Son?" Ian asked between forkfuls of Helsi's mushroom chicken and rice.

"Sean, why didn't we know about this sooner?" Helsi asked, getting up to start the coffeepot.

"He doesn't want us to know," Lucy piped. "He never wants his family there." She looked her brother squarely in the face. "I think he might be ashamed of us."

All eyes turned to Sean. A deep red moved up his neck and into his face.

"It's not that," Robbie stood to be heard. "He's not ashamed of us. He's ashamed of himself."

"Sit down, Robbie," Sean cried, his voice uneven.

"Well, that's what you said, Sean." Robbie looked accusingly at his elder brother.

"I told you I wasn't good enough to have the family come to my meets. That's what I said." He dropped his eyes, his body language screaming discomfort.

"Maybe Sean wanted to surprise everybody. You know, wait until he got really good then tell us. Right, Sean?" Dylan interjected.

"Is that right, Sean?" Ian asked, his voice tender.

"Sort of," Sean replied, scooping another helping of chicken onto his plate.

Sounds of the electric mixer rose above the conversation as Helsi beat egg whites at the counter.

Ian's voice rose above the noise. "You must have been on a rigorous training program, Sean, if you did well in the shot put." He looked at the boy.

"I did, Dad," Sean said. The mixer noise stopped abruptly and all eyes turned to Helsi. She scooped balls of ice cream into a bowl and covered them with meringue.

"I don't understand. When were you training?" Ian asked.

"All those times I said I was going to the library." Sean spoke with uncharacteristic bravado. "I was going to the weight room at school or to Joe-Joe's basement."

Sean opened up with details of his training, the sit ups, press ups, jump squats, and all the rest, engaging even the youngest Bradfords in the discussion.

Even Rachel contributed, standing to demonstrate wobbly jumping jacks she said her kindergarten class had learned.

Helsi switched off the chandelier and with a "tum-tum-ta-dum," march-stepped to the table, carrying a bowl in which sat a dome of toasted meringue, flaming with lighted cake candles. She led the family in singing congratulations to Sean, following the tune of Happy Birthday.

Sean grinned sheepishly, fighting feelings of delight with his mother's fanfare. She held the bowl in his face as he blew out the candles.

"What is this?" Lucy asked, staring into the bowl at the center of the table and removing the candles.

Helsi brought small cereal bowls and spoons. "Baked Alaska, sort of." She flashed a wide grin around the table. "It's all I could come up with on the spot."

Everyone enjoyed the chocolate ice cream with toasted meringue on top, Sean most of all.

He announced that the awards banquet would be next Tuesday at six thirty in the evening, and everyone whistled and cheered.

"But we get only four tickets per athlete," he said. "There's not enough space at the Eagles' Hall."

They agreed to decide later which Bradfords would use the tickets.

A joy-filled peace settled over the house that evening, and the children went quietly to bed as if savoring the essence of it.

Helsi tidied a kitchen cupboard full of plastic containers. She thought about the call from Sean's counselor, saying he was in danger of being ineligible for track next year if his grades did not improve. The news had not hit her in the stomach the way it would have before. Before Ian's overwhelming state of affairs.

She made neat stacks of same-size plastic lids and, with a small sense of satisfaction, closed the cupboard door.

Ian sat at his desk, writing on a legal pad.

Helsi glanced through the window at the Meadow house. The garage door was open, and the overhead lights were on. She saw Herb arranging boxes in the trunk of his car.

She slipped out the front door and hurried across the dark street.

"Hi, Herb," she called as she approached, not wanting to startle him.

"Hello, Helsi," he responded, his voice dropping flatly.

"Is everything all right with Mercedes?" She went to him and laid her hand on his forearm.

"Mercedes is well, thank you." His dark eyes bore into hers. "It's Phyllis who is in trouble. Big trouble." He slammed shut the trunk.

"How can I help you, Herb?" she asked.

"We're still in shock, Helsi," he said, walking away.

CHAPTER TWENTY-TWO—HOPE

Herb Meadow sat opposite Hope in her tiny office. His shoulders drooped; his wrists lay limply on the chair arms; his speech was labored.

Hope could think of nothing appropriate to say.

He had candidly explained to her the fact that his daughter Mercedes' doctor had filed strong charges against his wife, to the point that a criminal investigation was underway.

She wished for words that would make the man feel better, but none came. *How can I feel sympathetic toward a mother who would deliberately make her child ill? And a father who turns a blind eye?*

Munchausen by Proxy Syndrome, he called it. There's been a case in the papers recently. I believe the mother had a long history, lost two or three infants to mysterious deaths.

Hope rose and pulled two bottles of water from the shelf, handing one to Herb, who took it without a word. She sat down again.

We had a speaker on Munchausen at our principals' retreat last summer. Weren't we told that it takes longer than six months to establish a diagnosis? Mercedes hasn't been enrolled that long. If I remember correctly, she came some time after the holidays. Yes, that's right; we were a few weeks into the new semester. That was February or March, and this is May: two or three months.

"Those are strong charges, you know, Dr. Fleming," Mr. Meadow blurted, scrubbing his hands forcefully. "Highly libelous, I would say." He looked expectantly at Hope.

"The charges are horrifying," she said, meeting his eyes and seeing the deep pain they reflected. *Perhaps he did not know; he travels so much. But still…*

She looked at Mr. Meadow slumped in the chair, a broken man. Lost. Glancing at her desk, she winced at the stack of test-score reports she had arrived extra early to study.

Ray, on silent feet, strode through the outer office, into the clinic, waving as he passed her open door. Hope looked at the wall clock and saw that it was ten minutes past eight. Her first thought was to dismiss her visitor and spend a half-hour on the reports. *Who am I to dismiss a man so wracked with pain? I'm certainly not without sin here.*

"Mr. Meadow, Mr. Meadow," she said softly and waited for eye contact.

"Yes," he said finally in a weak voice, his eyes vacant.

Hope put her hand on his forearm. "Mr. Meadow, do you have a pastor? Or a close friend you might speak to this morning?"

"No, we're new in town. There's nobody but you."

Scraping noises drew her eyes to the corridor windows. Bluewave Stonecipher dragged a large art portfolio down the hall.

"Bluewave," she called. *I'm sure she's a trained lay minister.*

Bluewave came to Hope's door. "Ms. Stonecipher, aren't you a Stephen Minister?"

"Yes I am, Dr. Fleming," she said, her eyes taking in Herb Meadow and noting his body language.

Hope introduced them and watched as Bluewave worked her magic on Herb, readily convincing him to come to her classroom for a few "deep-breathing techniques and mental exercises guaranteed to soothe and relax his anguished soul."

Minutes later, she saw a slightly more energetic Herb Meadow glide past the office, clutching a pack of visualization cards and a tin of meditation tea.

Hope stepped into the hall and watched him enter the Latchkey Room, knowing he would say good-bye to Mercedes. She peeked into the large room and saw the child hugging her father tightly. Herb released the child, nodded to a staff member, and walked briskly through the lobby toward the main doors.

She walked back to her desk and scanned the weekly calendar. *I'm to meet Brad Kushner and Katrina Davis at eight fifteen to hear their ideas for punching up awards-day.*

She gathered a pencil and legal pad and stepped through the door, nearly colliding with Superintendent Ed Amiston.

"I have to see you, Dr. Hope," he said, entering the office and taking the nearest chair.

"One moment, please, Ed," she said and went to the public address system board. She turned on the intercom to the upstairs conference room and told Brad and Katrina she would be a little late. "The superintendent is here," she explained.

Ed Amiston told her he was taking a position upstate and would not be on board after June. "I wanted to personally inform each member of the administrative team," he said with sincerity.

They thanked one another for their service to district children and mutually wished good luck for the new school year.

Why is Ed leaving so abruptly?

Ed departed and a rather pale Helsi Bradford slipped into Hope's office for a quick word. She wanted to verify whether or not Herb Meadow had placed her name on Mercedes' emergency form. He had. Helsi thanked her and promptly departed.

Secretary Corinne Tompkins quietly handed Hope an official-looking envelope. "This is confidential, Dr. Fleming. I had to sign for it."

Hope folded it into her jacket pocket and hurried upstairs to the meeting where she sat down breathlessly. She perused the outline Brad and Katrina had prepared, trying her best to focus on it. Katrina explained the new category for academic awards.

Carmen Ricci joined them and handed each a one-page list of musical ideas for the awards assembly.

"Giving an award to third, fourth, and fifth graders for notable improvement in an academic area is a good idea, Katrina and Brad," Hope said, making eye contact with first one then the other. "And Poore Pond has traditionally done that."

"Still no academic awards for Kindergarten through second grade?" Carmen asked. Her eyes widened. "There will be disappointed teachers." She added gleefully. "I smell a lynching."

"And parents," Hope said, smiling. "But we don't put pressure for grades on primary students. They are in the throes of learning to read, and we must keep them focused on that complex task without undue pressure."

She could feel Carmen bristling to counterpoint.

"Most children that age, she continued, "are not developmentally ready for higher-level reading, reading to learn, as we say." She turned to Carmen.

"Some people believe they are, what with all the educational television, family outings, and preschool experience children have before kindergarten these days," Carmen said, stirring the pot in that way she had. "Parents need their kids' grades for their own reward. They've worked hard growing these little scholars."

"But then why are more and more kindergartners coming to us not ready to learn?" Brad said, taking Carmen's bait.

"And why do we need remedial reading and listening lab?" Katrina added.

A debate ensued. Hope, opting out, sat back and stretched her legs. Brad and Katrina defended their revised award categories to Carmen.

Remembering Corinne's envelope, she pulled it from her pocket, meticulously tore off the end, and discreetly read the official letter. It stunned her.

Hope stared in disbelief at the words on ivory bond paper:

> **Your name has been placed on the witness list for defendant Ian Bradford.**
>
> **You will be notified when you are scheduled to give testimony.**

Her heart froze. She was oblivious to the discussion going on around her.

Outside, buses and their air brakes made loud swooshing noises; but the group had no trouble hearing Carmen's clear voice excitedly describing her ideas for playing music as each recipient went forward to receive awards. Brad and Katrina joined in her delight and added ideas of their own.

"Why don't we invite the parents to escort their kids to the podium, give them an award, too? They deserve one." Brad said.

Hope looked at her watch. Five minutes to first bell.

She stood and made appropriate comments to the awards-day team, thanking them for their fine ideas and promising to assist in any way she could.

Carmen's quip followed her out the door: "And the step-parents, the grandparents, step-grandparents, favorite aunts and uncles, step-…"

Hope hurried downstairs, her head swimming with concern for the Meadow family, for Ed Admiston, for the Bradfords.

Corinne handed Hope a pink phone-message note as she entered the office. Robin Cutler had just called.

I wonder what Ms. Cutler wants. Our meeting went well, or so I thought. She seemed to understand that the consequence Mrs. Newhouse gave Terry was well intended.

She stood before her desk, mentally reviewing the conference she and Lou Ann had held with Ms. Cutler. She indicated she had understood the teacher's rationale, even said she had no doubt Mrs. Newhouse had her son's best interest at heart.

Hope stepped to the door. "Corinne, hold my calls, please, until further notice. I need a few minutes."

"Of course, Dr. Fleming," the secretary replied.

"By the way, what time did that letter arrive, the official letter?"

"The agent followed me in from the parking lot around seven-forty-five. She was obviously waiting for me in her car."

Backing into the office, Hope asked Corinne to get Ms. Cutler on the phone; she gently closed the door.

Ms. Cutler had vehemently disagreed when the teacher criticized her own judgment in this particular situation. "No, you understand my son; you were just trying to use a consequence that fit him and his weird obsessions." A model of understanding.

Hope lifted the receiver and greeted Robin Cutler. They chatted briefly about the weather and how the students benefited from outdoor recess so much more than indoor.

Anxiety grew in her stomach as she waited for Ms. Cutler to divulge her point.

"Actually, I wanted to speak to you, Dr. Fleming, about the conference with Mrs. Newhouse." Her serious tone put Hope on alert.

She gave her typical remarks about the "non-festering policy" Poore Pond encouraged parents to use, "no matter how small the concern may seem."

"I really respect Mrs. Newhouse. She's a good teacher." A dog began barking ferociously, and Robin excused herself to check the cause.

Sometimes this happens. Two of Hope's fingers rubbed dust from the leaves of a small acanthus plant on her desk. *A parent gives all the signals that the issue has been resolved to their satisfaction. Later, feelings of injustice consume them; and the entire process must begin again.*

Through the receiver, she heard a door slam and Robin's distant voice directing the dog.

Our culture fosters paranoia in all of us—but especially among parents. The media feeds it with all their advice segments.

"I am so sorry, Dr. Fleming," Robin said. "This animal of ours takes his watch-dogging very seriously." They both chuckled.

"Where was I? Oh yes. I could not help thinking, you know. I got so much out of that bullying workshop; I can't thank you enough for having it." She coughed lightly. "And the segment on teacher-bullying really enlightened me. I mean, I had no idea."

"Thank you, Ms. Cutler," Hope said, her voice flat.

"The irony in all this, of course, is that Mrs. Newhouse presented that lecture." Robin Cutler laughed sardonically. "She taught me about teacher-bullying, and now I seem to be accusing her of that very thing."

There it is; the other shoe has dropped. Hope waited. *I stifled similar feelings that Lou Ann's treatment of Terry may have been seen as teacher-bullying. But it's just so out of character for her to lose sight of the effect of her discipline on the child.*

Hope massaged her temples and breathed deeply. *I should never have let Lou Ann talk me into doing that segment at the workshop. But she kept lobbying to include it.*

"You know I don't see her as a bullying teacher, no, not at all," Ms. Cutler's voice warmed slightly. "But as she said in her talk, just as good children sometimes bully, and good parents may sometimes bully; the same can be true of good teachers."

Hope took a deep breath then exhaled slowly, searching for words.

"Do you know what really bothered me, Dr. Fleming?" Robin continued. "Through this whole thing, Mrs. Newhouse seemed focused more on what the class would think than on what was appropriate for Terry." She coughed softly. "Do you see what I mean?"

"Might we need another conference, Ms. Cutler? A phone conference perhaps?"

"No. No, I'll email her. I just want her to be aware of that one point. No further discussion is necessary."

Theodore raised his goblet and proposed a toast to the new homeless shelter on its two-month birthday. Hope and George raised their glasses as well, his spilling diet soft drink on the immaculate white tablecloth.

"I rarely drink soda from a wineglass," he chuckled, swabbing the cloth with his oversized napkin.

"May the foundation live on and do its work so well that one day we find very few homeless souls to shelter." Theo's rich voice reverberated through the dining room; faces of other diners turned their way.

"That'll be the day," Hope replied dryly. "Unless the human condition changes drastically, we will always have homeless classes." She sent a sidelong glance at George.

"You're absolutely right, Mom. But speaking of classes, we are seeing a new class of homeless now." Leaning forward, George lowered his voice. "We are seeing under-age youth."

"You don't mean under eighteen, do you, George?" Theo scarcely whispered.

"I should think not," Hope said, her face aghast. "Homeless of that age should be in foster care." Wanting to wash from her mind an image of twenty-year-old George living on the street, she took two large drinks of wine.

The waiter brought their salads and inquired whether they wanted ground pepper. All three said, "Yes please."

Theo narrowed his eyes at George. "George, you can't mean they've shown up at your shelter? Not that young?"

"Three of them arrived two days ago." He waved an open hand at the waiter, grinding away with the huge pepper mill. "That's fine. Thank you. Thank you."

"You cannot accommodate them." Theo shook his head quickly. "It's in the bylaws. Nobody under age eighteen is eligible for services. You know that, George."

"It's not so cut and dried, Theo," George said between large bites of greens. "They told Grace Ellen they were in their early twenties, even had photo-I.D. cards."

"You don't put much over on Grace Ellen," Theo scoffed.

"She does not believe they are that old." He rested the salad fork on the plate and pushed it aside. "And neither do I; they look about sixteen.

"So you've addressed their age with the staff?" Hope blotted the sides of her mouth with a napkin. "They're aware of the issue? It's out in the open?" She leaned out from the table to make way for a steaming plate of grilled salmon and asparagus.

"Oh they're aware of it all right." George looked happily at the sizzling steak the waiter placed before him.

"What is the next step?" Theo asked, his eyes on the small butter chafe the waiter delivered and lighted, all in one swift motion. His eyes looked skeptically at the rather withered scampi he deposited. He instructed him to bring plumper, fresher scampi; or, if not possible, then he would have the salmon.

The waiter apologized profusely and left with Theo's plate.

"Well, Grace Ellen went all soft on the boys, was ready to look the other way and accept their I.D.s as valid. 'They're just kids,' she said."

"Good way to buy time," Hope said, deftly cutting asparagus.

"But her attitude changed after Milan spoke to her." George said. "The minute he laid eyes on them, Milan knew they were homosexuals. He told Grace Ellen as much, and she flat out asked them if they were gay."

George further explained that they admitted they were gay and asked to stay just a few days until a friend who was going to take them in came back from New York.

"I talked to the director of Y-Haven at the YMCA over on Prospect." George said, impressing Theo and Hope with his take-charge approach. "They have both gay and heterosexual men in that program, so our boys would be welcome over there."

Relief spread on his mother's face as well as on Theo's.

"But they have no space now. 'Maybe later,' he told me."

Hope and George pushed their plates aside, and the three brought out their folders to go over the budget; but they simply went through the motions, so distracted were they by this perplexing new development.

Right after Theo finished his salmon, they went home.

Hope, still disturbed from last night's news of the latest complications at the shelter, became even more bothered by the conference she and Lou Ann had with Robin Cutler.

Watching the clock for a few minutes until time to monitor lunch lines, her mind seemed determined to seek other frustrations. She began to walk toward the cafeteria and wondered about the deposition, which was scheduled for late June, to hear Frederick Baldwin use yet another angle to file claim on his step-grandmother's estate.

Now that the audit he petitioned for was finished and no improprieties were found, what case could he have?

She would not let herself think about reasons why the audit had not revealed discrepancies. *Thank you, God.*

In fact, she could not, at this moment, bear to think about any part of her working years with Mary Baldwin. *That was so long ago. And I was such a foolish youngster. What's the good of looking back on days when I was at my stupid worst?*

Lou Ann deposited her class in the lunch line and stopped to speak to Hope. "How do you think the conference went, Dr.Fleming?"

Hope looked at Lou Ann with narrowed eyes. "Well, it seems to me, we all did a great deal of talking out of both sides of our mouths."

Hope redirected to the back of the line, both a child trying to cut into the middle and the generous classmate allowing it.

She rejoined Lou Ann.

"In retrospect, I cannot believe I let Ms. Cutler know how I fought to present that segment on teacher-bullying." She looked at Hope. "Was I nuts or what? 'It's our duty,' I kept saying. 'If we're going to talk about bullying in schools, we have to cover the whole gamut.'"

She watched Hope's shaking head. "I should not have allowed you to talk me into it, Lou Ann. It was so against my better judgment."

They concluded that Ms. Cutler may have wanted more than anything, her voice to be heard. Hope emphasized the point that Ms. Cutler did not want Mrs. Newhouse to apologize to Terry, just to try to keep future consequences more private.

"We both know she had a good point, Lou Ann," Hope said, her eyes tender. "You broke your own rule, didn't you?"

"That's the maddening part, Hope." She waved and headed to the teachers' lounge.

It was a rainy Friday and Hope could barely get out of bed.

She thought about indoor recess on a Friday when both students and staff would be in a weekend frame of mind. Add to that, the assembly culminating Poore Pond's Anti-Bullying Campaign.

Wayne-the-One-Man Band was coming as a treat for everyone's dedication to stamping out bullying. And the parent group was serving each assembly bags of caramel popcorn and box juice.

What was I thinking when I agreed to this? She dragged herself up and closed the side window, wiping rain spatters off the sill with her hand.

Ian Bradford was waiting in the parking lot when Hope arrived at school. He left his van and walked in with her, explaining that he needed a few minutes. Despite his serious face, he made small talk all the way.

Once in her office, she invited him to sit in the nearest chair.

"Dr. Fleming, I'm in a bit of bad trouble," he said, his eyes on the floor.

How can bad trouble be only a bit? She pondered whether or not she should tell him she had received a letter.

"I realize someone like you knows nothing about being in trouble with the law."

His eyes sought hers, but she was unable to give him full eye contact. *By the skin of my teeth, Ian.*

He scrubbed his hands, studying them intently.

She waited.

"I did a stupid thing." He looked at her and she returned his gaze. "It was illegal." He rubbed his elbows and stared out the window.

"My hours were cut. Helsi's working that little job, you know, trying to run the house the way she always did. I don't know."

He looked at Hope. "I needed to bring in more money. I just went crazy."

Hope leaned forward and touched his arm. "We've all done desperate things for money at one time or another. You're an honorable man, Ian Bradford. I will certainly appear as a character witness for you."

Their eyes met, his full of gratitude, hers – of guilt.

CHAPTER TWENTY-THREE—RAY

Ray had never seen their small bungalow so sparkling clean. Claire hung new white curtains over the blinds in the living room and yellow checked ones in the kitchen. Ray polished all the floors, shampooed the rugs, and washed windows. They stripped both rooms of odds and ends, leaving only chairs and necessary tables.

Ray's laid-off colleague, Marty, helped him install new clay tiles in the bathroom and a new blue countertop around the sink. Claire scrubbed the discolored wall tile antiseptically clean and applied whitener to the grout. She bought bright blue-and-yellow window and shower curtains.

"Everything looks just great, Claire. But you've spent so much money." Ray said, placing hot buttered toast in front of her.

"Well, it isn't every day my little brother gets engaged," she said before biting into the toast. She looked closely at the buttery wedge. "This is delicious, Ray. How'd you do it?"

"Cinnamon, but just a tiny bit."

"You'll be a great dad for Jeremy. He's going to love this tiny-bit-of-cinnamon toast." She looked at him with serious eyes that belied her joking tone.

I think I can be a great dad to Jeremy. I know I can. Ray stared into space. Ever since Heather had accepted his ring, he'd felt breathless, warm all over.

"I can't believe it's really happening, Claire." He turned and gazed at her with moist eyes."

For a moment, she returned his deep gaze.

"Oh don't go all dreamy eyed on me, Ray. You would think you were the only person ever to fall in love and get married, for gosh sakes." She stood and began clearing the table.

They heard rustling sounds on the baby monitor, and both hurried to Caroline's room.

She stretched her arm toward the rolling bed table without reaching it. Claire lifted the water glass, guiding the straw to her lips. She sipped thirstily.

Ray slid open the new curtains, wooden rings clacking softly. "Look Ma, it's a beautiful day!"

Claire hovered as Caroline eased herself up on one elbow. "A beautiful day for a beautiful couple's engagement party." She had barely enough breath to finish the words. Her chest rose and fell as she tried to breathe deeply.

"What time does it start, Claire?" She turned her shoulders to look at her daughter, rearranging the folds of the curtains.

Claire went to her and threw back the comforter, guiding her legs off the side of the bed. She took slippers from the floor and fitted them to Caroline's swollen feet.

"It starts at 4:30, Ma, but some people will show up earlier. So we all have to be dressed by three. "

Claire eased her slowly to a standing position.

"I'll start Ma's egg whites," Ray said and slipped out the door.

Ray left earlier than necessary to pick up bags of ice, wine and soda pop, the cake Claire had ordered, and folding chairs from the funeral home.

Caroline, clean and lovely in her azure blue lounging pajamas, sat serenely in her high-backed chair. Claire had moved it near the doorway between the kitchen and living room, so she could supervise all the preparations.

Ray lifted the lid on the cake box and lowered it for her to see. "Is that the cassata cake, Ray? Oh look at the beautiful lettering. And those intertwined rings!" Overcome with emotion, she dabbed at her eyes with a thick wad of tissues.

Ray—too choked up for words— smiled at her with furrowed brows. *I hope all this excitement is not a bit much for her. Wait until she sees Aunt Peggy. Maybe we should not keep it a surprise that she's coming up from Florida again.*

Claire came in with folded tray tables under each arm.

"Did you bring the chairs, Ray? Let's set them up before we place these trays." She leaned them against the kitchen table.

"I have to hurry to get the ham before I go to the airp—." He interrupted himself. "—deli for the bread and salads." He and Claire exchanged knowing glances.

"Anyway, Marty and Rosie will be here in half an hour. They want to help; let them set up chairs, Claire. That's why they insisted on coming early." Ray showed the cake to his sister before placing it in the center of the table.

"Perfect," she said, half-looking at it. "Rosie's bringing Seven-Layer Salad, isn't that right, Ray? "And fruit gelatin, I believe." She moved the cake slightly to the left.

"What the heck is gelatin, Claire?" Ray quipped.

"Jello, Ray. J-E-L-L-O."

"Calm down; calm down." Ray patted her arm. "You're trying to do too much." He took the pack of paper napkins she was trying to open with her teeth and slit the cellophane with a paring knife. "I'll do the napkins; you take a break."

"Have a cold drink, Honey," Caroline said, taking a swallow of lemonade from her glass.

A loud knock at the front door stopped all conversation. Ray hurried toward a figure whose face was hidden by an over-sized bouquet of spring blossoms, and opened the storm door.

"Delivery for Ray and Heather," the man said and handed the enormous vase to Ray.

His arms reached only part way around the wide container, and he could barely carry it. He managed to make it to the kitchen counter where they could really see the gorgeous flowers.

"Who sent it?" Caroline asked as Ray searched for a card.

He pulled on a white envelope, bringing up the long plastic clip which held it.

Claire took a damp paper towel to bits of soil dropped on the floor.

"It's from everyone at school," Ray announced, smiling from ear to ear. He handed the card to Caroline.

"Congratulations to our favorite couple from all the Poore Pond School family," she read, her uneven voice full of pride.

"What a wonderful gift, Rayley." She looked at him with misty eyes. "It shows how much they think of you." Out came the tissues again.

"Let me see," Claire said, taking the card. She read it slowly. "That's nice, Ray. I'll find the right thank-you card to send them. That's really nice."

After much discussion, the flowers were placed on the child's chair that had belonged to Ray and Rory. Claire brought it from Ray's bedroom and put it dead center in front of the fireplace.

Caroline applauded when she and Ray lowered the bouquet carefully onto the chair. It seemed to transform the entire room.

"Now Rory will be with us at the party," Claire said. She saw Caroline pull out the tissues and added, "That little squirt always loved a party. Remember, Ma, how he'd drink himself sick from all the soda pop."

"That's the only time we had soda pop in the house, when you and Dad had a party." Ray laughed. "We were deprived kids."

Caroline laughed and cried and kept her smile for a long time.

Ray worried about Heather. She had not been herself at the party. Though obviously delighted with the festivities, she seemed to have little energy and even less appetite for most of the delicious food.

Before all the guests had gone, she asked Ray to take her home. Aunt Peggy managed to postpone her leaving by guiding her to sit on the front porch swing and engaging her in idle conversation. She propped her up with cushy pillows from the sofa and told stories about Ray and Rory as boys. She even managed to interest her in eating more food.

Soon after, Heather asked again to be taken home. She was so obviously exhausted that Ray left immediately. Claire and Aunt Peggy assembled portions of food in plastic containers for Heather and Jeremy, bagging them neatly for Ray to carry.

Caroline suggested she leave Jeremy with them for awhile, and Claire offered to bring him home in a couple hours. But Heather wanted him with her.

Ray settled them into their apartment, putting the food in the refrigerator and gifts in the living room. Jeremy went into his room to play with the set of soldiers Aunt Peggy had given him.

Ray took Heather by the hand and led her to the sofa.

He encircled her thin shoulders with his arms and sat holding her, neither speaking.

"Did I tell you I've been offered a full-time job at the pharmacy, Ray?" She told him, her voice so weak it frightened him.

"That's wonderful, Heather. But first we need to get you to a doctor. It's not like you to be this tired."

"I just need a good night's sleep, that's all. All this excitement and everything." She nestled into his neck. "I'll be fine in the morning."

He let her sleep in his arms for awhile. Then reluctantly he eased her into a prone position, covered her small figure with a chenille throw, and went to look in on Jeremy.

He did not leave the apartment until Jeremy, bathed and in clean pajamas, was sleeping soundly in his bed.

After writing a note asking her to call him when she awoke—no matter how late, he left Heather sleeping comfortably on the sofa.

The party was the main topic at the Sellers' breakfast table early Sunday morning. Everyone had a positive comment.

"I stayed up longer than I've been able to for months," Caroline said, her voice still uncharacteristically energetic.

"Well, I enjoyed meeting your Hope, Ray," Aunt Peggy said. "She was not at all what I expected; she's a nice person. And that son of hers—George—what a friendly, natural guy." She lifted her cup to meet the coffeepot Claire carried. "Are Hope and Theo a couple or what? He's a nice man, too. Sophisticated, but nice."

"Hope surprised me as well," Claire said, meeting Aunt Peggy's gaze. "She gave me an idea for a job I didn't know I was qualified for." Claire replaced the coffee carafe on its base and sat down again at the table.

"What job is that, Claire?" Caroline asked in a hopeful voice.

"Substitute teacher." She turned toward her mother. "Hope said there's a shortage of good subs, and all you need is a degree in anything to apply. It doesn't have to be an education degree."

Ray tried to envision Claire getting along with the kids at Poore Pond. "Do you think you might do it?"

"I think I might. The pay's not bad. And Hope said I could use her name as a reference." Claire smiled around the table.

Aunt Peggy answered the ringing phone and handed it to Ray. "It's Jeremy."

Ray, consumed with foreboding, carried the phone into the living room. "Hi Sport. How are you doing after all those cupcakes yesterday? How's your mother?"

"I'm fine, Ray."

The silent pause was deafening. Ray waited.

"My mom's okay. She wanted me to ask you to come over for lunch. Today. Around noon, she said. Can you make it?"

"Let me speak to Mom, Jeremy."

"She can't; she's in the shower." He chuckled.

"Just tell her I'll be there. I'll be there before noon." His heart pounded. "Tell her that, Jeremy. Bye Sport."

Heather seemed more her energetic self when Ray went to the apartment for lunch. She had fussed a lot with ham and turkey wraps and milkshakes, which she ate heartily, finishing in short order.

She offered chocolate mint candies for dessert and ate two of those.

Ray was relieved. He celebrated by insisting on clearing the table for her.

"I've definitely decided to take the job at the pharmacy," she announced as they sat at the clean kitchen table, enjoying the warm breeze blowing through the open double windows.

"When will you start?" Ray asked, folding and refolding his paper napkin.

"They need me to start as soon as possible." She drank from her glass of iced tea. "But I want to spend a week with Jeremy before I get bogged down with work."

"We were going to try to go fishing one of those days, remember?" Ray asked. "I'll be on summer hours, so I'll be free at three. We could go then." He peeled the paper off another chocolate mint and popped it into his mouth.

"Let's just plan on it then," she said, standing. "Let's sit on the sofa, Ray. I'm a little beat."

A feeling of dread came over him as he followed her into the living room. The apartment, though clean and full of sunlight, grew dull and dreary. *I wish Jeremy hadn't gone with the Bradfords to Robbie's game. We need him here cheering up the place.*

Heather lifted Ray's arm from her shoulder and stood.

"Oh, I almost forgot." She went to the kitchen and pulled a packet of papers from a drawer. "Here is Jeremy's day-camp schedule, Ray." She handed him the packet and sat down again.

"The camp bus comes at seven forty-five, and I leave for work at eight fifteen; so it's perfect." She turned to him and smiled.

"So you need me to meet his bus on Fridays and stay with him until six? Right?" Ray laughed. "That'll be great dad practice."

He picked up the television remote, and she slid his arm around her shoulder again.

I'll take Wednesday off; it's supposed to be sunny and in the seventies. Ray surfed to the History Channel and stared at old movies of Prohibition and bathtub gin. He took Heather's hand in his, intertwining their fingers. The place seemed bright again.

Monday was a typical last day of school, emotional and hectic. Many students asked to come back in the following weeks to help Ray carry the mounds of trash each classroom generated, to the huge dumpster.

Fifth graders, not only his former helpers but also others, came to say good-bye, promising to come back and visit him as middle-schoolers.

"You won't be too cool to come back to your elementary school?" he would ask.

"We will be, but we'll come anyway," they laughed.

Numerous children brought small gifts including: cupcakes, drawings, their faces in tiny school photographs, flavored coffees, key rings, pens, markers, packets of seeds.

Younger children hugged him; older ones shook his hand.

Fourth-grader Martin Purdue came to shake his hand, lost in his autism and saying nothing; but smiling genuinely the entire time.

Emmylou Parks, fifth-grader, came to give Ray a miniature molded figure of a shaggy-haired dog who resembled Ringer. She had made a tiny paper wreathe to hang around its neck and attached a thin, glue-stained ribbon banner that read: Never forget.

Ray stifled an urge to warn her to stay off the internet.

Jeremy came with a classmate to the office in the boiler room, proudly pointing out the framed photographs of himself and his mother. "Mr. Sellers is going to be my dad," he boasted, making Ray feel important.

The entire fifth-grade class was clapped out of the building, leaving the principal, teachers, staff members, and parents who had come to help honor the school and the students, both poignantly sad and tiredly happy.

After dismissal and good-bye waves to every busload and all the student walkers, Ray went to his office and sank into the desk chair to catch his breath. He checked his watch. Let's see. Did I tell Heather I would pick her up at 5:30 or 6:00? He scoured his desk for a note he may have written while he had her on the phone.

I know the ceremony starts at 7:00. But do the graduates have to be there at 6:00 or 6:30?

He dialed her apartment number. No answer. He dialed her cellular phone. No answer. *She's waiting outside for Jeremy's bus.* His palm slapped his forehead. *What was I thinking?*

I'll just be there at 5:30.

At four o' clock sharp, Ray walked through his door, stopping as Corinne's serene voice called him on the speaker. He headed to the office.

"Dr. Fleming needs to see you, Ray. That was such a lovely engagement party your family gave. They really are wonderful." She rose and stepped to Hope's door, opening it for him.

"Hi, Ray," Hope said, her voice sounding as weary as he felt. "I've changed my mind about the staff meeting tomorrow." She motioned for him to sit across the table from her, shifting stacks of report cards and teachers' goal reports to clear space between them.

"But it's all set up in the cafeteria, Hope." He glanced at her wall clock; his stomach tensed.

"But it's going to be hot tomorrow, ninety degrees. And it will be a long meeting." Her eyes bored into his. "We need an air-conditioned room." Her voice had a note of finality he had come to understand as a signal that this directive was not up for discussion.

"I'll see to it, Hope, early tomorrow morning, if you don't mind."

She rose, opening her mouth to speak.

He spoke before she could begin. "I have to get out of here right away. Heather graduates tonight." He stood, not looking at her.

"Oh heavens, Ray." She cupped her cheeks in both hands. "I had it in my mind that the ceremony was next week." Rummaging for her pocket calendar, she added, "I know I marked it on my calendar." She thumbed through the pages. "Here it is, plain as day, Monday, June sixth."

"I am sorry, Ray," she said, turning pleading eyes to his. She waved him away with her hand. "Go on; we'll worry about meetings tomorrow." Grabbing her purse, she followed him out the door.

Thirty-eight graduates in their crisp white lab coats sat on the stage in the small auditorium at Riverwalk Community College.

Ray and Claire sat on either side of Jeremy, who held the new coloring book and box of markers Claire had given him. Claire had Ray's dozen long-stemmed red roses on her lap. They watched people still filing in and taking seats although it was nearly seven o'clock.

Hope slipped into a seat at the back of the room, her arms full of long-stemmed white roses. Ray and Claire, watching her, exchanged smiles.

"Look!" Jeremy cried. "Dr. Fleming has the same flowers we have. Only they're white!" He poked Ray, then Claire.

The house lights went down, leaving the stage warmly lit.

Two men in suits closed the entrance doors.

Ray kept watching Heather in the front row, reading her body language. *She seems nervous.* He tried to send a subtle wave, but she did not seem to see it.

She studied the program.

The college president spoke briefly, then the dean of the health careers department. Ray felt too excited to focus on their words. The director of the pharmacy assistant program spoke next, engaging Ray and most of the audience with her easy-going style and personal anecdotes about the students.

"These pharmacy assistants can count pills with the precision you hope coin counters in the U.S. Mint can match." Everyone laughed and applauded.

"They understand those twenty-syllable names of drugs and know the generic equivalents." More applause. "And most amazing of all, they can pronounce them."

Ray found himself laughing along though his mind was busy picturing Heather performing each task the director described.

She announced the presentation of diplomas and began to call names.

Fairly consumed with excitement, he followed the program, tracing with his finger each person's name who came forward to receive a diploma. As his finger moved closer to Heather's name, he could barely breathe.

She stood, smiled broadly, and walked to the podium with her old energy. Wearing unstoppable smiles, Ray, Claire, and Jeremy applauded exuberantly.

Jeremy and Ray held the double doors for Heather and Claire and a few others following them. Waiting graciously, Ray glanced into the street where a line of cars filed out behind a black limousine, their tail lights glowing like pairs of dragons' eyes. Ray noticed the lavish fins on the limousine. *There's a vintage car like Davey's.*

To celebrate the occasion, Ray stopped at Bumper's for ice cream. They each ordered the house specialty, hot-fudge-pistachio sundaes.

Some of Heather's fellow-graduates came in with their families, and they engaged in happy conversation across the room. Pop Bertie, picking up on their celebratory mood, applauded the graduates and offered them free sundaes. Still grinning, he fed quarters into the player piano; and the moving keys played ragtime music.

One of the graduates, a young bearded man, pulled his wife onto the floor, and they began a lively dance. Another took the floor with her teen-aged son.

Heather's eyes met Ray's invitingly; he looked at the dancers and shook his head. They laughed.

"May I have this dance, Mrs. Baker?" a deep voice called from behind the corner booth. Everyone at the table turned as a pair of black cowboy boots extended onto the floor, and a tall figure unfolded himself to a standing position.

"Oh no," Heather whispered, her face contorted, her eyes on Claire.

Claire took in a rush of air. Jeremy stared at his mother. Ray's chest burned.

Davey sauntered over to them. "I understand congratulations are in order here." He looked at Ray and offered his hand. Ray ignored it and stood.

"Mom graduated, Dad!" Jeremy cried from his seat beside Claire. "She's a pharmacist now."

Claire sat stiffly, staring at the floor.

A new song began; Davey glanced at the dancers. He turned to Heather. "What about it Heather? Will you honor me with a little dance?" He leaned past Ray to get closer.

Ray and Heather, taking in his smoky breath, made eye contact. *There is no alcohol on his breath.*

Davey stared at her. "For old time's sake?" He waited. "For best wishes in your new career?" He reached inside his jacket and pulled out a white envelope, handing it to her.

Heather looked away. Davey turned to Jeremy and handed the envelope to him. "Give this to your mom, Son."

He went to the counter, folded his long torso onto a stool, and placed an order with the clerk.

A pall fell over the Sellers' table. Jeremy tried to start a conversation. "Look, Pop Bertie is playing more songs."

Heather kept glancing toward Davey.

Ray looked sadly his way.

Claire continued to stare at the floor, but her body softened. The sound of tinkling piano keys filled the room.

Heather rose and looked into Ray's eyes. "Excuse me, Ray. I'll just go settle this." She nodded toward Davey.

Ray stood and watched her go. Claire looked aghast.

They watched her sit down next to him, shoulder to shoulder, their heads bobbing as they talked.

Ray's heart pounded. *I should go over there. This is my business, too.* He watched as they stood and began to dance tentatively, Heather distancing her body from his.

Heat rose in Ray's chest. He could not bear to see Davey's arms around her.

The music stopped; they hugged briefly. Heather turned and beckoned to Jeremy who ran eagerly to them. Davey bent down and hugged his son. Jeremy hugged him back, giving his all.

Davey will always be there in the background, intruding on our lives.

Ray looked at his sister, watching the scene with warm eyes.

Heather led her son and his father to the table. Glancing at Davey, she stepped back.

"Ray, I understand you and Heather are engaged to be married."

Abruptly Ray stood. "That's right, Davey."

He offered his hand to Ray. "Congratulations, Buddy." They managed a genuine handshake.

He looked squarely at Ray. "She loves you. Jeremy idolizes you."

Davey adjusted his shoulders. Breathing deeply, he exhaled and said. "I'm going to honor that. I'm sorry I was such a jerk."

"And Claire," he leaned toward her. "I'm sorry I was so rotten to you. You didn't deserve it."

Claire, though taken aback, looked at him with soft eyes. "I forgive you, Davey. I wasn't always the most cheerful date in town." She smiled, extending her hand; he grasped it briefly.

"How's Caroline?" he added. "Give her my best."

Giving a small salute, he turned on his heel and left.

"Bye, Dad," Jeremy called after him.

A cloud of poignant relief hung over the little party. They gathered their things, waved goodbye to Pop Bertie and the remaining graduates.

No one spoke as they walked to the van. Heather slipped her arm around Ray's waist; he held her closely, feeling her diminished energy.

Claire held Jeremy's hand and kept her arm around his shoulders as they drove home.

CHAPTER TWENTY-FOUR—THE BRADFORDS

Helsi, pulling on cropped jeans and T-shirt, heard the phone ring twice. *That's Jake's daily call.* She ignored the tiny knot in her stomach. *When is this thing going to settle?*

She stepped into thong sandals and looked in on the children to see which ones were still sleeping. Rachel and Robbie's beds were empty.

She found them downstairs on the living-room floor, facing the television, bowls of dry cereal in their laps.

"Dad's on the phone with that lawyer guy again," Robbie announced, searching his mother's eyes. "Why does he have to call every morning?"

"He's helping Dad fix his mistake," Rachel said, looking authoritatively at her brother.

Helsi dropped onto the sofa. *Where did she get that?* Her mind began to fill with terrible images of Ian behind bars and the children crying inconsolably.

"What does that mean, Dad's mistake?" Robbie asked defiantly, grimacing at his sister.

Rachel tilted her head toward him and, hand on hip, set him straight. "Dad wasn't thinking about the law and he broke it. Now he has to work hard to fix things."

"What things?" Robbie looked at Helsi with wide eyes. "Which one did he break? Did he drive too fast?"

Where did Rachel get that? Did Ian tell her that?

"We can't talk about it now, Sweetie." Helsi took the child's empty bowl. "Let's go to the table and have a proper breakfast. Come on, Rachel, you too."

She heard Ian say goodbye on the phone and sighed with relief. Stepping into the laundry room, she found him perched atop the washer like a teenager, dialing another number.

Minutes later, Ian rushed past Helsi who was scrambling eggs for a still-sleepy Dylan sitting silently at the table.

"I have to go, Babe," Ian said, brushing her cheek with his lips. "The chief wants to see me now."

She quickly scooped the eggs onto a plate and handed it to Dylan.

"What about?" she asked, following him out the door.

"He met with the prosecutor yesterday, wants to fill me in."

"Did he give you any clues?" She stood next to the van, and he lowered the window.

"No. None." He waved as he backed out the drive.

"Toast, please, Mommy." Dylan said when she entered the kitchen. She put two slices of bread in the toaster oven.

What did Jake tell us? Ian could give up a jury trial and still have a trial? Or he could plead guilty or no contest and then do a plea bargain? But didn't he say that meant the prosecutor would really throw the book at him?

Her head was spinning. She stared out the window at the Meadow house and thought of Mercedes and Herb.

The toaster oven's signal buzzed; she removed the toast and buttered it, placing it before Dylan without a word.

"Mommy, I don't feel so good," said Dylan, his voice smaller than usual.

She brewed a cup of weak tea, added honey and lemon; and taking the boy on her lap, she held him while he sipped it.

After drinking half the tea, he slid to the floor and smiled at her.

"I feel better now." He placed the cup in the sink, headed to the staircase. "I'm getting dressed, Mom. Where are my shorts?"

Dylan's picking up on the tension here; he just needed a little TLC. Anxiety rose in her stomach.

"There's a box of summer clothes in the hall, Dylan. I just took it down from the attic yesterday. Look in there."

He dashed upstairs. Within minutes he returned, wearing wrinkled, too-tight cargo shorts, his skinny, white legs crying for the sun's touch.

"Is Jeremy coming over today?"

"Not this week; his mom's on vacation. He's staying with her," Rachel shrilled from the next room.

Helsi looked at Rachel, shaking her head. *I hope Heather is all right. She did not look well at her graduation. And she left the engagement party early.*

Dylan found his catcher's mitt and opened the side door. "Come on, Robbie. Let's go outside." Robbie and Rachel ran upstairs to dress.

Helsi rinsed dishes at the sink. Looking out the window at the Meadow house, she thought she saw Phyllis quickly gather the paper from the front step. *She must be home now. I should visit her, take a dish of food or something.*

Herb came out the door, his arms around a large, obviously heavy carton. She watched him open the trunk of his big car and place the box inside. Then Phyllis reappeared, carrying a similar-sized carton, which she placed in Herb's trunk.

Curious, Helsi wiped her hands and ran outside. She crossed the street, waving at Herb and Phyllis who did not seem to see her.

"Hello, Herb, Phyllis," she called.

They turned and hurried into the house.

Helsi walked toward their front door, stopping at the first step. *No, this is probably a bad time. I'll check back later.*

Sounds of the children at their games floated up through the open bedroom window where Helsi sat at the computer, enjoying a rare moment of normalcy.

Sean and Lucy were both at the junior high school; he helping inventory and organize track equipment, she, cleaning files in the school newspaper room.

Thoughts of sticky summer days when all five Bradford children would complain of boredom made this moment more wonderful.

Ian could be joining them in the boredom department if the chief suspends him all summer. Or worse yet, lets him go.

Arching her back and stretching her shoulders, she then gave full attention to the list of websites for cleaning companies. She scrolled down until she found a site that looked like the kind of service she planned to start and clicked on it.

After visiting more than twenty sites and taking pages of notes, she sat back and mentally reviewed the business plan she'd been carrying around in her mind. *I think I'm ready to write it out now. But I don't really know what a business plan looks like.*

Ian did not appear for lunch, so she and the children had grilled-cheese sandwiches and tomato soup without him. She left portions for him in the microwave and cleaned the kitchen.

The phone rang early in the afternoon. Helsi finished folding the towel she had pulled from the dryer and went to answer it.

She put the receiver to her ear and heard Robbie call out loudly, "Mom, Dad's on the phone."

"I have it, Robbie." She waited. "Ian?"

"I'll be home soon, Son." A click told them the boy had hung up the phone.

"Where are you, Ian?" Helsi asked, flooded with fear.

"I'm just leaving Jake's office, Helsi." A chill went through her when she heard his disheartened voice.

"We missed you at lunch. Come home as soon as you can, Ian."

"I'm leaving now, Helsi. Save me some lunch, will you?"

Robbie, Dylan, and Rachel carried recycled milk jugs filled with lemonade down the street where the Omar kids had set up a stand on their corner lot.

Placing a legal pad on the kitchen table, Helsi returned to her business plan, trying to write as fast as thoughts came to her. She preferred to clean houses but kept having nagging thoughts about cleaning offices instead. Rates were higher for offices than homes, at least on the websites she visited. She believed schedules were more fixed as well.

And I certainly would not have to worry about fitting in with the family. There would be no personal relationship at all. I don't know.

She heard Ian's car in the drive and went to the door.

"I hope you have food for me, Hon," he said, kissing her cheek. "My stomach is roaring."

He seemed calmer than she expected.

She sat across from him and watched him eat his lunch, straining to comprehend the bits of information he gave her between swallows.

He told his wife that Jake said the judge would accept a plea bargain if he pleads guilty, and he would be fined and sentenced to prison or a jail term.

Helsi, horrified, moaned and closed her eyes. *Here it comes. We have to face it now.*

Finally, she looked into his eyes but saw none of the pain he had to be feeling.

"Prison or a jail term? Oh Ian." She took his hand.

"It's not what you think, Helsi." He took the last bite of his grilled cheese sandwich, scooped the soup bowl dry, and sat back, swallowing.

"Jake says I won't be locked up. The judge will put me on community supervision."

"What does that mean?" she asked, her ears acutely attuned.

"Probation, Hon. Probation. Community supervision is just a nice word for probation." He mopped his mouth with a paper napkin and crumpled it onto his plate.

"So you have a probation officer you have to meet with regularly?"

"That's only a small part of it." He looked around the kitchen. "Do you have any dessert? I'm still hungry."

Helsi brought him the last serving of banana pudding from the refrigerator. "I was secretly saving this for myself, Ian. Enjoy."

She smiled and sat back down. "What else?"

He explained the rules of probation, including: being prohibited from leaving the state, being required to notify the probation officer before changing addresses, attending counseling, etc.

"If I fail any of the requirements, off to jail I go." He smiled sardonically.

Helsi was afraid to ask about his job although she felt desperate to talk of money. *How big a fine? Now's not the time.*

"I'll be suspended from my job until probation is over," he said, the anguish he'd kept at bay now creeping into his voice. He did not look at her but scraped the bottom of the pudding dish with a spoon, studying it intensely.

Helsi stood. "We don't have to talk about this now, Ian. You should relax. We'll talk about it later."

"Where are the kids?" Helsi told him and wondered aloud why the little ones weren't back from selling their lemonade.

At that moment, Robbie burst in with two empty jugs and asked for refills. "The daycare kids are buying us out. And the teachers," he announced, laughing with delight. "Hi, Dad." He went to his father and hugged him.

"Where'd you find them, Son?" Ian asked, looking less tense.

"They're walking. The whole class all over the sidewalks." He watched his mother shake the jugs, mixing the lemonade. "The teacher said they're on a walking field trip to the park."

He carried a jug in each hand, stopping at the door. "There's another class coming. They told us to be ready." Ian held the door open for him.

He smiled up at his father. "Already we have twelve dollars and thirty-two cents." Bending under the weight of the jugs, he hobbled happily through the door and down the street.

Helsi lay awake thinking in dollar figures. She and Ian had talked at length after the children went to bed. Not only would the family be living on her paltry income alone, there were probation charges as well as the fine. *I cannot believe Ian must pay fifty dollars a month service charge to be on probation. Twenty-two dollars per visit to a counselor—and he's required to go every month?*

She looked over at her husband, sleeping soundly, breathing evenly.

I don't have a choice now; I've got to start that cleaning business. Right away. And pray that Dr. Fleming will pay me to keep working for Heather a little longer.

She tried to calm herself by counting her blessings, starting with the hope that Ian would not go to jail. She prayed softly that he wouldn't. *At least Chief said the formal report and reprimand would be expunged from Ian's file once he successfully completed probation.* She whispered prayers of gratitude for that.

Ian woke her with a mug of coffee. She felt as if she had slept only minutes.

"It's still dark, Ian. What time is it?" She sat up and took the coffee from him, glancing at the clock. "Three forty? It's the middle of the night! Why are we up?" She sipped the hot coffee.

Ian sat on the bed. "Helsi," the seriousness in his tone frightened her. "There's something strange going on across the street," he whispered.

"Across the street? You mean at the Meadow house?"

"Yes. Cars keep going and coming. They don't turn on their headlights, sort of creep down the street."

"Can you see who's driving? Is it Herb? Or Phyllis?" She rose and went to the window. The house was completely dark. There were no cars in the drive.

She turned and sat on the bed beside Ian. "Just today, Ian, I saw Phyllis and Herb outside and started over there. I called out to them, but they ignored me and hurried into the house."

"There's something crazy going on over there." Ian went to the window. "It's all dark." He stared. A small, white mass floated across the front lawn. "Snowball's out there running around."

"Snowball? Phyllis's cat?" Helsi joined him at the window. "She hovers over that cat almost as much as she hovers over Mercedes. I can't believe she let Snowball out this late."

Later that morning, they found Snowball stretched across their front step. Ian opened the door to get the paper, and the cat crept inside. "Look, Ian, she's lost her red collar."

Three days later the suspense ended. Ian and Jake met at length with the prosecutor and worked out the terms of the plea bargain.

Jake had strategically scheduled the meeting, so that they would go before a judge known for his loaded docket and ability to cut through red tape; thus, speeding up the process.

The judge readily accepted the plea offer they had negotiated with the prosecutor. Ian received a five-hundred-dollar fine, an order to pay three-hundred dollars in court costs, and six- months' probation.

Terms of the plea bargain required him to disclose names of individuals he associated with in his brief dealings with Argosy: his classmate, Gene Galbraith; operations manager, Lawrence—whose last name turned out to be Metcalf—according to a police file photograph Ian identified; and warehouse supervisor, Wally. There were no file photographs resembling Wally, so Ian gave a description of him and his dog Ripper.

Probation terms and costs matched those Jake had outlined for him and he had shared with Helsi.

Helsi had spent the three days jump-starting her business. She used their credit card to purchase cleaning supplies and was relieved to learn she could also use it to place an ad in a local business publication mailed in bulk to all area businesses.

With no time to be creative, she applied for a business license for Helsi's Cleaning Service. Later, she would think of a more unforgettable company name.

Sean helped her design a logo on the computer and print out rather professional-looking flyers, which he and his friends placed on windshields in parking lots around town.

By court day, she had two firm accounts to clean small office buildings, the keys and one-year contracts in her hand.

Both Ian and Helsi felt a sense of relief once his sentence had been imposed and conditions were clear. Tension drained from them as they sat in lawn chairs and watched the children play volleyball in the backyard. Lucy and Sean had pounded the unsubstantial stakes in the ground and raised the equally flimsy net, a ritual marking the beginning of summer at the Bradford house.

It was obvious that the children sensed the absence of tension in their parents. They seemed content to be together as a family, enjoying the warm weather and bickering little.

When the ice cream truck sounded its bell down the street—another summer ritual, Lucy proudly used her babysitting money to treat everyone.

Snowball, the Meadow family's cat, planted himself at their feet and watched them lick their cones. Helsi had given in to the children and bought cat food, agreeing to look after him until his owners returned from wherever they had gone.

Ian, wiping ice cream from his chin with his hand, looked at Helsi and smiled. "I'm proud of you for stepping up with that business so soon, Hon."

"I've been planning it for months, Ian. This tragic event gave me the courage I needed to finally just do it." She furrowed her brow and looked across the lawn at the kids.

"Well, I can help you, you know." Ian said. "With the cleaning." His eyes shone with good intentions.

"But Ian, I need you to be home with the kids when I'm on a job." She turned to look at him. "You weren't thinking we would leave Sean or Lucy in charge, were you?"

"Well, yes. I kind of thought that. They do all right babysitting now and then." He rubbed his bare leg and smoothed his khaki shorts.

"That's now and then. We're talking about several nights a week, hopefully five once I get going." Their eyes met, and she saw the hurt in his.

"Just a thought," he said, looking away.

"I'm not worried at all about the cleaning end of it. I know how to clean." She touched his forearm. "What really scares me is the business end. I know nothing about that."

"You're smart, Helsi; you can learn," he said, his voice flat and distant.

"I'm going to read the paper, maybe find some odd jobs I can do." He rose and went into the house.

She ran into the house after him. "Ian. Ian, this is the perfect opportunity for you to take extra classes this summer."

"What would be the point?" He looked at her with cold eyes. "A convicted felon wouldn't have a chance of getting hired as a physician's assistant." He turned his back to her.

"You could take daytime classes and be home at night when I'm cleaning offices," she pointed out, ignoring his fatalism. She caught his arm. "It would be smarter to focus on bettering yourself than to shrivel with self-pity." Surprised at her mercilessness, she shot him a sidelong glance.

"I'm not sure I could concentrate on studying, Helsi, with all my underbelly obligations, all the legal hoops I'll be jumping through with the other low-lifes." He looked away, his chin quivering.

"Ian, you have five children. What choice do you have?"

Their eyes locked and held.

CHAPTER TWENTY-FIVE—HOPE

Hope felt the chill of the empty building now that the school year had ended. She could not stop thinking about Mercedes Meadow. She did not understand how the child could have missed school the day of the special assembly completing the months-long, school-wide Anti-Bullying Campaign.

It was her idea to include the skits. They were such a perfect addition; and since they were written by small groups of students, they were a perfect way to see how much the children understood about bullying and their part in stopping it.

In her mind's eye, Hope could see the small girl at dress rehearsal in a new blue, pleated skirt and grown-up dress shoes.

How could she have been absent that day? She wrote the skit for her class. She had the lead part. She was the narrator.

I should think Herb would have made every effort to get her here. If that were not possible, why wouldn't he at least call in? Surely, he doesn't want any more trouble than he already has.

Corinne, routinely following district absence-verification policy, had tried all morning to reach the family; but the only response was a busy signal every time.

"How could the line be busy all morning?" Corinne asked, furrowing her brow. "Unless someone had taken it off the hook."

In compliance with the policy directive, she had notified police and reported that the absence could not be verified though many attempts had been made.

The assembly had gone on without Mercedes, classmate and co-writer Patti Densford replacing her as both narrator and a character in the class skit.

Though Patti did not display the captivating stage presence everyone admired in Mercedes, she did a fine job, pleasing the audience with her gift for spontaneous humor.

While she waited for a follow-up visit from police, Hope recalled that the Bradfords lived across the street from the Meadow family and dialed their home number. She thought of the day Helsi Bradford came to verify that her name was on Mercedes' emergency list.

Ian's deep voice greeted her, reminding Hope of his brush with the law. She was relieved that he had not been incarcerated.

"Hello, Mr. Bradford—Ian," she said and asked him if he knew what had happened to Mercedes' family.

"Helsi tried to phone them and just kept getting busy signals." Ian offered. He told her about the strange goings on one night and how he had seen no signs of life over there since. "Their cat is still in the neighborhood." He chuckled. "Our kids have been feeding him."

Hope—pondering the situation—kept silent.

"The police were here a few minutes ago," Ian continued. "I told them what little we knew."

Corinne stood at her door mouthing the words: The police are here.

"Thanks anyway, Ian. Goodbye."

"Oh, Dr. Fleming. I'll stop in to see you next week," he said, his voice suddenly tense. "I want to update you on my day in court."

"All right, Ian. Goodbye."

"Obviously, they left in the night, Dr. Fleming," Officer Gregory said as they sat in Hope's office. "All the signs point to it."

Crackling sounds came from his mobile receiver; he stepped out to talk to his colleague who sat in the cruiser, receiving radio information from Champion City.

Preoccupied, Hope sauntered to Corinne's desk and stared vacantly as the secretary put away files and papers, preparing to end her workday.

Where is Phyllis? Herb was so upset that day.

Both officers returned and walked into Hope's room ahead of her. She closed the door, and they all sat down at the small table.

Officer Kelly looked at his colleague.

"It seems that Champion City authorities have been trying to locate Phyllis Meadow," Officer Gregory began. "They closed in on her just a few days ago. They had her in for questioning." He looked at Hope's glazed eyes and chose his words carefully.

"Doctors there accused her of doing harm to her child." He lowered his voice. "They have actually filed charges."

He stood. "The woman's in big trouble. I can't believe you folks didn't get wind of it."

Hope felt her face color and lowered her head.

Officer Kelly rose and followed his colleague to the door. He turned to Hope and said, "The school will get a report."

She watched them leave then said goodbye to Corinne.

Now she stood frozen in the quiet office. *Did Herb take Mercedes away because Phyllis was in custody, perhaps to a relative's house?*

I should have done more for him that day in my office.

She straightened the contents of her inbox and placed stray pens and pencils in their cup. She drew her purse from the desk drawer.

All I did was pass the poor man onto Bluewave. She's the one who tried to help him. But what could I have done?

She locked the office and walked past rows of trash cans overflowing with end-of-year discards. Debris swept into piles littered the lobby, annoying her. *Why can't Ray and Rosie follow through and lift those piles into the trash? Just because classes are over doesn't mean the school cannot look tidy.*

Theo gave Hope just the sort of Saturday night that would calm her. He prepared a simple, three-course, pork-tenderloin dinner for them in his elegant apartment and, sensing her emotional overload, banned any talk of problems.

Sipping exotic, fruity cocktails that he had chosen to compliment the pork dinner, they laughed playfully at every subject that arose, even breaking their own rule against making unkind remarks about the less fortunate.

They toasted the staff at the shelter. They toasted the clients.

"We should give the place an impressive name, Hope," Theo said as he drew the chilled shaker from the refrigerator. "Something that makes it sound first rate."

"Do you mean a euphemistic name? A name that implies it is something other than what it is?" Hope asked, a smile spreading across her face.

"Exactly. Just like you educators do." He smiled back at her, his eyes twinkling. "For example, take the word academy. It typically implies a prestigious school, either one with a rigorous, classical course of study or one with a specialized training program." He refilled their glasses.

"But you educators brazenly began using it to name your alternative schools where students with conformity problems were sent." He returned the shaker to the refrigerator. "Millwood Academy sounds like an exclusive institution. Much pleasanter than Millwood School for Incorrigibles" They both laughed.

"Or Millwood School of Last Resort," he continued. They laughed uproariously.

Hope rose from the sofa and moved to Theo. Suddenly serious, she said, "But you know those names are an attempt to dignify a situation, present a positive image." Her eyes challenged him to disagree.

"How about calling the shelter Fresh Start Academy?" she asked.

"Or Face-Yourself Factory," Theo said, ignoring her sincerity.

She studied his face. *I'm not sure I like this side of Theo.*

In the end, they had made irreverent jokes, not only about schools and their politics, but also about boards of trustees and homelessness as a lifestyle choice.

Poking fun at themselves, they mocked control-freak school principals and smoke-and-mirrors consultants. They abandoned themselves to the therapy of laughter gone wild.

Physically spent, they reclined on Theo's red velour sofa and propped their feet on the glass-topped cocktail table.

Theo brought a tray of cappuccino and tiny, rich pastries into the living room where they nibbled and drank without speaking, both savoring the moment.

He put on a new album of The Metropolitan Opera performing Don Quixote and settled into a soft embrace with Hope, letting the beautiful voices wash over them as they drew pleasure and strength from the closeness of their bodies.

Finally, she asked to be taken home. They kissed in the car and reluctantly said goodbye at her front door.

At last in bed, blanketed by a silken duvet and the warm glow of her feelings for Theo, she fell deliciously to sleep.

Hope needed a lazy Sunday. The entire week she had been deluged with serious problems of other people—people she cared about deeply.

Still basking in the glow of a magical Saturday night with Theo, she tried to hold on to that mood.

The day became a blur of resting, reading, snacking, and ignoring the house phone. She would have answered her cellular phone in case George or Theo called, but she never heard it ring.

Monday morning Hope and Corinne tended to various end-of-year duties, greeting the occasional teachers who came to finish closing their classrooms.

Ray and Rosy passed through the office from time to time, joking about how easy their jobs would be if Hope could just keep the teachers and kids away all year.

Everyone laughingly agreed, knowing in their hearts that the teachers and the children gave real meaning to their jobs. Because of them, they felt that what they did was honorable work.

The week passed in a flurry of year-end tasks and preparation for the new academic year.

Friday, Corinne had gone home for the day. Ray and Rosie's shift ended at three. There were no teachers' cars in the parking lot.

Hope looked at her watch and decided to put in a few hours of work before meeting Theo.

Just last evening he had called George and her to tell them the president of the board of trustees had contacted him about a few concerns. He suggested the three of them gather for an early dinner to discuss those issues, so he could take their input to the six-thirty trustees' meeting.

But George was en route to a PolyFlem customer in Sebring with a rush delivery of essential materials to duplicate the order that had been lost in transit.

They would meet without him.

Hope sat at her desk and signed a stack of purchase orders for supplies and textbooks to use at the start of next school year. She completed the stack and carried it to Corinne's desk.

She walked to the table and surveyed the piles of student folders, grouped according to next year's classes and teachers. She scanned the student rosters atop each pile, looking for last-minute changes made after she had approved the lists.

Vicki Perry's name had been neatly lined out and Bluewave Stonecipher's written next to it in Corinne's precise manuscript.

I'm so glad the school board decided to give Bluewave a full-time contract. She's an outstanding teacher. Even Vicki said she would feel better about giving up her class to be a full-time mom if Bluewave could be her replacement.

She noted the names of two pairs of students who had been traded from one class to another, recognizing them from teacher-request notes parents had sent in. She had seen the notes atop papers filling her inbox.

The teachers—knowing how Hope felt about allowing parental requests to skew the carefully constructed, collaborative lists—were careful to place question marks after the changes. They also included short profiles of the students to help her with final decisions.

She sorted through damaged books in the rebind box, looking for any that might hold up for one more year. Finding none, she looked at the clock.

She had just enough time to stop in the faculty lavatory and freshen up.

As Hope approached the table in the dimly lit restaurant, Theodore stood to greet her. His kiss, though quick, was fervent. It sent a fleeting thrill through her entire body.

"How was your day, Hope?" he asked as she took the chair he held for her. He slid it effortlessly toward the table.

"It was a picnic compared to the week as a whole," she said flatly. She placed her hand on his forearm. "What is all this fuss about the board?"

Theodore sat down and arranged his napkin on his lap. He released the lower button of his jacket.

"It seems they want more accountability from the center," he said, his eyes meeting hers.

"What? Financial accountability?" Hope shrilled. "They're getting regular financial statements, aren't they?"

"Yes, they are." Theo looked toward the waiter and nodded briefly.

"They want accountability on the success rate: the progress with clients who are receiving all those psychological services."

"So the trigger was that forty percent of the budget for fifteen people." Hope said. "Is that what caught their attention?" She smiled at the waiter.

"Exactly," Theo said. "Are you having the salmon again, Hope?"

She chose the almond-crusted scrod, Theo, prime rib.

The waiter left and they sat back with their wineglasses.

"We've been operational only a few months, Theo. What sort of progress could be measured in that brief a time?" Hope asked, placing her wineglass on the table.

"None at all, of course." He leaned toward her. "The board wants to make sure we have assessment procedures in place, that's all." He sat back to allow the waiter to place a salad before him.

Hope looked approvingly at her greens and agreed to a smattering of flaked cheese. She positioned her fork to begin and looked again at Theo.

"Then they are just doing their job," she said.

"That's right. They are just doing their job," Theo echoed.

Throughout the dinner, they chatted about many things; but the conversation always made its way back to the center.

"Belva wants to volunteer this summer," Hope said, toying with her fork at the salad remains. "She has a background in guidance and counseling, actual experience—not just the few courses principals are required to take."

"Then we should quickly sign her up before she changes her mind. We certainly don't need any more paid staff," Theo remarked with a smile.

Their plates arrived and they ate at a leisurely pace, chatting about safe, pleasant matters throughout the meal.

Hope finished the rich dessert; she placed her spoon on the saucer and sat back, sighing deeply.

Theo signaled the waiter to bring coffee. Momentarily, he came with a pot of steaming brew—Theo's special preference—and filled their cups.

She added a raw sugar cube and droplet of cream, stirred them in, and drank blissfully.

Touching Theo's forearm, she looked at him with soulful eyes. "Theo, I must tell you how I appreciate your friendship, your presence." Her voice thickened.

He took her hand. "I would like to think that what we have is more than friendship, Hope." He stared into her eyes.

"Oh, it is. Much more," she said, her eyes moist. "But you make everything seem all right—bearable. You would not believe the day I've had. The week I've had. It has been hellish." She looked away.

Turning back to him, she added, "And just to be here in this lovely setting with you looking after me so well—it's wonderful."

"Exactly what has been the most hellish event in your week?" he asked, still holding her hand tightly.

She told him about Mercedes, the charges against Phyllis, and her fears for the family.

She described Ian's cut in pay and hours, his turning to illegal avenues to bring in more income, how he and Helsi worked so hard for their children.

She could not stop the flow of words. Every problem she had recently faced spilled onto Theo.

He continued listening with full attention, looking at her with patient, loving eyes.

"I feel dreadful when people I know personally fall into the hands of law enforcement," she said. "How do they ever get out? How do they ever get their lives back?" She pulled a folded tissue from her bag and dabbed her eyes.

She looked at the ceiling. "How will I ever get my life back if Frederick's lawyers manage to file charges against me?"

She turned and faced him squarely. "That's what they're trying to do, you know. Charge me with embezzlement."

Theo shifted his hips and raised his chin.

Her eyes desperate, she continued, "I'll be forever trapped in the legal system!"

"What are you talking about, Hope?" He furrowed his brow. "What embezzlement? You? How could anyone charge you with embezzlement?"

"Because I am an embezzler!" She moistened her lips and met his eyes briefly. "A long time ago when I was very young, I—acquired money—fraudulently." She dropped her chin. "A lot of money." She buried her face in her hands.

The silence was deafening.

Finally, she looked up, and her eyes met Theo's withering face. He gently let go her hand.

What have I said? Oh, what have I done?

Hope slept little, if at all. She rose well before dawn; showered; dressed in well-fitting, white-gabardine pants and a colorful rich-girl-print tee-shirt and leather sandals.

Arriving at the homeless center before the residents' breakfast had begun, she went to the kitchens. The two cooks were preparing food and offered her coffee and hot cinnamon buns.

Ignoring her usual strategic eating habits, she took both. She sat on a stool at one of the stainless-steel prep tables and with uncharacteristic abandon, ate two of the cinnamon buns.

Hearing the shuffle of feet behind her, she turned and saw George. He wore rumpled khakis with a shapeless polo and slip-on sandals; his hair was disheveled.

"Hi, Mom. Why are you here so early?" He leaned to kiss her, sending waves of putrid breath at her face.

"George, you look as if you just rolled out of bed?" She fanned out her hands, palms up, for emphasis. "Are you all right?"

"I'm fine, Mom." He rubbed his unshaven chin. "And actually I did just roll out of bed." His eyes twinkled mischievously above his smile.

She sent him a stricken look and abruptly stood. "Don't tell me, George Michael Fleming, that you slept here on the premises—with the residents!" She flung her arms toward the floor.

She sighed heavily, a pained expression covering her face. "I cannot bear this," she said, her voice fading as her chin dropped.

She took a moment to gather herself. Then nose in the air, she said sharply, "What earthly reason could you have for sleeping in this shelter with these dangerous derelicts?"

George stared at her, his face blank. He took the stool next to her.

What if he's had a falling out with his father? Heat rose in her chest. *It would be just like Michael to throw him out. For no good reason.*

Her eyes softened, and she placed her hand gently on his arm. "What's happened, Son?" She rose, hovering over him. "Has your father dismissed you?"

"Nothing's happened, Mom." He stood. "And if by dismissed you mean thrown me out, no, Dad has not thrown me out." He looked away.

"Come on, I'll show you where I sleep—where I slept last night." He started toward the back hall, Hope following him with scorn in her steps.

He led her past the classrooms, past the dining room, and to the locked door of the front office. She waited while he pulled keys from his pocket and unlocked it.

She saw at once, protruding from behind the massive desk, the tip of a folding cot and rumpled bed linens. She walked briskly to it and instinctively began straightening a blanket, a sheet, plumping a pillow.

George watched in silence until she finished.

She smoothed the fitted sheet, covered half of it with the folded blanket; then sat down on it and stared up at him.

"All right. Let's have it, George, the whole story." She patted the mattress beside her. "Sit down."

He rolled the desk chair near the cot and sat in it.

"You are not going to like the story, Mom." He looked deeply into her eyes. "I don't like it either."

He told her, as passively as if he were telling her the time of day, that Brooke Ferris had moved into Michael's condominium.

"You can't mean Brooke, our social worker?"

"The very same," he said, his face unreadable.

Hope lifted her chin, her eyes moving sideways though her face remained fixed on his. *How on earth did those two hook up? What would macho Michael see in that intellectual, earth-mother, exotic creature?*

He could see her taking it all in, trolling her mind for small details that would give a sinister explanation for this new development.

A vision of Brooke's willowy form filled her mind's eye: her classic face and sleek, black hair with the antique silver clip anchoring it on her graceful neck.

No. What would that poised, accomplished, compassionate beauty see in Michael? That's the big question. Michael with all his rough edges?

George broke her thoughts. "Brooke and I were having dinner at Mario's one night, and Dad came in." His eyes panned the room.

He glanced furtively at his mother and continued, "I introduced them, and Dad really turned on this—this magnetism."

He rose from the chair and began pacing slowly around the desk. "I've never seen Dad so charming, Mom. He turned on perfect manners."

He stopped moving and looked at her. "He made super-suave small talk and kept looking into Brooke's eyes."

He scrubbed his hands. "I had never seen that side of Dad." A smile broke his lips. "He was such a little puppy. When he sat down in the booth next to her, I became invisible. Totally invisible."

A vision of the crusty Michael acting the totally smitten romantic threw them into gales of laughter.

Forgetting her dismay at George's sleeping in the office, she stood and said with rare openness, "If any woman could revive his long-dormant heartstrings, Brooke could. I've seen her soften the most grisly derelict, fresh off the streets."

"As have I," George agreed."

They heard the distant movement of residents gathering in the dining hall for Saturday breakfast. Grace Ellen's bossy voice sounded above the din as she admitted non-resident arrivals for the open breakfast held once a week. While she escorted them, she barked the house rules one by one without stopping for breath.

They opened the office door, admitting wonderful cooking smells from the dining-room buffet.

"I'm famished, Mom. I'll just," he motioned toward the breakfast.

Her brow furrowed at his scruffy appearance.

"Oh, right. Mom. Could you just bring me something?"

She hurried out the door, calling back to him, "I certainly hope you have clean clothes here."

George sat at the desk with his tray of bacon and eggs. His mother joined him with another mug of coffee and a fruit cup.

They discussed ways to assess the progress of residents who were seeing A.J.—Dr. Case—on a regular basis.

George informed her that A.J. completed psychological profiles of each client the first month of treating them.

"I remember looking at a few." He took the last bite of egg and toast. He looked at Hope's fruit cup. She shook her head and placed it in front of him. "Thanks, Mom."

Together, they considered the fact that some clients saw Brooke and Father Eli as well as Dr. Case and decided that they, too, should work up their own profiles.

"A.J. plans to complete periodic profiles of each client to look for change or best-case scenario; any sort of growth," George said excitedly."

"So we do have assessment procedures in place," Hope said with finality. "Good."

She spent the morning inspecting the physical plant, checking all areas for cleanliness, order, and safety. She was appalled to find a basket of soiled bed sheets in the laundry room.

Tracking down Grace Ellen and taking the issue up with her as they walked down the hall, she insisted that laundry staff were to finish all the bed linens before leaving work on Friday.

"And make sure all sheets are washed in hot water, Grace Ellen. I noticed a bottle of cold-water detergent in the basket with the sheets, and both washers were set for cold water washes."

"Who knows what kind of vermin come in on the skin of these poor creatures." Hope's eyes met the residents' manager's, and she wanted to put the words back in her mouth.

"Damn those street people and their sloppy hygiene," Grace Ellen said, her voice flat.

They reached the laundry room where Hope showed her the washer dials, pointing to the cold-water settings on both.

"I just meant to say that the residents deserve clean, sanitary beds, Grace Ellen."

Hope lifted the bottle of detergent and handed it to her, their eyes meeting. "That's the least we can do for them." She looked away. "Get rid of that. I cannot think of any laundry we would have here that should be done in cold water. "Can you?" she added, wanting a response.

Grace Ellen began loading the dirty sheets into one of the large, front-loading washers, making a big show of turning the temperature dial to hot and measuring powdered detergent from a super-sized box on the shelf. She closed the door on the washer and turned to Hope.

"Some of the residents might have a fairly good sweater or hundred-percent-cotton sweatshirt, Dr. Fleming." She brushed stray soap powder from the floor with a paper towel. "Hot water would destroy things like that."

"I didn't think of that." Hope said sheepishly. "Keep it then." She sniffed the air. "I'm glad to see you measure the detergent you use. That's one of the ways we can keep costs down."

Hope, exhausted, left the center at 2:30. As she pulled out of the parking lot, she saw Theodore's black town car pull in. She stopped, ready to lower the window; but he gave her a weak wave and kept going.

Heartsick and with tense stomach, she drove on.

How can he treat me like that? I thought he truly cared. But a part of her was not surprised by this change in him.

After a long shower and a short nap, she ate a light supper of melted cheese over chopped tomatoes on whole-wheat pita bread. She poured herself a second glass of white wine and switched on the television in the family room.

Surfing channels, she found an old Jimmy Stewart movie, the one about an honorable young senator who discovers the unholy workings of Congress his freshman term.

She brought a box of dark chocolates from the kitchen and settled on the sofa, determined to get lost in the film.

Sunday, haunted by silent telephones—both house and cellular—she rattled around the rooms, finally digging into the cupboards at the lower part of the bookshelves in the living room.

Sorting, tossing, poring over the contents in every box and album, she emptied the cupboards.

Cleaning them with oil soap and replacing the contents she deemed worth keeping took most of the day. Carrying the piles of discards to trash cans in the garage filled the rest.

Old photographs, certificates, and mementos she saved for George filled an empty, copy-paper box she had brought from school. She pushed it to the back hall.

The house phone rang, flooding her with excitement. She hurried to the kitchen to answer, her mind racing with options for the best disposition to show toward Theodore.

"Hello, Hope speaking."

"Hi Hope. I'm sorry to interrupt your weekend." Her heart sank as she recognized Ray Sellers' voice.

"Oh, that's not a problem, Ray." Feeling suddenly tired, she perched on a stool at the counter. "What's on your mind?"

"Your note, Hope. Your beautiful note about the early wedding gift; it came yesterday." His voice fairly sang with joy.

"She was surprised by your decision. Well, flabbergasted actually." He chuckled. "She said nobody's ever done anything that generous for her."

"Well, Heather certainly deserves it, Ray." Hope willed herself to rise above the indifference she felt at the moment. "She has worked so hard to meet her goals."

"And she appreciates the help, Hope, really she does." His voice thickened. "She could never have done it without you. Thanks to you, she has a good-paying career ahead of her."

"You and I both know that her work has only just begun." Hope replied, barely managing to keep up her side of the conversation.

"Right," Ray said. "Once you qualify for a job and get hired, then you have to fight to keep it. She'll find that out later."

He cleared his throat. "But what I really called about was to tell you that Heather insists on paying you back for hiring Helsi to work at the apartment all those months. She appreciates your being so generous. But it's just not right, she says."

He began to talk faster and faster, and Hope wondered if he were reading his speech.

"Heather said that when you paid her tuition, it was a lot like giving her a scholarship, a big scholarship. Even that's too big a wedding gift to give her. But she accepts it and is most grateful."

"How is Heather, Ray? I know she hasn't felt well." Hope began to warm to this exchange. She was oblivious to her cell phone ringing in the background.

"She would have called you herself, but she's not feeling that well yet. The doctor gave her some pills; they make her sleep all the time." Hope heard the concern in his voice. "She'll talk to you later. Anyway, she'll pay you back in installments for what you paid Helsi. She knows just how much it adds up to. And she thanks you very much for canceling the tuition loan you gave her. It's the best wedding gift in the world."

Later that evening, Hope recalled the conversation with Ray and allowed herself a few warm feelings from his words. She thought of Mary Baldwin.

I understand how she must have taken pleasure in helping me at a time when I needed it. Having Heather to help has been a godsend. Mentoring a principled young woman like her has—well, it has been balm to my wretched soul. She has helped me see what's really important.

The ring of a telephone sounded; but Hope, lost in her thoughts, did not hear it.

Struck with the realization that had she asked her, Mary Baldwin would quite likely have given her the money for the semester in Europe and for all those other expenses, Hope's heart throbbed with self-hatred. She willed the past out of her mind.

She hurried upstairs where she changed into her most comfortable pajamas, faded pink paisley pants and a soft, pink tee-shirt with long sleeves.

She switched on the news

Again, the telephone rang. Again, it went unanswered.

The usual stories of murders, robberies, accidents, and the like flashed across the screen. Hope leafed through a magazine from the bedside table and barely noticed.

"The George Fleming Foundation for the Homeless has been hit by activists," the broadcaster announced, sending her attention squarely at the television set.

Footage came on the screen of young parents picketing in front of the shelter. They carried signs saying:

Not in this Neighborhood

Give Them Jobs not Handouts

House these Unfortunates Someplace Else

Keep this Neighborhood Family Friendly.

Hope glued her eyes to the screen, watching the sidelines for George or some of the staff members. She thought she saw Milan's face peering out a window of the building but could not be sure.

"Interesting side note on the Fleming Foundation," the broadcaster continued. "Founder George Fleming, son of local educator Dr. Hope Fleming, is reportedly a new multi-millionaire and was formerly homeless himself."

Hope cringed. "What does that have to do with anything? She said aloud. "And how do they know all this?" *It could be fodder for Frederick Baldwin's legal case. I hope he's not watching.*

Why are they objecting now? Why wasn't there opposition when we were renovating the building? We had a sign out front.

She wondered if this action had anything to do with Adelaide's new habit of walking the block after lunch on nice days, looking theatrical in full makeup and scrubwoman dress.

Could the open breakfasts every Saturday be attracting attention? Some of the clientele are not very respectable looking.

I should ring Theo. He'd know just what words to use to help put this into perspective.

She lifted the phone to dial but glanced at the clock and stopped. It was nearly 11:00; she knew he tended to be in bed by that hour. Her heart ached to hear his voice.

Why didn't George call from the center when this protest began?

Suddenly exhausted, she checked all the doors, turned off lights, and dragged herself upstairs. Tears of anger and humiliation spilled down her cheeks. Tomorrow's appointment with Bernard McElson loomed large and daunting.

The distinguished attorney looked at Hope, his serious eyes penetrating hers from across the enormous desk. "Have you engaged your own legal counsel, Dr. Fleming?" he asked.

"Of course, Mr. McElson. I took your advice immediately. Do you not recall meeting my attorney, Megan McGillicuddy, last March?"

He spoke on the intercom to his secretary, who arrived in a matter of minutes with a file. Hope watched silently as he opened the folder and looked through its pages. *I cannot believe he does not recall seeing Megan. She's so drop-dead gorgeous.*

Finally, he looked up at his client. "Yes, yes I do, Hope." He rubbed his temple. "I see so many people in the course of a week that I don't always have quick recall." He smiled weakly.

"Well, I cannot believe you don't remember Megan, Bernard." She leaned into the desk. "She is a rare beauty, a real thoroughbred."

"Yes, I remember her now, a dark-haired, classic type." Bernard did not look up from his papers. "She had amazing self-confidence for her young years." He looked at Hope, who nodded.

"I'm afraid we're in for a long fight, Hope." He sat back in his chair and removed his glasses. Frederick is now formally contesting the will."

"On what basis? The audit found no improprieties." Hope arched her back and looked at him with worried eyes.

"Frederick is a very determined young man, Hope. He wants a share of this estate and will probably try every legal avenue in the book to get it." He began replacing the contents of the folder.

"On what basis?" Hope asked again. *Why won't he look at me?*

"We will meet with Frederick's attorney—you, Ms. McGillicuddy, and I—before the deposition." He closed the folder and stood.

Hope rose as well. They shook hands across the desk.

"On what grounds, Bernard? Just give me that." Hope's innocent eyes belied her attempt to bend the rules.

"We'll discuss all that at the pre-meeting, before the deposition." He walked her to the waiting room.

Hope felt unsettled and agitated when she left the law office. She considered whether to pick up food to take back to school or to get a quick lunch at home.

She passed Canterbury Road, changed her mind, and pulled into the parking lot of a drycleaner. Shifting the gear into park, she paused to think. *I am so fragmented today.*

I'll just have a proper lunch at home. A little quiet relaxation might calm my nerves. She pulled out and headed back toward her street.

Hope found Corinne typing the last few class lists into a database. All but two groups of student folders had been neatly filed away to await the opening of the new school year.

She stopped typing and greeted the principal.

"The purchase orders are all ready for your signature, Hope. They are on your desk. The catalogs are there, too. I did not want to file them until you went over the P.Os, in case I ordered the wrong items."

"Good, Corinne. Those reading kits are confusing with all those levels under one catalog number." Hope opened her office door. "Tomorrow's your last day, isn't it?"

"Yes, it is." Corinne smiled. "We leave for the coast the next morning."

"That will be just what you need after this backbreaking year. Initiation by fire," Hope said. They laughed together.

"You have two messages, Hope. Brad Kushner left you a note, and Mr. Bradford called. He'll stop by around three o'clock."

Hope read Brad's note and it cheered her. He wrote that the Purdues had "taken their neurologist's advice and were sending Martin to a summer camp in Lakemore for kids with Pervasive Developmental Disorder." The teacher's delight shone through his words.

That's a good camp. It's been recognized again and again for success with students like Martin.

I needed a little good news today.

"Hello, Martha. You're looking very well," Corinne's voice broke Hope's thoughts.

Hope turned toward the door as the secretary entered.

"Mrs. Poynter is here, Dr. Fleming. Will you see her now?" she asked in a low voice.

"Of course, Corinne." Hope rose.

Martha Poynter, looking rested and fit, shook hands with Hope. "I want to thank you, Dr. Fleming, you and Theodore—Mr. Keller—for letting me teach literacy at the homeless center." She took the chair Hope nodded toward.

"Those poor people try so hard to read. They get all excited when they have even the tiniest success." She looked at Hope with earnest eyes.

"That's wonderful, Mrs. Poynter. How many students do you have now?" Hope took the chair opposite her.

"Three now that Milan is working with me. I help two young women who dropped out of school in primary grades, and now Milan." She smiled proudly. "Milan reads a little; he's very smart. I'm sure he'll rise through the levels fairly fast."

"He has a long shift; when do you work with him?" Hope asked.

"Eleven o'clock," she said promptly.

That's during his workday. What's going on here? Hope opened her mouth to speak.

"It's his lunch hour. He brings his lunch and eats while we work." Martha looked at her sheepishly. "I bring him dessert sometimes, little home-baked cookies, cupcakes." She shrugged her shoulders and smiled. "And he does his homework."

"That's noble work you are doing, Martha. Everyone at the center appreciates it." Hope stood. "I hope we're not imposing on you though, with your tutoring here and over there."

"Oh no," she rose. "Now that I'm working in Mrs. Thorpe's classroom, she has everything laid out for me. So I don't spend much time on preparation." She smiled broadly. "I don't want to give up the children. I love them. I'll miss them over the summer."

Hope thanked her for stopping in and watched her cross the lobby.

"Be sure to thank Mr. Keller for me," she called to Hope from the door.

"I don't know what's happened to Mr. Bradford, Hope. It's after three now," Corinne said, handing Hope a pink message sheet. "I'm leaving; I'll see you tomorrow."

Hope reminded her of their luncheon date and watched her go.

I almost want Ian Bradford to be a no show. I don't think I'm up to hearing about his day in court.

She looked at the message in her hand.

> Bernard phoned. Case on continuance until early next
> year due to Franklin Baldwin's impending surgery.

She reread it and sighed. She read it again and felt reprieve.

She sat at her desk, partly longing to call Theodore but unwilling. Another part of her resolved against ever talking to him again.

The clock showed 3:35. She looked at the piles of purchase orders and class lists, aching to go home but unable to act. She sat frozen, staring out the window, shutting out all thought.

"Are you in there, Doctor?" A male voice pierced her detached mind. Ian Bradford poked his face around the door frame.

Hope managed an energetic smile and invited him into the office. They sat at the table and chatted about weather, about Dylan, about Helsi's new business, about the recall of city workers.

She noticed the strain around his eyes and secretly winced.

"Well Dr. Fleming, you've always taken such a big interest in my family and me." He spoke haltingly. "It's only fair that I give you a full account of my court case." He looked away and swallowed.

"It's not easy for me—you've always treated me fairly and with respect," He took a deep breath, "and I let you down."

His eyes met hers. "But I owe you this, so here goes."

You don't owe it to me. I do not want to hear it. Any of it. I cannot bear to know about your crime or your punishment. The devastation they've wreaked on you, on your family. The humiliation. The power the courts now wield over you, a private citizen. A man just trying to take care of his family. The fines they imposed. The dignity they stripped from you. The shame. The pound of flesh.

Father God, please spare me this.

Ian's voice droned on for minutes, but Hope heard not a word.

A man's pride shall bring him low:
but honour shall uphold the humble in spirit. Proverbs 29:23

DISCUSSION QUESTIONS

1. Discuss personality traits of Hope and her sister Frances and their impact on the relationship. Why does Hope say it would have been easier to cope with Frances' untimely death if Frances had stayed at home? What do you think?
2. In different scenes, Hope displays different, often opposing character traits. Discuss scenes that reveal them. What sort of flawed thinking does Hope reveal in the last scene of the book? How did you react?
3. What does the reader learn about Hope's leadership styles from her interaction with teachers? With support staff? With students? With parents? Do you see her as a positive or negative force at Poore Pond School? Explain.
4. In this book, there are graphic examples of the multi-level responsibilities of principals. It has been said that the role is largely one of "putting out fires." How well does Hope put out these fires? Give examples.
5. To what extent does Hope respect teachers? How do you know?
6. Several individuals help Heather complete her Pharmacy Assistant training. Who were they and how did they help? What can you infer about Heather from her ability to accept this help?
7. Why do you think Ray waits so long to propose to Heather? What characters help him finally decide and how do they do it?
8. What element in Ian's nature allows him to break the law?
9. Ian refers to Helsi's determination as "I-am-woman" behavior. What impact does her strong independence have on her husband? On the family?
10. Discuss scenes in which Hope deals with parents' concerns. Do you agree or disagree with her actions?
11. Discuss scenes in which particular teachers deal with parents' concerns. Do you agree or disagree with their action?
12. Which character(s) change(s) the most? In what ways?

REFERENCE NOTES

Chapter 1	*Establishing a Nonprofit Organization,* The Foundation Center, 2002. http://fdncenter.org
	Elusive Dreams We homeless people are just looking for safe places to sleep, The Plain Dealer, Cleveland, Ohio (February 19, 2006) pp. H-1,3
Chapter 4	*Police Troll Net in Underage-Sex Stings,* The Plain Dealer, Cleveland, Ohio (November 16, 2003) pp. A-1,8
Chapters 10, 16	*Autism Speaks It's time to listen,* Autism Coalition for Research and Education. http://autismspeaks.org
Chapter 19	*Bullied by the Teacher,* Better Homes and Gardens (September, 2003)pp.170-177
Chapter 21	*Track and Field,* Track City Track Club.
	http://www.trackcity.org
Chapter 22	*Munchausen by Proxy Syndrome.* http://ho,e.coqui.net *Munchausen Syndrome,* Jon Donavon Mason, MD,FACEP, FAA. http://www.emedicine.com
	Counting Gay Youths Who Are Homeless, The Plain Dealer, Cleveland, Ohio (January, 17, 2006) p. B-2
	Discovering God's Vision for your Life, Kenneth C. Haugk's Stephen Ministries, 2045 Innerbelt Business Center Drive, St. Louis, MO 634114-5765
Chapter 24	*What is Probation and What Happens to an Individual who Gets Probation as Part of a Plea Bargain?*
	http://www.pbs.org/wgbh/pages/frontline/shows/plea/faqs
Chapter 25	law.com Law Dictionary.
	http://dictionary.law.com/default2.asp?selected

ABOUT THE AUTHOR

Ruth Harwell Fawcett is a retired educator turned writer, publisher, and consultant. She writes about her favorite place to be—a school. Always fascinated by the rich mix of personalities in a school, she creates composite fictional characters from observations gathered in what she calls "that laboratory of human behavior."

Dr. Fawcett left her place in education earlier than planned in order to live her writing dream. Having become a published writer and now leading other writers toward their publishing visions, she has become acutely aware of what a thrill and a privilege it is to be a part of the birth of a book.

Ruth lives with her husband and son, dividing her time between Cleveland and Atlanta where her two daughters reside with their husbands and her ten grandchildren (including three grandchildren-in-law), all providing more fodder for fictional characters.

ABOUT THE COVER ARTIST

Pamela Dills, cover artist for the Poore Pond Series, has had a diverse career in the field of art. She earned a BFA from Kent State University and began her career as a graphic artist in Washington, DC., with an advertising firm. She continued in advertising in Cleveland, directing major and varied accounts.

After a sabbatical to raise her two sons, now in college, she has returned to her field as a free-lance artist specializing in acrylics and pastels. She shows her work in galleries throughout Cleveland and southern Florida.

Pamela lives in Cleveland with her husband and three dogs.

PRAISE FOR HONOR IN THE HEART

"I turned down p. 153...[depicting] a parent telling the principal her son's version of an incident in P.E. class...a great example of how children go home and tell their parents something that is their interpretation...but there may be more to know."

—*Ginger Williams, Director of Field Experience, Oglethorpe University*

"The school and teaching philosophy in this book are consistent with what we know about excellent schools where the most effective learning occurs."

—*Beth Roberts, Ph.D., Professor of Education, Oglethorpe University*

"Now on my suggested reading list for aspiring principals, this book teaches important lessons about school administration from the inside out. It helps graduate students to examine themselves and to discover the real meaning of becoming educational leaders."

—*Frederick Hampton, Ph.D., Professor of Education, Cleveland State University*

QUICK ORDER FORM

Honor in the Heart **(Book I) and *Honor Me Honor You* (Book II) are both good choices as Book Club selections as well as supplemental reading for Teacher-Education Classes and Graduate Programs in administration. Discussion questions are included.**

Copies may be ordered using a photocopy of this convenient form.

Honor in the Heart Book I	Honor Me Honor You Book II
Hardcover $23.95 plus $1.50 tax	Hardcover $22.00 plus $1.38 tax
Paperback $14.95 plus $0.94 tax	Paperback $14.00 plus $0.88 tax

Save 15%, order a box set of both books:
Hardcover Set (I and II): $39.00 plus $2.44 tax
Paperback Set (I and II): $24.65 plus $1.55 tax

Add $4.00 shipping for single copies, $2.00 each additional book.

Discounts are available for multiple copies:

6 – 10 copies:	10% discount
10 – 20 copies:	20% discount
More than 20:	**Contact Ambrosia Press LLC** **PH: 440-951-7780** **FAX: 440-951-0565** **ambrosia03@earthlink.net**

Send check with order form below to:

AMBROSIA PRESS
P.O. BOX 7226
EASTLAKE, OH 44097-7226

Name: ____________________

Address: ____________________

City: ____________ **State:** ______ **Zip** ____________

Your email address for updates: ____________________

QTY.		Tax	Total
____	**Hardcover Honor in the Heart @ 23.95**	**$1.50**	**$** ________
____	**Paperback Honor in the Heart @ 14.95**	**$0.94**	**$** ________
____	**Hardcover Honor Me Honor You @ 22.00**	**$1.38**	**$** ________
____	**Paperback Honor Me Honor You @ 14.00**	**$0.88**	**$** ________
____	**Hardcover Box Set Books I and II @ 39.00**	**$2.44**	**$** ________
____	**Paperback Box Set Books I and II @ 24.65**	**$1.55**	**$** ________
	Shipping		**$** ________
	Total including tax and shipping		**$** ________